# JOURNAL FOR THE STUDY OF THE OLD TESTAMENT
## SUPPLEMENT SERIES
# 120

Editors
David J.A. Clines
Philip R. Davies

JSOT Press
Sheffield

# THE
# REFORMING
# KINGS

## Cult and Society in
## First Temple Judah

## R.H. Lowery

Journal for the Study of the Old Testament
Supplement Series 120

For Mom, Sharon, Bethany, Christopher and Gary

Copyright © 1991 Sheffield Academic Press

Published by JSOT Press
JSOT Press is an imprint of
Sheffield Academic Press Ltd
The University of Sheffield
343 Fulwood Road
Sheffield S10 3BP
England

Printed on acid-free paper in Great Britain
by
Billing & Sons Ltd
Worcester

British Library Cataloguing in Publication Data

Lowery, Richard H.
    The Reforming kings: cult and society in first
    temple Judah.—(JSOT supplements, ISSN 0309-0787;
    v. 120)
    I. Title. II. Series
    222.15

ISBN 1-85075-318-0

## CONTENTS

## PREFACE

This book is a revision of my PhD dissertation. I deeply appreciate the encouragement and advice of faculty and student colleagues at Yale University, especially my advisor, Professor Robert Wilson.

Professor Walter Rast, of Valparaiso University in Indiana, was a helpful dialogue partner while I wrote the manuscript. I am grateful for the support of my faculty colleagues at Phillips University and wish to acknowledge the invaluable contribution of my student research assistant, Brian Gerard. I am especially indebted to Professor David Dungan and my mentor, Professor Lee Humphreys, of the University of Tennessee, who introduced me to the critical study of the Bible and inspired me to teach.

The support of my family was the key to the completion of the book. I especially thank Professor Keith Watkins of Christian Theological Seminary in Indiana, and my wife, the Reverend Sharon Watkins, for their advice and assistance in the production of the manuscript.

I deeply appreciate the support of Sheffield Academic Press, especially the careful editing and useful suggestions of Professor David J.A. Clines and Dr J. Webb Mealy.

Richard H. Lowery
June 10, 1990

## ABBREVIATIONS

| | |
|---|---|
| AASF | Annales Academiae Scientiarum Fennicae |
| AB | Anchor Bible |
| *ANEP* | *The Ancient Near East in Pictures Relating to the Old Testament* (ed. J.B. Pritchard; Princeton: Princeton University Press, 1969) |
| *ANET* | *The Ancient Near Eastern Texts Relating to the Old Testament* (ed. J.B. Pritchard; Princeton: Princeton University Press, 1969) |
| ATD | Das Alte Testament Deutsch |
| ATANT | Abhandlungen zur Theologie des Alten und Neuen Testaments |
| *AusBR* | *Australian Biblical Review* |
| *BA* | *Biblical Archaeologist* |
| *BAR* | *The Biblical Archaeologist Reader* |
| *BASOR* | *Bulletin of the American Schools of Oriental Research* |
| BBB | Bonner biblische Beiträge |
| BDB | *Hebrew and English Lexicon of the Old Testament* (ed. F. Brown, S.R. Driver and C.A. Briggs; Oxford: Clarendon Press, 1952 [orig. pub. 1907]) |
| *Bib* | *Biblica* |
| BFCT | Beiträge zur Forderung christlicher Theologie |
| *BJRL* | *Bulletin of the John Rylands Library* |
| BWANT | Beiträge zur Wissenschaft vom Alten und Neuen Testament |
| BZAW | Beihefte zur Zeitschrift für die alttestamentliche Wissenschaft |
| *CBQ* | *Catholic Biblical Quarterly* |
| *CMHE* | F.M. Cross, *Canaanite Myth and Hebrew Epic* (Cambridge, MA: Harvard University Press, 1973) |
| ConBOT | Coniectanea Biblica, Old Testament Series |
| *EncJud* | *Encyclopaedia Judaica* |
| *EvT* | *Evangelische Theologie* |
| FRLANT | Forschungen zur Religion und Literatur des Alten und Neuen Testaments |
| HKAT | Handkommentar zum Alten Testament |
| HSM | Harvard Semitic Monographs |
| *HTR* | *Harvard Theological Review* |
| *HUCA* | *Hebrew Union College Annual* |
| ICC | International Critical Commentary |
| *IDB* | *The Interpreter's Dictionary of the Bible* |

| | |
|---|---|
| *IDBSup* | *The Interpreter's Dictionary of the Bible, Supplementary Volume* |
| *IEJ* | *Israel Exploration Journal* |
| *JANESCU* | *Journal for the Ancient Near Eastern Society of Columbia University* |
| *JAOS* | *Journal of the American Oriental Society* |
| *JBL* | *Journal of Biblical Literature* |
| *JCS* | *Journal of Cuneiform Studies* |
| *JNES* | *Journal of Near Eastern Studies* |
| *JSOT* | *Journal for the Study of the Old Testament* |
| JSOTSup | Journal for the Study of the Old Testament Supplement Series |
| *JSS* | *Journal of Semitic Studies* |
| KHAT | Kurzer Hand-Commentar zum Alten Testament |
| *KS* | A. Alt, *Kleine Schriften zur Geschichte des Volkes Israel* (ed. M. Noth; Munich: Beck, 1953) |
| NCB | New Century Bible |
| NW | Northwest (Semitic) |
| OTL | Old Testament Library |
| *OTS* | *Oudtestamentische Studiën* |
| *PEQ* | *Palestine Exploration Quarterly* |
| RSV | *Revised Standard Version* |
| SAT | Die Schriften des Alten Testaments |
| SBL | Society of Biblical Literature |
| SBLMS | Society of Biblical Literature Monograph Series |
| *SBLSP* | *Society of Biblical Literature Seminar Papers* |
| SBT | Studies in Biblical Theology |
| SHANE | Studies in the History of the Ancient Near East |
| *SJT* | *Scottish Journal of Theology* |
| *TRu* | *Theologische Rundschau* |
| *TynBul* | *Tyndale Bulletin* |
| *TZ* | *Theologische Zeitschrift* |
| *UF* | *Ugarit-Forschungen* |
| *ÜS* | M. Noth, *Überlieferungsgeschichtliche Studien* (Tübingen: Niemeyer, 3rd edn, 1968 [orig. pub. 1957]) |
| *VT* | *Vetus Testamentum* |
| VTS | Supplements to Vetus Testamentum |
| *WHJP* | *The World History of the Jewish People* (ed. A. Malamat; Jerusalem: Massada, 1979) |
| WMANT | Wissenschaftliche Monographien zum Alten und Neuen Testament |
| *ZAW* | *Zeitschrift für die alttestamentliche Wissenschaft* |
| *ZDPV* | *Zeitschrift des deutschen Palästina-Vereins* |
| *ZTK* | *Zeitschrift für Theologie und Kirche* |

# INTRODUCTION

The anti-monarchical 'manner of the king' (1 Sam. 8.11-18) is a highly polemical but basically accurate characterization of life under Israel's and Judah's monarchies. 'A king', Samuel reportedly told the people, 'will take your sons and put them in war chariots and make them foot soldiers. He will appoint them commanders of regiments and brigades, overseers to work his plantations, reap his harvest and build his weapons of war. He will make your daughters perfumers, bakers and cooks. He will take the best of your produce, a tenth of your crops and give it to his officers and bureaucrats. He will draft your best servants, young men and cattle and put them to work for the crown. He will take a tenth of your flock. You will be slaves.'

The monarchy had an enormous impact on the economic and social life of the nation. Providing material support for the court and its cult pushed already vulnerable Israelite farmers to the edge and over the cliff. Royal policies put a double burden on working people. Taxation and forced labor requirements brought economic changes which left increasing numbers of people landless, alienated from their means of subsistence. Then history added insult to injury. As if the burden of supporting a national monarchy were not enough, the people soon found themselves producing surplus for an imperial military and administrative bureaucracy as well. This straw broke the camel's back. Out of burdensome conditions of Assyrian imperialism grew social protest, in some cases led by social insiders, from court advisors like Isaiah to the landed wealthy such as Amos.

Judah was increasingly restless, uneasy about foreign domination. Even among the religious and political elites, a desire for change began to take hold. Not change merely for the sake of righting economic wrongs, but change for the sake of a restored national identity. On these winds of change came a new approach to Judah's national life, a comprehensive way of looking at the world which integrated different traditions of the past and varied interests of the present. This deuteronomic world-view carried Judah into its brief freedom between the periods of imperial domination. In the disaster of exile, it became the springboard for new theologies by which Israel understood its historical experience as God's people. All along the way, it sought to integrate the whole life of the people—economic, social, political, religious.

To understand how deuteronomic thought functioned for Judah, this study seeks to trace the forces of change in Judah after Solomon's kingdom split and before the Babylonians ended Davidic rule in Jerusalem. It looks first to the material conditions of life in monarchical Judah before Assyria entered the picture. It moves to a discussion of cult reform in the pre-Assyrian period. A chapter each for the three reforms reported during Assyrian rule, along with discussions of imperial obligations and their impact, set the stage for a chapter on Josiah's reform. Taking all this discussion into account, the final pages try to pull together a broad-sweep social history of deuteronomic theology in the monarchical period.

A number of recent trends in various quarters of Old Testament research are converging to reopen questions about the relationship between the Judean monarchy and First Temple cultic organization and practice. Newer literary research has thrown into question earlier assumptions about the delineation and dating of sources, particularly in the Pentateuch. Recent archaeological discoveries and fresh examinations of biblical and extrabiblical written sources indicate the existence of a closer link between cult and court in Judah than was formerly believed. In light of newer research, the involvement of Judean kings in cult reformation requires investigation anew.

Oestreicher's thesis[1]—that political concerns generated Josiah's reforms—prompted nearly 50 years of debate, which by the end of the 1960s had produced a strong consensus that the deuteronomic religious reformation was part of a more general rejection of Assyrian imperial authority. The consensus was broken, however, by two dissertations which appeared almost simultaneously at the end of the 1960s.

J. McKay[2] closely examined the cultic innovations and reforms

---

1. T. Oestreicher, *Das deuteronomische Grundsetz* (BFCT, 47.4; Gütersloh: Bertelsmann, 1923).

2. J. McKay, *Religion in Judah under the Assyrians 732–609 B.C.* (London: SCM Press, 1973).

from Ahaz to Josiah. On the basis of the biblical texts, he finds no reason to believe that the reforms of Hezekiah and Josiah were designed to expel Assyrian deities from the Judean cult. Since the 'consuming interest of the Deuteronomistic historian in recounting Hezekiah's reign is the relationship between Palestine and Mesopotamia', it is

> almost unbelievable that, if the worship of Assyrian gods in the Temple was a central feature of this relationship, the Deuteronomist should have passed it over in silence and have preferred to record such trivialities as the removal of an otherwise unknown bronze serpent, or to summarize the reforms in terms of Canaanite cult symbols.[1]

McKay draws on religious-historical evidence from Northwest and East Semitic cultures to argue that the 'various deities worshipped in Judah during the period of Assyrian domination lack the definitive aspects of the Assyrian gods and generally exhibit the characteristics of popular Palestinian paganism'.[2] Though he considers dubious at best the Akkadian texts adduced by Gressmann[3] to argue Assyrian imposition of cultic obligations on its vassals,[4] McKay nevertheless concedes that Mesopotamian gods were very probably worshipped in Judah after 732, when Ahaz brought Judah into the Assyrian imperial orbit. This, however, he attributes to Assyrian cultural hegemony and a general eclipse of pure Yahwism by popular superstition, which increased in Judah when Samaria fell and Judah's own independence from Assyria seemed impossible.[5] To summarize, McKay sees a correlation between the cultic reforms of Hezekiah, Manasseh and Josiah on the one hand, and the rising and falling hopes of independence from Assyria on the other. But the relationship is indirect, with resurgent nationalism contributing to demands of purity in the national cult and political despair fueling superstitious paganism and respect for the gods of the conquerors.

M. Cogan[6] has reached similar conclusions, primarily investigating

1. McKay, *Religion*, p. 15.
2. McKay, *Religion*, p. 67.
3. H. Gressmann, 'Josia und das Deuteronomium', *ZAW* 42 (1924), pp. 313-27.
4. McKay, *Religion*, pp. 60-66.
5. McKay, *Religion*, p. 69.
6. M. Cogan, *Imperialism and Religion: Assyria, Judah and Israel in the Eighth and Seventh Centuries B.C.E.* (SBLMS, 19; Missoula, MT: Scholars Press, 1974).

the Assyrian evidence. He attacks the standard assumption[1] that Assyria imposed worship of imperial gods on all its subject peoples. To the contrary, Cogan distinguishes two fundamental categories of domination and a third, 'intermediate stage'.

First, the Assyrians administered provinces.[2] These formerly independent countries, annexed to and governed by Assyria, were considered Assyrian in all matters. Depending on the relative strength or weakness of the indigenous gods, native provincial deities sometimes were excluded from the reorganized official pantheon;[3] however, the installation of the Assyrian cult within the provinces 'did not preclude the continued practice of local native cults'.[4] In Cogan's view, the 2 Kings 17 description of Assyrian religious policy is plausible.

Second, the Assyrians were allied to vassal states. These relatively independent states paid tribute, publicly proclaimed their allegiance and occasionally supplied a troop quota for the Assyrian army operating in the area. However, Cogan's reading of the Assyrian sources reveals no religious impositions on vassals, neither sacrificial dues required nor religious symbols erected.[5] Vassals 'were free of any cultic obligations toward their master'.[6] Having established the Assyrian evidence, Cogan turns to the apostate cultic practices recorded in Kings and Chronicles and, like McKay, argues for their Palestinian origin. But Cogan is less willing than McKay to correlate, even indirectly, Hezekiah's and Josiah's religious reforms with nationalistic assertiveness against Assyria. Rather, he argues that Assyria had long since lost imperial influence in the West by the time of Josiah's reform.[7] Like McKay, however, Cogan sees a general demoralization during Manasseh's reign which hastened Judah's acculturation to Assyria and reversion to non-Yahwistic indigenous beliefs and practices.

Finally, Cogan rejects the notion that Hezekiah's and Josiah's

1. E.g. A.T.E. Olmstead, *History of Assyria*, III (Chicago: University of Chicago Press, 1968).
2. Cogan, *Imperialism*, pp. 42-60.
3. Cogan, *Imperialism*, p. 47.
4. *Ibid.*
5. Cogan, *Imperialism*, pp. 56-60.
6. Cogan, *Imperialism*, p. 60.
7. Cogan, *Imperialism*, p. 71.

reforms are motivated by political rebellion against Assyria, agreeing instead with the deuteronomic view of the Manasseh era as 'an age of unprecedented abandonment of Israelite tradition'.[1] Thus, the reforms of Hezekiah and Josiah were genuine religious reforms whose motivations are best sought in 'the spirit of repentance and soul searching which took hold in Judah during the recurring crises of the eighth century BCE'.[2]

The studies of McKay and Cogan met with general approval and set the terms of scholarly discussion until the appearance of two German dissertations at the end of the 1970s.

The first published, H.-D. Hoffmann's *Reform und Reformen*,[3] examines cult reformation in the Deuteronomistic History in an effort to prove M. Noth's theory[4] of the history's single authorship. Hoffmann in a sense agrees with McKay and Cogan that there is no textual evidence for a political motivation of Hezekiah's or Josiah's reform, either from the available Assyrian sources or from Kings.[5] But Hoffmann's conclusion derives from a radically skeptical evaluation of Kings' historical worth, an orientation markedly different from that of McKay or Cogan. In Hoffmann's view, the cult reforms of Manasseh and Josiah are very closely bound and serve as summaries, combining nearly all the motifs and themes of previous cult reforms.[6] As such, these two accounts are particularly untrustworthy as historical sources. His evaluation of cultic vocabulary and literary structure in the Deuteronomistic History leads him to conclude that the historian's authorial activity is much deeper than usually thought, so that it is no longer possible to separate the historian's creative work from his annalistic source. Indeed, the detailed precision of passages usually taken as annalistic is only a skillful literary device which gives 'local color' to the account, thereby underscoring its (fictitious) reliability.[7] While Hoffmann

1.   Cogan, *Imperialism*, p. 113.

2.   *Ibid.*

3.   H.-D. Hoffmann, *Reform und Reformen. Untersuchungen zu einem Grundthema der deuteronomistischen Geschictsschreibung* (ATANT, 66; Zürich: Theologischer Verlag, 1980).

4.   M. Noth, *The Deuteronomistic History* (JSOTSup, 15; Sheffield: JSOT Press, 1981).

5.   Hoffmann, *Reform*, pp. 318-19.

6.   Hoffmann, *Reform*, p. 46.

7.   Hoffmann, *Reform*, p. 315.

believes that cultic changes undoubtedly occurred, he concludes that Kings' account of Josiah's reform yields no clue for a tradition-historical or literary-critical reconstruction of the actual reform or its relation to a supposed rejection of Assyrian influence. He further argues that there is a unified, literarily-conceived cultic history in the narrative of the Deuteronomistic History which stretches from Deuteronomy to 2 Kings. Hoffmann's study intends to confirm Noth's view of single authorship of the Deuteronomistic History and to undermine any attempt to retrieve from Kings historical information about the First Temple cult.

H. Spieckermann's dissertation[1] was published two years after Hoffmann's, though both were accepted for degree in 1979. It consists of two different studies which Spieckermann ties together in a brief concluding chapter.

The first part examines the major cultic reform accounts from literary and historical-critical perspectives. Since he dismisses the historical value of Chronicles, he focuses attention primarily on Kings. Building on the redactional analysis of R. Smend,[2] W. Dietrich[3] and T. Veijola,[4] he detects a number of deuteronomistic editorial hands, as well as pre- and post- deuteronomistic elements.

1. H. Spieckermann, *Juda unter Assur in der Sargonidenzeit* (Göttingen: Vandenhoeck & Ruprecht, 1982).

2. R. Smend, 'Der biblische und der historische Elia', *VTS* 28 (1975), pp. 167-84; *idem, Die Entstehung des Alten Testaments* (Stuttgart: Kohlhammer, 1978); *idem*, 'Das Gesetz und die Völker: Ein Beitrag zur deuteronomistischen Redaktionsgeschichte', in *Probleme biblischer Theologie* (FS von Rad; ed. H.W. Wolff; Munich: Kaiser Verlag, 1971), pp. 494-509; *idem*, 'Das Wort Jahwes an Elia. Erwägungen zur Komposition von I Reg. xvii–xix', *VT* 25 (1975), pp. 525-43.

3. W. Dietrich, *Prophetie und Geschichte. Eine redactions-geschichtliche Untersuchung zum deuteronomistischen Geschichtswerk* (FRLANT, 108; Göttingen: Vandenhoeck & Ruprecht, 1972); *idem*, 'Josia und das Gesetzbuch (2 Reg. xxii)', *VT* 27 (1977), pp. 13-35.

4. T. Veijola, *Die ewige Dynastie. David und die Entstehung seiner Dynastie nach der deuteronomistischen Darstellung* (AASF, 193; Helsinki: Suomalainen Tiedeakatemia, 1975); *idem, Das Königtum in der Beurteilung der deuteronomistischen Historiographie. Eine redaktionsgeschichtliche Untersuchung* (AASF, 198; Helsinki: Suomalainen Tiedeakatemia, 1977); *idem*, 'Salomo—Der erstgeborene Bathseba', *VTS* 30 (1979), pp. 230-50; *idem, Verheissung in der Krise. Studien zur Literatur und Theologie der Exilszeit anhand des 89ten Psalms* (AASF, 220; Helsinki: Suomalainen Tiedeakatemia, 1982).

Part 1 concludes with a complicated, admirably creative reconstruction which may be summarized as follows. The essentially accurate details of Josiah's reform lie at the heart of the Kings account of his reign. This account then generates the literature backward, projecting the persona of Josiah onto previous royal history as the standard of judgment. As the literature moves further into the past, monarchs tend to fall into a rather shallow pattern of alternating good and evil. The evaluations of Hezekiah, Manasseh and Josiah form a closely bound literary triad which serves to enhance the stature of Josiah. Manasseh is pictured as the completely evil opposite of the faithful reformer Josiah. This portrait of corruption, however, requires the fiction of an extraordinarily good predecessor to highlight Manasseh's wickedness. Hezekiah becomes the anti-type of Manasseh who is the anti-type of Josiah. Hezekiah's evaluation must be positive because it functions literarily to negate a negative. The Kings account of Hezekiah's reign thus yields little historical information. Only the removal of the bronze serpent has the ring of truth.[1]

Part 2 re-examines the Assyrian evidence cited by Cogan and introduces other texts to show that Assyria did impose cultic obligations upon vassals as an integral part of imperial policy.[2] Spieckermann rejects Cogan's assertion that Assyria distinguished between vassals and provinces when imposing cultic obligations,[3] but argues that Judah's generally cooperative demeanor made unnecessary many of the empire's more repressive measures.[4] In light of the Assyrian evidence, he re-examines the biblical texts and concludes that Ahaz masterfully engineered a cultic compromise which sensitively resolved the conflict between Yahwistic practice and religious duties to the Empire. Against Kings' fictitious account, Spieckermann asserts that Hezekiah continued the cultic compromise of Ahaz, in spite of his rebellion against Assyria. Manasseh likewise carried forward the compromise and skillfully secured over 50 years of peace and prosperity for Judah. Here, Spieckermann makes the surprising and promising proposal that a priestly group in the Jerusalem temple, at the very heart of royal and imperial power in Judah, became unsettled with popular gravitation toward the exotic and seemingly efficacious magic

1. Spieckermann, *Assur*, pp. 170-75; cf. Hoffmann, *Reform*, p. 154.
2. Spieckermann, *Assur*, p. 369.
3. Spieckermann, *Assur*, p. 370.
4. Spieckermann, *Assur*, p. 371.

and ritual of the Assyrian overlords. The keystone of their own cultic ideal became an emphasis on the uniqueness of Yahweh. The implications of such an ideal for Judah's vassalage to Assyria were obvious. Thus, for discretion's sake, these priests embedded their program in a fiction, set in antiquity and attributed to no less an authority than Moses. They hid the book in the temple and waited for a propitious moment to go public. That moment came with the decline of Assyrian power in the West, a development which occurred around the time of Josiah's accession to the throne. The 'discovery' of the book inaugurated a sweeping top-down religious reform which had little popular support, except perhaps in its political dimensions. After Josiah's death, the cult quickly reverted, only now the compromise worked to the service of neo-Babylonian rather than Assyrian overlords. The priestly ringleaders of the Josianic reform faded into the background of their ritual duties, silent until the hindsight of the exile prompted them to organize past events into a coherent and meaningful explanation of their present.[1]

This brief survey of the major recent studies prompts several observations. McKay, Cogan and Spieckermann all correctly assume the biblical texts have some value in reconstructing First Temple era history. Spieckermann's more skeptical orientation balances the earlier authors' easy acceptance of the biased picture offered by the biblical texts. Cogan accepts at face value the the Deuteronomists' presentation of the royal cult. Thereby, he adopts the romantic and mistaken view that developments in the royal cult had purely religious motivations. Both McKay and Spieckermann are closer to the mark, appreciating the dialectic between religious and political factors in the official cult. This dialectical relationship, however, deserves greater analysis and elaboration than either author gives it.

Cogan and McKay quite rightly see potential historical value in Chronicles. While Spieckermann correctly resists the optimistic claims of recent Chronicles enthusiasts, he too hastily dismisses the document's utility as a source for historical reconstruction. Spieckermann has the upper hand in the debate about imperial religious policy, strengthening the earlier scholarly consensus built on the hypothesis of Oestreicher. Apart from his treatment of Hezekiah's reign, his reconstruction of Judean royal cult history is compelling,

---

1.  Spieckermann, *Assur*, pp. 377-79.

unlike those of McKay and Cogan. Spieckermann's literary recon- | struction is interesting but finally unconvincing. His lack of clarity about dating and situating the complex redactional activity he discerns offers little historical or sociological explanation for the process of literary formation. This is a problem since his treatment of the Hezekiah–Manasseh–Josiah triad depends on an exilic setting. Furthermore, his evaluation of Hezekiah's cult reform as a fictitious positive foil for Manasseh does not square with the dissimilarities between this account and those of Manasseh's and Josiah's reigns. Spieckermann's own interpretations of the Assyrian evidence and of the 'foreign cults' make especially likely Hezekiah's reform of the cult along the general lines indicated in Kings. Hezekiah is, after all, the only Judean king whose rebellion against Assyria is attested in both biblical and Assyrian texts. What is called for is a critical historical orientation which balances the optimism of McKay and Cogan and the skepticism of Spieckermann.

As the above discussion already implies, Hoffmann's rejection of Kings' historical value is problematical. The difficulty itself of disproving such radical skepticism demonstrates its limited usefulness as a scholarly orientation. I raise only two objections here. First, the discernment of theological bias and even a rather heavy patterning of history does not rule out the historical value of the texts. It is possible to correlate the biblical accounts with extrabiblical evidence and make educated conjectures about actual events underlying the biblical accounts. Second, Hoffmann's case is weak that the Deuteronomistic | History is the product of a single creative genius. Though | Spieckermann's redaction-critical model is too complex to be supported by the text, it does demonstrate a number of literary tensions which are not adequately described by Hoffmann's theory of authorship. Divergent Kings accounts of Sennacherib's siege (2 Kgs 18–19) illustrate the problem. Viewing the author(s) as partly compiler(s) of older sources provides a more plausible explanation of these striking units than does Hoffmann's view of the historian as free-handed artist. Neither his theory of authorship nor his historical skepticism is warranted.

A new investigation is in order—one which incorporates Spieckermann's conclusions about Assyrian imperial policy, and moves on to a closer examination of the relationship between government-sponsored cult reforms and other social-political developments. Such a study must assume the appropriateness of the historical-critical enterprise, and it must focus on the emergence and development of deuteronomism, clarifying its effect upon the First Temple cult.

Recent scholarly trends make this project timely. Growing consensus against Alt's theory of kingship in the South and North,[1] the current disfavor toward Noth's amphictyonic theory,[2] the decline of form-critical approaches to historical books and the general rejection of von Rad's credal hypothesis[3] undermine many of the assumptions upon which tradition-historical reconstructions of deuteronomism have been built. New questions about the literary development of the Pentateuch cast doubt on the past correlation of (presumably Northern) Elohistic traditions with deuteronomic ones. The presumption of an antimonarchical bias in Deuteronomy and other deuteronomic literature is challenged. Recent research into the institutions of royal administration in Judah[4] sheds new light on the royal-bureaucratic function of the cult, its rural sanctuaries and its priestly officials, making the idea of cult centralization as a royal-sponsored program all the more intriguing. Finally, the explosion of interest in deuteronomic literary activity in the exile[5] raises anew the issue of the pre-exilic roots of this theological tendency.

A few remarks are in order about the deuteronomic literature and

1. T. Ishida, *The Royal Dynasties in Ancient Israel: A Study of the Formation and Development of Royal Dynastic Ideology* (BZAW, 142; Berlin: de Gruyter, 1977). See also B. Halpern, *The Constitution of the Monarchy in Israel* (HSM; Cambridge: Harvard University Press, 1981); T.N.D. Mettinger, *King and Messiah. The Civil Legitimation of the Israelite Kings* (ConBOT, 8; Lund: Gleerup, 1976).

2. M. Noth, *Das System der zwölf Stämme Israels* (BWANT, 4.1; Stuttgart: Kohlhammer, 1930; repr. 1966). N.K. Gottwald (*Tribes of Yahweh. The Sociology of the Religion of Liberated Israel 1250–1050 BCE* [New York: Orbis, 1979], pp. 345-86) gives a detailed critique of Noth's amphictyonic model.

3. G. von Rad, *Deuteronomy* (OTL; Philadelphia: Westminster Press, 1966), pp. 11-30. Contrast N. Lohfink, 'Die Bundesurkunde des Königs Josias', *Bib* 44 (1963), pp. 261-88, 461-98; M. Weinfeld, 'Deuteronomy—The Present State of Inquiry', *JBL* 86 (1967), pp. 249-62.

4. G.W. Ahlström, *Royal Administration and National Religion in Ancient Palestine* (SHANE, 1; Leiden: Brill, 1982).

5. E.g. H.H. Schmid, *Der sogenannte Jahwist: Beobachtungen und Fragen zur Pentateuchforschung* (Zürich: Theologischer Verlag, 1976); R. Rendtorff, *Das überlieferungsgeschichtliche Problem des Pentateuchs* (BZAW, 147; Berlin: de Gruyter, 1977).

the post-exilic revisionist history of the Chronicler.

## Kings

Contemporary discussion about the authorship, dating, redaction, structure, intent, and historiographical utility of Kings rightly begins with Noth's groundbreaking work on the Deuteronomistic History.[1] His theory and two major modifications by F.M. Cross,[2] on the one hand, and Smend, Dietrich and Veijola, on the other,[3] define three basic approaches taken by most recent writers.[4] The following brief comments are intended not so much to summarize[5] as to highlight difficulties and important insights offered by each of the three schools of thought.

Noth's proposal that Deuteronomy, Joshua, Judges, Samuel and Kings together constitute a single historical *magnum opus* (the Deuteronomistic History), which chronicles the entire history of Israel in the land, signaled a new era in the scholarship of these books. Three of his contributions still enjoy wide consensus. First, Noth finally put to rest older attempts to trace pentateuchal sources beyond Deuteronomy. Second, he convincingly argued that the Deuteronomistic History begins with the historical narrative in Deut. 1.1–4.43 and incorporates the deuteronomic code. Third, he asserted the fundamental unity of the Deuteronomistic History. Although the

---

1.  Noth, *The Deuteronomistic History*.

2.  F.M. Cross, 'The Themes of the Book of Kings and the Structure of the Deuteronomistic History', in *Canaanite Myth and Hebrew Epic* (Cambridge, MA: Harvard University Press, 1983), pp. 274-89.

3.  See the bibliographic notes above.

4.  Hoffmann (*Reform*) is one of the few who continue to support Noth's single authorship theory. Many of the older commentaries adopt a dual redaction model: e.g. I. Benzinger, *Die Bücher der Könige* (KHAT; Freiburg: Mohr, 1899), pp. xiii-xv; A. Šanda, *Die Bücher der Könige* (Exegetisches Handbuch; Münster: Aschendorff, 1911), I, pp. xxxvi-xl; J. Gray, *I and II Kings* (OTL; Philadelphia: Westminster Press, 3rd edn, 1977), pp. 6-9; cf. also O. Eissfeldt, *The Old Testament: An Introduction* (New York: Harper & Row, 1965), p. 299. These predate Cross's essay and differ in their dating of the pre-exilic original edition. Outside of Germany, Smend and his students have found little following for their redactional theories. Only one of the major English-language commentaries to appear since Smend and his students proposed their model adopts their reconstruction: G.H. Jones, *1 and 2 Kings* (NCB; Grand Rapids, MI: Eerdmans, 1984), I, p. 44.

5.  Jones (*1 and 2 Kings*, pp. 28-46) gives a brief but thorough summary.

degree of literary unity exhibited by the Deuteronomistic History remains a point of controversy,[1] with most finding it much less unified than Noth would have it, few dispute that the books from Deuteronomy through Kings, as presently structured, constitute a loosely coherent literary complex. More comments about the literary unity of Deuteronomistic History follow below. I assume the basic soundness of the first two points and question the third.

A fourth, closely related hypothesis has suffered widespread criticism. Noth's conviction finds little agreement that a single exilic author or editor conceived and produced, from beginning to end, a tightly cohering Deuteronomistic History.[2] Different editorial techniques evident in the various books of the Deuteronomistic History have formed the basis of one important challenge to the single authorship proposal.[3] A second challenge arises from thematic and theological divergences within the Deuteronomistic History.[4] The widespread conviction that Noth's proposal oversimplified the matter has led to important modifications which specifically address the redaction of Kings.

Cross has revived an older theory,[5] given most recent articulation

1. See the discussions in G. Fohrer, *Introduction to the Old Testament* (Nashville: Abingdon Press, 1970), p. 194; R.A. Carlson, *David the Chosen King. A Traditio-Historical Approach to the Second Book of Samuel* (Uppsala: Almqvist & Wiksell, 1964), p. 29; J.R. Porter, 'Old Testament Historiography', in *Tradition and Interpretation* (ed. G.W. Anderson; Oxford: Oxford University Press, 1979), pp. 125-62, 135-37.

2. G. von Rad, *Old Testament Theology* (New York: Harper & Row, 1962), I, pp. 346-47; Fohrer, *Introduction*, p. 194; M. Weinfeld, *Deuteronomy and the Deuteronomic School* (Oxford: Clarendon Press, 1972); Porter, 'Historiography'.

3. See von Rad, *Old Testament Theology*; Fohrer, *Introduction*; but note G.W. Trompf, 'Notions of Historical Recurrence in Classic Hebrew Historiography', *VTS* 30 (1979), pp. 219-24; R.D. Nelson, *The Double Redaction of the Deuteronomistic History* (JSOTSup, 18; Sheffield: JSOT Press, 1981), p. 14.

4. A. Weiser, *Samuel. Seine geschichtliche Aufgabe und religiöse Bedeutung* (FRLANT, 81; Göttingen: Vandenhoeck & Ruprecht, 1962), p. 25; contrast Nelson, *Double Redaction*; Jones, *1 and 2 Kings*, pp. 38-39.

5. See the commentaries of Benzinger, Šanda and Gray on Kings, and O. Eissfeldt's OT introduction; also A. Kuenen, *Historische-kritische Einleitung in die Bücher des Alten Testaments* (Leipzig: Schulz, 1885–94), pp. 88-100. Good histories of dual redaction hypotheses are found in A.N. Radjawane, 'Das deuteronomistische Geschichtswerk: ein Forschungsbericht', *ThR* 38 (1974), pp. 177-216; Nelson, *Double Redaction*.

by G. Fohrer,[1] which postulated the existence of two major editions of the Deuteronomistic History, a pre-exilic original and an exilic revision.[2] The brief essay in which Cross broadly outlines his proposal offers little detailed exegesis. R. Nelson,[3] however, applies Cross's theory to several passages throughout Kings.

Nelson correctly identifies Cross's most important contribution to the dual redaction hypothesis as his provision of a reasonable motive for the production of each edition.[4] The pre-exilic Deuteronomistic History was propaganda for the Josianic reform. Two themes, the promise to the house of David and the sin of Jeroboam, unify the history and climax in Josiah's reign and cult reform.[5] The exilic second edition updated the original history, transforming its theological import by inserting material meant primarily to explain the exile.[6]

Cross and Nelson's argument that a pre-exilic edition of the Deuteronomistic History served the purposes of Josianic reformers is convincing. Kings' consistent emphasis on cult centralization, for example, does not make sense as an originally exilic theme. As a practical proposal, it is intelligible only if the temple is standing and its cult is functioning. Of course, neither condition existed in the exile.

On the other hand, cult centralization in Kings may never have been a real proposal.[7] In such a case, an exilic setting is plausible. Then, cult centralization as a criterion for judging monarchs would generate cumulative evidence in the case against exiled Judah. The past failure of Judah to centralize worship in Jerusalem would be an important factor in Yahweh's decision to punish them with exile.

This reconstruction has two problems. First, while removal of the high places is the most consistent and apparently most important criterion of judgment for Judean kings down through Josiah, its violation

---

1. Fohrer, *Introduction*, p. 194.
2. Cross, *CMHE*, pp. 274-89.
3. Nelson, *Double Redaction*. See also J.D. Levenson, 'From Temple to Synagogue: 1 Kings 8', in *Traditions in Transformation: Turning Points in Biblical Faith* (ed. B. Halpern and J.D. Levenson; Winona Lake, IN: Eisenbrauns, 1981), pp. 143-66; R.E. Friedman, 'From Egypt to Egypt: Dtr[1] and Dtr[2]', in *Traditions in Transformation*, pp. 167-92.
4. Nelson, *Double Redaction*, p. 28.
5. Cross, *CMHE*, pp. 278-87.
6. Cross, *CMHE*, pp. 285-86.
7. G. Hölscher, 'Komposition und Ursprung des Deuteronomiums', *ZAW* 40 (1923), pp. 161-255.

never is presented as a sin worthy of exile. Except in the cases of
arch-villains Ahaz and Manasseh, high place worship is not even
mentioned in the negative evaluations of Judean kings (1 Kgs 15.3; 2
Kgs 8.18, 27). Elsewhere, with the exception of 1 Kgs 14.22-24, the
untypical description of popular practice in Rehoboam's Judah, only
good kings are criticized for failure to remove the high places.

Second, the high place theme climaxes in the reform of Josiah. The
final word on the high places is that Josiah removed them. After
Josiah, cult centralization drops as a standard of judgment for Judean
kings. Yet Ezekiel indicates that high place worship continued in
Judah right up until the destruction of Jerusalem (6.2-14; 16.24, 25,
31, 39; cf. 18.6, 11, 15; 20.28-29; see also Jer. 2.20; 3.6, 13; 17.2).
The abrupt disappearance of high place worship as a central
theological problem in Kings, despite other biblical evidence that the
practice continued, suggests that this theme found its fulfillment in
Josiah's cult reform. It also supports Nelson's contention that the final
four regnal summaries are written by an exilic editor, since cult
centralization would be moot under such circumstances. The
Deuteronomists might have drawn explicit links between high place
worship and the exile, as Ezekiel did. Yet none of Kings' apparent
predictions of Babylonian exile makes any mention of high place
worship as a contributing factor. Why should a cult practice so
prominent in the deuteronomic explanation of the North's fall (2 Kgs
17.9-11) and so important in the earlier evaluation of Judean kings
nowhere appear as an explanation of Judah's exile? The
straightforward answer to that question is that high place worship
functions as a criterion of judgment only in a pre-exilic edition of
Kings. It intends to explain the destruction of the North and to justify
the cult reforms of Hezekiah and Josiah. As a corollary, it also legiti-
mates the northward expansion of Judah under these monarchs.

Another possibility must be considered. A late exilic or early post-
exilic origin for the cult centralization theme may be argued.[1] Its
motivation could be found in the political-theological discussions
which preceded the building of the Second Temple. Kings' failure to
connect high place worship with exile would make sense, if the book
were oriented primarily toward the future of the restored community
in Jerusalem. Josiah, whose persona dominates the book, would func-

---

1.    Hölscher, 'Komposition and Ursprung'; Oestreicher, *Grundsetz*.

tion as the ideal type for a reconstituted monarchy. Cult centralization, coupled with a ringing condemnation of First Temple
'syncretism', would make sense, as the faithful prepared to start over
again from scratch. Advocacy of centralization and repeated warnings
about 'the abominations of the nations whom Yahweh your God
dispossessed before the Israelites' might share the social context and
outlook of Ezra–Nehemiah, for example. An immediately pre-Second
Temple setting is attractive.

Such a proposed setting has its problems, however, for the literary
question concerning the closing chapters of Kings remains. A rather
smoothly running narrative suddenly begins to sputter when it gets to
Josiah's untimely demise. In the end, it simply runs out of fuel altogether. Such an awkward ending is especially curious if Kings is
conceived of as having been produced as a post-exilic whole. Furthermore, the Chronicler's use of Kings, especially the adaptation and
simplification of such key themes as high place abolition, implies some
temporal distance between the two works. From Kings to Chronicles,
substantial thematic and theological development is evident. An early
post-exilic dating of Kings would require a much later dating of
Chronicles than most commentators are willing to grant.

Positing an exilic or post-exilic setting for the first appearance of
the cult centralization theme in Kings creates more problems than it
solves. A setting in the midst of Josianic reform, however, presents
cult centralization as a real, though extraordinary, proposal advocated
by the authors. It also explains the theme's climax in Josiah's reign
and the authors' curious failure to connect high place worship with
predictions of the Babylonian exile.

It is indisputable that Kings comes to an important climax in its
presentation of the reign and reform of Josiah.[1] It remains possible,
though unlikely, that such a history was first produced by a later,
exilic admirer of the king.[2] The weight of the evidence, however,
supports the view that one major edition of Kings appeared as
'propaganda', justifying Josiah's radically unorthodox reorganization
of political-religious life in Judah.

While the Josianic edition appears to be the definitive pre-exilic edi-

---

1.  Cross, *CMHE*; Nelson, *Double Redaction*, p. 28.
2.  Spieckermann (*Assur*, pp. 160-99) sees the whole book as generated in the
exile from a basically accurate pre-exilic account of Josiah's reform (pp. 30-71, 153-
60).

tion of Kings, it is not necessarily the first. H. Weippert's suggestion that Kings has a substantial pre-Josianic redactional history[1] has met with little support. Apart from the perceived shortcomings of Weippert's analysis,[2] two widely held opinions make an earlier edition difficult to imagine. First, most assume that Kings is literarily dependent upon the legal core of Deuteronomy. Add the second widely held belief that an *Urtext* of that deuteronomic code (D) is the lawbook discovered during Josiah's reform (c. 621), and you have a firm date before which no edition of Kings could have been written.[3]

Other considerations weaken this argument, however. Most importantly, though 'discovered' toward the beginning of Josiah's reformation, the lawbook probably had been written and first preserved in the temple prior to Josiah's accession. An edition of Kings directly dependent upon D could have been written earlier, in the time of Amon, Manasseh or even Hezekiah. One also might question whether Kings actually is dependent upon a text of D. Does Kings' use of laws and themes given literary expression in D mean the code was already written when the first author of Kings began work? Finally, the distinction between D and the supposedly later material of the Deuteronomists is increasingly difficult to maintain. Evidence of 'redactional activity' throughout D[4] blurs the distinction between the two. Clearly Deuteronomy contains legal material, some of which is ancient, now imbedded within narrative prose and poetry closely akin to materials in Kings and elsewhere in deuteronomic literature. However, the differences within Deuteronomy between narrative and legal code may be explained as differences of genre. Furthermore, supposed terminological and thematic 'developments' from D to the Deuteronomists[5] correspond to different periods addressed by the books and therefore may be explained as skilled literary technique. It is hardly surprising, for example, that D should resist the anachro-

---

1. H. Weippert, 'Die "deuteronomistischen" Beurteilungen der Könige von Israel und Juda und das Problem der Redaktion der Königsbucher', *Bib* 53 (1972), pp. 301-39.

2. Nelson, *Double Redaction*, p. 31; Jones, *1 and 2 Kings*, p. 42.

3. Jones, *1 and 2 Kings*, p. 31.

4. See the 'secondary hand' in the deuteronomic core: Noth, *Deuteronomistic History*, p. 27, 112 n. 34.

5. Weinfeld, *School*, pp. 320-65; E.W. Nicholson, *Deuteronomy and Tradition* (Oxford: Clarendon Press, 1967), pp. 107-14; Porter, 'Historiography', pp. 139-41; Jones, *1 and 2 Kings*, pp. 29-31.

nistic identification of Jerusalem as Yahweh's chosen place or David as Yahweh's chosen king.[1] The reader should expect such attention to detail from authors who so carefully varied their treatment of high place worship before and after the building of the Temple (cf. 1 Kgs 3.4 with subsequent condemnation of high place worship).

Cross's Josianic 'propaganda' edition, followed by an exilic revision, is plausible. The possibility of a pre-Josianic edition of Kings cannot be excluded, however.

Jepsen[2] theorized that Kings had a pre-deuteronomistic redactional history, beginning with an eighth-century synchronistic chronicle meant to contrast the stable Judean monarchy with its unstable, recently fallen Northern counterpart. Separate annalistic materials were collected by seventh century Jerusalem priests. Early in the exile, a priestly redactor ($R_1$) merged and supplemented the two pre-exilic sources, creating a cultic history of monarchical Israel and Judah. Later in the exilic period, a Mizpah-based disciple of Jeremiah ($R_2$) added prophetic legends and recast the work as a deuteronomic interpretation of the monarchical period.

Jepsen's reconstruction has a number of flaws[3] and few supporters.[4] However, his view that Kings has a complex redactional history, possibly including pre-deuteronomic edition(s), continues to have an impact, especially in Germany.

R. Smend[5] identified in Joshua both the foundational work of the Deuteronomistic Historian (DtrG; more recently, he and his students have used the designation DtrH) and a legally oriented revision by a 'nomistic' redactor (DtrN). Smend's students, W. Dietrich[6] and T. Veijola,[7] proposed the existence of a third redactional layer, chronologically situated between DtrH and DtrN. The work of a 'prophetic' redactor (DtrP), this revision introduced prophetic stories, themes and forms. Subsequent refinements of this model, such as those of Spieckermann,[8] have discerned layers within the layers, envisioning

1. Jones, *1 and 2 Kings*, p. 30.
2. A. Jepsen, *Die Quellen des Königsbuches* (Halle: Niemeyer, 2nd edn, 1956).
3. Jones, *1 and 2 Kings*, pp. 41-42.
4. Weippert, 'Redaktion'.
5. Smend, 'Gesetz', pp. 494-509.
6. Dietrich, *Prophetie*.
7. Veijola, *Dynastie*; *Königtum*.
8. Spieckermann, *Assur*.

a very complex network of finely nuanced revisions and additions.

The Smend model is strongest in its portrayal of a redactional process which occurred over time, but within a tradition circle or 'school' which maintained a degree of literary-theological continuity.[1] Its greatest problem arises from the dissection of the layers. In the final analysis, its proponents commit the same kind of logical error by which Jepsen's reconstruction fell: they assume that 'legal', 'prophetic' and 'historical' concerns are so incongruous that their appearance in the same document necessarily indicates literary layering. These incongruities, however, exist more in the minds of the critics than in the social consciousness of exiled Judeans, as the book of Ezekiel testifies.

The strength of the Smend analysis is undermined by a practical confusion about the nature of theological-literary development. His method helps to the extent that it recognizes the theological-literary enterprise as an inherently social process which incorporates different interests and perspectives. It is legitimate and useful to pursue the various social experiences and interests which underlie the received texts. It is wrong, however, simply to assume that divergent interests represent different redactions. In practice, Smend and his students make that assumption. The result is a thoroughly top-heavy redactional structure which threatens to topple the literature upon which it is built.

Greater appreciation of theological-literary production as a social-historical process discourages such complicated literary reconstructions. As a social process, theological reflection always mediates a variety of interests and perspectives. In Israel's case this mediation took literary and non-literary forms. A more or less precarious coherence of divergent interests and perspectives occurs throughout the theological process, in all of its literary and non-literary contexts. Thus, written theology necessarily reflects various interests. Original editions express the tensions inherent in socially developed theology. Occasionally, biblical literature shifts style, vocabulary or content in such a striking way as to indicate literary layering. But more often than not, it is difficult to ascertain whether the tensions existed on a 'pre-literary' level of tradition, or whether they first appeared as the result of editorial activity. In this regard, both form and redaction

1.    Jones, *1 and 2 Kings*, pp. 40-46; Weinfeld, *School*; Carlson, *David*, p. 29; Porter, 'Historiography', p. 135.

criticism exhibit a key weakness, though each is partially correct in its intuition about biblical literature. Social-historical analysis can be more relaxed about perceived tensions and contradictions within the literature, recognizing that theology, by its social nature, brings together divergent interests. Whether they are brought together through successive editorial revisions or through a process of theological reflection preceding the original edition is not as important as the fact that the present literature expresses different interests and holds them in tension. Lowering the stakes in the discernment of redactional layers acts to check the proliferation of redactors, a tendency inherent in Smend's model.

The Smend–Dietrich–Veijola reconstruction has found limited support outside of Germany.[1] G.H. Jones,[2] for example, adopts their model, but English-language scholars, as a rule, accept some form of the dual redaction hypothesis.

The two schools of thought represented by Cross, on the one hand, and Smend, on the other, both encounter difficulty when they try to peel away relatively intact redactional layers. Each, however, raises important challenges to Noth's theories about the Deuteronomistic History. Cross and Nelson's research successfully questions the exilic origin of Kings. Smend and his students do uncover greater complexity in the literature than Noth's single authorship theory allows. Yet, none of the above scholars questions the essential coherence of the Deuteronomistic History. A detailed discussion of this matter requires another forum, but a few remarks are pertinent to the study of official cult reform in Judah.

Deuteronomic language and themes run throughout the corpus which Noth designated the 'Deuteronomistic History'. However, they also appear in literature outside its boundaries. A major deuteronomistic revision of the book of Jeremiah has long been recognized. Furthermore, the last decade has seen a growing 'pan-deuteronomic' tendency particularly among German redaction critics. O. Kaiser's fifth edition of the Isaiah 1–12 commentary[3] envisions an exilic deuteronomistic editing so extensive as to make eighth-century

1. Among Germans, see, for example E. Würthwein, 'Die josianische Reform und das Deuteronomium', *ZTK* 73 (1976), pp. 395-423.

2. Jones, *1 and 2 Kings*.

3. O. Kaiser, *Das Buch des Propheten Jesaja. Kapitel 1–12* (ATD, 17; Göttingen: Vandenhoeck & Ruprecht, 1981).

Isaiah material virtually unrecoverable. H. Schmid[1] and R. Rendtorff[2] both find a definitive deuteronomic stamp on the overall structure of the Pentateuch. It is unlikely that exilic deuteronomistic editors are responsible for everything currently being attributed to them; however, the scholarly discernment of deuteronomic language and themes widely dispersed in the biblical literature raises the question of whether the repetition of such themes in the historical books from Deuteronomy to Kings is sufficient grounds for assuming that these books comprise a unified historical work.

The question is all the more pressing in light of differences between the books. Von Rad's attack on the stylistic and thematic coherence of the Deuteronomistic History[3] has been tempered by subsequent research. For example, Richter's study of cycles in Judges[4] blunts the force of von Rad's distinction between the literary-historical sensibilities evident in Judges on the one hand, and Kings on the other.[5] Still, differences abound. Judges shows minor deuteronomistic editing of a previously existing work, unlike Kings, whose definitive authorship is deuteronomistic. Samuel and Kings incorporate source materials differently.[6] In fact, Samuel shows little deuteronomistic editing at all.[7] The content and overall intent of Joshua does not smoothly fit Judges. Obviously, some effort has been made to connect these books. The conclusion of Deuteronomy and the introduction of Joshua editorially link these two books, as does the covenant renewal ceremony at Mt Ebal (Josh. 8.30-35). The opening verse of Judges implies continuity with the Joshua narrative. The Succession Narrative bridges Samuel and Kings. Surface linkages, in other words, do exist. As such, Noth's claim of a unified historical narrative is not outrageous. It is, however, finally inadequate to explain serious differences between the books. The fundamental coherence of the Deuteronomistic History, as Noth conceived it, is in serious doubt.

---

1. Schmid, *Sogenannte Jahwist*.
2. Rendtorff, *Problem*. Issue 3 of *JSOT* (1977) is devoted to a discussion of Rendtorff's work. It includes a response by Schmid and a review of Schmid (*Sogennante Yahwist*).
3. Von Rad, *Theology*, I, pp. 346-47.
4. W. Richter, *Die Bearbeitungen des 'Retterbuches' in der deuteronomistischen Epoche* (BBB, 21; Bonn: Hanstein, 1964).
5. Trompf, 'Recurrence', pp. 219-24.
6. Though note Porter, 'Historiography', p. 137; Jones, *1 and 2 Kings*, p. 39.
7. Fohrer, *Introduction*, p. 194.

Fohrer[1] best accounts for the divergences with his suggestion that a series of originally independent books with different redactional histories now loosely comprise the deuteronomic literary complex. He prudently rejects the notion of a unified Deuteronomistic History *magnum opus* and restricts consideration of the Deuteronomist's authorial work to Kings alone. His position requires modification, however, in light of the close literary relationship between Kings and Deuteronomy.[2]

Kings is inextricably bound with Deuteronomy. Both in its legal core (chs. 12–26) and in the surrounding narrative, Deuteronomy raises concerns and uses language central to the Kings evaluation of monarchical history. In fact, key units in Kings appear to be modeled on particular passages in Deuteronomy—for example, the Manasseh narrative (2 Kgs 21) and Deuteronomy 18. Kings and Deuteronomy are closely bound by language, theme and structure. De Wette's hypothesis[3] offers an important insight. Whether or not it is right about the historical facts of the case, it correctly reads the intended message of 2 Kings 22–23 that Deuteronomy and the discovered lawbook are one and the same document. It is unnecessary here to determine precisely the nature of the process by which Deuteronomy and Kings evolved. I suspect they exerted mutual influence on one another and grew in a somewhat dialectical fashion, probably from the time of Hezekiah down through the exilic period. The close connection of the two books transcends mere speculation, however. Therefore, this research moves cautiously but freely between them in order to discern the nature and development of deuteronomic theology. Clearly, deuteronomic passages occur elsewhere, both within and outside of the corpus Noth designated as the Deuteronomist History. This study utilizes such deuteronomic material, but proceeds on the assumption that Deuteronomy and Kings together constitute a distinct literary complex. Questions about the origins and development of Joshua through Samuel are bracketed, except to say that these books originally developed outside the literary-theological process by which

1. Fohrer, *Introduction*, p. 194.
2. Weinfeld, *School*, pp. 320-65.
3. W.M.L. de Wette, *Dissertatio critica exegetica qua Deuteronomium a prioribus Pentateuch libris diversum, alius cuisisdam recentioris opus esse monstratur*, 1805; repr. in de Wette, *Opuscula* (Berlin, 1833).

Deuteronomy and Kings evolved, only later to be reworked along deuteronomic lines.

## Chronicles

S. Japhet[1] raised anew A.C. Welch's objection[2] to the prevailing view that Chronicles and Ezra–Nehemiah constitute the coherent, unified work of a single author (the 'Chronicler').[3] H.G.M. Williamson,[4] most notably, has built upon Japhet's work. Williamson summarizes, as follows, the main considerations upon which the common authorship model is built:[5]

1. the almost verbatim parallel between the end of Chronicles and the introduction of Ezra,
2. the content of 1 Esdras which begins at 2 Chronicles 35 and continues into Ezra, and
3. a supposed similarity of outlook, interests and theology between the two collections.

The first point supports common authorship only by assuming a dubious process of canonization: an originally continuous work was

1. S. Japhet, 'The Supposed Common Authorship of Chronicles and Ezra–Nehemia Investigated Anew', *VT* 18 (1968), pp. 330-71.

2. A.C. Welch, *The Work of the Chronicler. Its Purpose and Date* (London: Oxford University Press, 1939); *idem, Post-Exilic Judaism* (Edinburgh: Blackwood & Sons, 1935), p. 186.

3. L. Zunz, *Die gottesdienstlichen Vorträge der Juden, historisch entwickelt. . .* (Berlin: Ascher, 1832), p. 19; E.L. Curtis and A.A. Madsen, *A Critical and Exegetical Commentary on the Books of Chronicles* (ICC; New York: Scribner's 1910), p. 3; A. Bentzen, *Introduction to the Old Testament* (Copenhagen: Gad, 1948), p. 205; G.W. Anderson, *A Critical Introduction to the Old Testament* (London: Duckworth, 1959), p. 215; W.O.E. Oesterley and T.H. Robinson, *An Introduction to the Books of the Old Testament* (London: Oxford University Press, 1934), p. 110; P.R. Ackroyd, *I and II Chronicles, Ezra and Nehemia* (London: SCM Press, 1973)— though he considers the question open; K.-F. Pohlmann, *Studien zum dritten Esra. Ein Beitrag zur Frage nach ursprünglichen Schluss des chronistischen Geschichtswerkes* (FRLANT, 104; Göttingen: Vandenhoeck & Ruprecht, 1970).

4. H.G.M. Williamson, *Israel in the Books of Chronicles* (Cambridge: Cambridge University Press, 1977); *idem, I and II Chronicles* (NCB; Grand Rapids: Eerdmans, 1982).

5. Williamson, *Israel*, pp. 5-6.

split in two as the larger canon took shape.[1] The canonizers left an overlapping section at the end of Chronicles and the beginning of Ezra to preserve an awareness of the now divided history's original unity. The likelihood of such a process is highly questionable.[2] Furthermore, Welch's common sense observation that editors 'do not take the trouble to stitch together two documents, unless they have been originally separate',[3] remains convincing.[4]

M. Haran offers an interesting variation on the theme.[5] He sees the overlap as a scribal technique made necessary by the length of scrolls in antiquity. The scribe could not fit the entire Chronistic work (Chronicles–Ezra–Nehemiah) on one scroll. In the absence of a natural break in the history, the scribe added a 'catchline' to the end of 2 Chronicles, duplicating the first verses of what is now the book of Ezra, in order to make plain the integral connection of the two scrolls. As Williamson notes,[6] however, there is an excellent 'natural break' in the history just before the 'catchline'. 2 Chron. 36.21 concludes with the monarchy ended, Jerusalem destroyed, the Temple burned, the people deported, and the land desolate. Ezra 1.1 (= 2 Chron. 36.22) begins an entirely new era, both politically and religiously. Williamson's own suggestion that the duplication derives from liturgical use of Chronicles—the desire not to end a reading on a negative note—is not wholly convincing, but it seems more likely than Haran's proposal.

The second consideration in support of common authorship requires that 1 Esdras reflect a text tradition more original than the Masoretic Text of Chronicles and Ezra. K.-F. Pohlmann[7] offers the most thorough recent argument that 1 Esdras contains the original ending of the Chronicler's work. Williamson[8] counters that it is a secondary compilation. The text-critical arguments on either side are inconclu-

---

1. Curtis and Madsen, *Chronicles*, p. 3.

2. Williamson, *I and II Chronicles*, p. 5.

3. Welch, *Post-Exilic Judaism*, p. 186.

4. Williamson (*Israel*, p. 13) refutes in detail the use of this overlap to argue common authorship. See his more recent article 'Did the Author of Chronicles Also Write the Books of Ezra and Nehemiah?', *Bible Review* 3 (1987), pp. 56-59.

5. M. Haran, 'Explaining the Identical Lines at the End of Chronicles and the Beginning of Ezra', *Bible Review* 2 (1986), pp. 18-20.

6. Williamson, 'Also Write'.

7. Pohlmann, *Studien*.

8. Williamson, *Israel*, pp. 12-36; summarized in *I and II Chronicles*, pp. 4-6.

sive, but Williamson casts sufficient doubt on the priority of 1 Esdras to render highly questionable its use in the debate about authorship of Chronicles and Ezra–Nehemiah.

Third, the alleged similarity of syntax and vocabulary[1] has been successfully challenged.[2] R. Mosis[3] and P. Welten[4] criticize Japhet's lexical and syntactical study;[5] however, she correctly notes several examples of wide divergence in the language of Chronicles and that of Ezra–Nehemiah.[6]

Finally, the common outlook, interests and theology of the two collections has been disputed recently by a number of scholars.[7] Shared interests in genealogy, temple and temple worship, as well as the prominent role of clergy in the whole life of the community do not provide firm evidence for common authorship. While such a commonality of interest yields important information about the focal concerns of the post-exilic religious community in Jerusalem, it cannot be adduced to argue the unity of Chronicles and Ezra–Nehemiah. That similar interests characterize the Priestly writings and the book of Malachi[8] indicates that such were not unique in post-exilic Jerusalem.

More interesting than the similarities are the divergences of theology between Chronicles and Ezra–Nehemiah. Most striking is the

---

1. E.g. J.M. Myers, *I Chronicles. Introduction, Translation, and Notes* (AB; Garden City, NY: Doubleday, 1965), p. xviii.

2. Japhet, 'Common Authorship'; Williamson, *Israel*, pp. 37-59; updated in light of critical response, *idem, I and II Chronicles*, pp. 6-9.

3. R. Mosis, *Untersuchungen zur Theologie des chronistischen Geschichtswerkes* (Freiburg: Herder, 1973), p. 214.

4. P. Welten, *Geschichte und Geschichtesdarstellung in den Chronikbüchern* (WMANT; Neukirchen–Vluyn: Neukirchener Verlag, 1973), p. 4.

5. Japhet, 'Common Authorship'.

6. Japhet, 'Common Authorship'.

7. S. Japhet, 'The Ideology of the Book of Chronicles and its Place in Biblical Thought' (PhD dissertation, Hebrew University; Jerusalem, 1983 [Hebrew]); Williamson, *Israel*, pp. 60-70 and *I and II Chronicles*, pp. 9-11; R.L. Braun, 'A Reconsideration of the Chronicler's Attitude toward the North', *JBL* 96 (1977), pp. 59-62; *idem*, 'Chronicles, Ezra, and Nehemiah: Theology and Literary History', *VTS* 30 (1979), pp. 52-64; J.D. Newsome, 'Toward a New Understanding of the Chronicler and his Purposes', *JBL* 94 (1975), pp. 201-17; D.N. Freedman, 'The Chronicler's Purpose', *CBQ* 22 (1961), pp. 436-42; F.M. Cross, 'A Reconstruction of the Judean Restoration', *JBL* 94 (1975), pp. 4-18.

8. Williamson, *I and II Chronicles*, p. 9.

absence in Chronicles of Ezra–Nehemiah's polemic against inter-marriage. The nine-chapter genealogy which prefaces Chronicles contains numerous references to mixed marriages, with no negative comment (2.3, 17, 34; 3.1; 4.17; 7.14; 8.8). Other notations include 2 Chron. 2.13; 8.11; 12.13; and 24.26. Furthermore, as Williamson observes,[1] Chronicles omits 1 Kgs 11.1-8, an explicit condemnation of Solomon's foreign marriages. This would be an odd omission for the author of Neh. 13.26: 'Did not Solomon king of Israel sin on account of such women? Among the many nations there was no king like him and he was beloved by his God; nevertheless foreign women made even him to sin.' Related to this important difference is the varying treatment of Samaritans/Northerners. J.D. Newsome[2] is followed by R.L. Braun and others[3] in showing that Chronicles actually has a rather favorable view of foreigners in general and Northerners in particular, an attitude markedly different from that of Ezra–Nehemiah. Other differences have been noted, including the absence of the doctrine of immediate retribution in Ezra–Nehemiah,[4] the centrality of prophecy for Chronicles and its insignificance in Ezra–Nehemiah,[5] and differing attitudes between the two works toward history and historiography.[6] The numerous differences considerably weaken the case for common authorship.

Thematic continuity does exist between the works, however, with regard to the temple and the organization and execution of its cult. Additionally, the prayers in Ezra 9 and Nehemiah 9 seem consciously to adopt the Chronicler's retribution and remnant language.[7] These and other similarities support Braun's suggestion that the later authors and editors of Ezra–Nehemiah (and sections of Chronicles) 'considered themselves as following faithfully in the train of the author of Chronicles...'.[8] One need not accept, as Braun does, Cross's detailed reconstruction of the redactional history of

1. Williamson, *Israel*, p. 61.
2. Newsome, 'New Understanding'.
3. Braun, 'Reconsideration'; *idem*, 'Chronicles', pp. 53-56; Newsome, 'New Understanding', pp. 205-207; Mosis, *Untersuchungen*, pp. 169-72.
4. Williamson, *Israel*, pp. 67-68; Braun, 'Chronicles', pp. 53-56.
5. Newsome, 'New Understanding', pp. 203-204, 210-12.
6. Newsome, 'New Understanding', pp. 207-10; Williamson, *Israel*, p. 68; *idem*, 'Also Write', p. 57.
7. Braun, 'Chronicles', p. 63.
8. Braun, 'Chronicles', p. 64.

Chronicles and Ezra–Nehemiah[1] to agree with the basic insight that the latter books build upon an independent and prior text of Chronicles.

It is unnecessary here to settle definitively the debate over the authorship and redaction of Chronicles and Ezra–Nehemiah. However, the interpretation of Chronicles does depend, in part, upon one's view of the literary relationship between these books. The common-authorship model has encouraged a skewed reading of Chronicles. Themes and tendencies of Ezra–Nehemiah, such as its anti-Northern and anti-foreign bias, are—inappropriately—transferred to Chronicles, with the result that important characteristics of the literature are missed or misconstrued. While leaving open the questions of authorship and redactional history, I will treat Chronicles as a distinct unit, separate from, though now related to, Ezra–Nehemiah. The term 'the Chronicler' refers throughout to the author of Chronicles, whether or not the same person or group also wrote Ezra–Nehemiah.

Several important characteristics of Chronicles have direct bearing on the study of cult reform in Judah.

The Chronicler draws heavily from a text of Kings which will have been very similar to the version of that book preserved in the Masoretic Text. Yet there are key divergences. These may be explained in three ways: (1) the Chronicler's text of Kings differs from the Masoretic Text, (2) the Chronicler has other sources which correct the Kings record, (3) the Chronicler adds to, deletes from and revises Kings freely to fit his own literary-theological project. Each can be argued strongly at various points in Chronicles.

Factual variance between Chronicles and Kings raises poignantly the question of the biblical records' accuracy. Historical proximity generally favors Kings when the two histories disagree. However, Kings has its own strong tendencies which shape its presentation of history. For this reason, evaluation must proceed on a case by case basis. Where a different Chronicles reading clearly fits a larger tendency of the book, the report is dubious. A different Chronicles account is most

---

1. F.M. Cross, 'Restoration'. His reconstruction may be summarized as follows: The first edition ($Chr_1$), c. 520, incorporates 1 Chron. 10–2 Chron. 34, plus Ezra 1–3. $Chr_2$, c. 450, added Ezra 5.1–6.19 and the Ezra narratives. $Chr_3$, c. 400, edited out some material about Zerubbabel and added the genealogies of 1 Chron. 1–9.

probable in terms of historicity when it fits no larger literary-theological pattern, while the corresponding Kings narrative is demonstrably tendentious. In the case of divergence, neither a text-critical judgment that the Chronicler's *Vorlage* of Kings varies from the Masoretic Text, nor a conclusion that the Chronicler has a different source by which to correct Kings finally settles which account has greater historical value.

Even the Chronicler's verbatim repetition of Kings warrants critical attention to the larger designs of the authors. Throughout the book, the Chronicler takes liberties with the Kings record. Therefore, a decision to reproduce a passage word for word may be just as important as a decision to depart from Kings.

Both Kings and Chronicles present history as a theological construct. As social historical records, they both are suspect. Neither can be dismissed, however, as historically useless. Coordinating their portrayals with other literary and archaeological data and avoiding conclusions which require greater precision and certainty than the evidence can offer, the social historian may profitably use Kings and Chronicles to reconstruct pre-exilic social history.

## Summary and Overview

How can the programmatic tensions within deuteronomic reform theology be explained? The answer begins with the transition from a decentralized 'tribal confederacy' to a more unified monarchical state. The monarchy came to dominate the social life of the nation. The first two chapters of this book describe the commanding social role of the monarchy in the economic (Chapter One) and cultural (Chapter Two) life of the people. Economically, the monarchy shifted the decentralized subsistence agriculture toward surplus production for the support of the monarchy. Culturally, the monarchy legitimated its social role through an official cult which presented the king as the divinely chosen earthly representative of Yahweh, the true owner of the land and sovereign of the people. The social dominance of the monarchy carried a high price, however. Supporting a monarchical state was too much for many Judeans who could barely produce enough to support themselves. Though opposition to the monarchy grew, Davidic political and religious authority kept the lid on things.

The economic and cultural demands of Assyrian imperialism threat-

ened social cataclysm (Chapter Three). Social tensions introduced by
the establishment of a monarchical state were exacerbated under the
strain of Judah's imperial obligations. Social problems became clearer
and less acceptable to more people. Out of this imperial era ferment,
deuteronomic reform theology began to emerge (Chapter Four). Born
of social unrest, deuteronomic theology bears a family resemblance to
antimonarchical protest. It incorporates popular discontent with the
monarchy but transforms it, directing its force outward against
Assyria. Deuteronomic theology thus shows a curious mixture of con-
tempt for the royal cultic status quo (Chapter Five) and support for
the monarchy. After the disintegration of the Assyrian empire,
deuteronomic reform became the basis of a crown-initiated cultural
revolution meant to reconstitute a national identity for Judah, now
free of imperial domination (Chapter Six and Conclusion).
Deuteronomic theology exhibits seemingly irreconcilable tensions,
because under the pressure of foreign domination, deuteronomists
found a way to reconcile irreconcilable social interests.

Chapter 1

MONARCHY AND ECONOMY

The social context of First Temple cult reform is defined in part by
the way Judah organized its people and resources for material
production. Detailed analysis of Judah's productive system over time
is beyond the scope of this study. However, useful generalizations are
possible. Long-term trends are discernible. Combined with other
historical and sociological information, broad comments about the
productive system are valuable components of a social reconstruction.

Judah's mode of production did not change fundamentally over the
course of the monarchical period. Within overall stability, however,
the productive system was dynamic. It evolved, sometimes in fits and
starts, but usually very gradually. It was affected by external forces
and events—most notably imperial subjugation and war. It was filled
with internal contradictions which fueled revolts and reforms,
adjustments and retrenchments. It produced social problems which it
could not resolve. But Judah's mode of production remained
essentially the same from the beginning of the monarchy until its end.

If the productive system was constant over time, so were its
contradictions. Tensions between classes, within classes, between
various occupations and strategies of production, all were present in
varying degrees and combinations throughout the period of the
monarchy. These tensions found expression in the challenges and
compromises of Judah's ongoing political and religious life.

The task of this chapter is to paint a broad picture of Judah's system
of production during the monarchical period and to draw out some of
its social and political implications. This social-economic canvass will
form the backdrop for subsequent analysis of cult reform in Judah,
particularly deuteronomic cult reform.

## Agriculture

D.C. Hopkins[1] looks at land-use strategies, especially the 'intensity' of cropping over time,[2] to help reconstruct the social-economic make-up of monarchical Judah and Israel. Land-use strategies are determined above all by environmental factors. Climate, soil and geography make water availability the decisive environmental constraint on agriculture in Palestine. High-intensity rain on a limited number of days means that precipitation (when it comes) usually outstrips water saturation into the soil. Quick surface water collection and runoff periodically lead to flooding, waterlogged bottom lands and swamp conditions. In addition, an extremely high evaporation rate drains the summer soil of almost all moisture, threatening winter plantings. Conserving and controlling water, then, is a high agricultural priority in the Palestinian environment. In monarchical Israel, farmers controlled water by various field techniques, irrigation and drainage and terracing.[3]

Terracing has received a great deal of attention in the last 20 years.[4] This farming technique creates a series of step-like terraces along the slopes of hills otherwise too steep to be cultivated with much success. Besides giving the farmer level ground to work, terracing prevents soil erosion and significantly reduces water runoff, allowing increased infiltration into the soil. Fairly steep slopes can support crops without terracing 'so long as pressures on production are not too great', Hopkins says.[5] However, by conserving soil and managing water

1. D.C. Hopkins, 'The Dynamics of Agriculture in Monarchical Israel', *SBLSP* 22 (1983), pp. 177-202; *idem*, *The Highlands of Canaan: Agricultural Life in the Early Iron Age* (Social World of Biblical Antiquity Series, 3; Sheffield: Almond Press, 1985), pp. 235-61.

2. Cf. E. Wolf, *Peasants* (Foundations of Modern Anthropology Series; Englewood Cliffs, NJ: Prentice-Hall, 1961), pp. 19-34.

3. Hopkins, 'Dynamics', p. 180; *idem*, *Highlands*, pp. 173-86.

4. G. Edelstein and M. Kislev, 'Mevasseret Yerushalayim: the Ancient Settlement and its Agricultural Terraces', *BA* 44 (1981), pp. 53-56; G. Edelstein and S. Gibson, 'Ancient Jerusalem's Rural Food Basket', *BAR* 8 (1982), pp. 46-54; G. Edelstein and Y. Gat, 'Terraces around Jerusalem', *Israel—Land and Nature* 6 (1980), p. 73; L.E. Stager, 'The Archaeology of the East Slope of Jerusalem and the Terraces of the Kidron', *JNES* 41 (1982), pp. 111-21; C.H.J. de Geus, 'The Importance of Archaeological Research into the Palestinian Agricultural Terraces, with an Excursus on the Hebrew Word *gbi*', *PEQ* 107 (1975), pp. 65-74.

5. Hopkins, 'Dynamics', p. 181.

better, terracing in Iron-Age Israel significantly increased agricultural productivity in highland areas otherwise little farmed.

Terracing enhanced the land's productivity, but also required a substantial shift in labor patterns. Terrace construction and maintenance 'was a complex operation demanding a staggering investment of time and labor', Edelstein and Gat write.[1] The labor power and level of cooperation required could not have been met by a production unit as small as the household or extended family (*bêt 'āb*).[2] Large-scale cooperation between families (household and extended) was necessary. The appearance of terrace agriculture in the Judean and Northern highlands, then, indicates increasing social-political integration just before rise of the monarchy.[3] A centralizing tendency emerged which counterbalanced the natural tendencies of small-scale agriculture toward social fragmentation and decentralized production.[4]

The labor requirements of terracing have prompted some to question whether this strategy necessarily utilized some kind of compulsory labor.[5] Forced labor on such a scale would have required a centralized political authority substantial enough to impress laborers and sustain work on these time-consuming projects. The corvée, of course, was widely used by monarchical states of the ancient Near East, including Israel and Judah. If terracing required corvée labor, how was this farming technique related to the emergence of the Israelite monarchical state in Iron IIA?

De Geus's study[6] indicates there was widespread use of terracing in the Palestinian hill country in Iron I. Stager[7] cites excavations at Iron I 'Ai (c. 1100) which reveal terrace farming techniques 'typical of the nearly 100 new settlements founded in the hills at that time'. De Geus sees terrace farming as occurring in Palestine no earlier than c. 1200.

---

1. Edelstein and Gat, 'Terraces', p. 73.
2. Hopkins, 'Dynamics', pp. 182-83; *idem, Highlands*, pp. 177-88, 252-61; F. Frick, *The Formation of the State in Ancient Israel* (Social World of Biblical Antiquity Series 4; Sheffield: Almond Press, 1985), p. 139.
3. Hopkins, *Highlands*, pp. 178-86; de Geus, '*gbi*'.
4. Frick, *Formation*, p. 137.
5. Cf. P. Barlett, 'Adaptive Strategies in Peasant Agricultural Production', *Annual Review of Anthropology* 9 (1980), pp. 553-61; Hopkins, *Highlands*, p. 178.
6. De Geus, '*gbi*', pp. 65-74.
7. Stager, 'East Slope', p. 116.

Stager, however, argues on the basis of Ugaritic texts[1] that agricultural terracing was introduced in the Levant as early as the Late Bronze Age (LB). As he shows, architectural terracing in Jerusalem dates from the fourteenth century,[2] but agricultural terracing was probably a later development.[3]

Terrace farming began to flourish in the Palestinian hill country in the Israelite period just prior to the establishment of the monarchy. A strong centralized monarchy with powers to raise a corvée, then, was not the *sine qua non* of terrace farming in Israel.[4]

The labor requirements of terrace farming did, however, play an important role in the social conditions which gave rise to the monarchy. The institutions and conventions of highland agricultural society continued to have an impact on royal policy long after the monarchy was an accomplished fact.

The techniques of highland agriculture required a high level of cooperation and a diversified strategy to limit risk. Small cattle herding provided a hedge against crop failure, but horticulture was the backbone of highland agriculture. Tree and vine crops—olives, grapes and figs—were staples.[5] Cereal, wheat and barley ordinarily are open-field crops.[6] Open fields, of course, were in shorter supply in the highlands than in the lowlands. Terracing may have given highlanders more flexibility in crop strategies, but the rather narrow terrace strips were better suited to fig, grape and olive cultivation.[7] Both terrace farming (horticultural and agricultural) and (non-terrace) orchard and vineyard keeping are labor-intensive strategies involving long-term capital investments.[8]

These techniques of production had social implications. The rapid spread of agricultural terracing techniques in the premonarchical Israelite period indicates some form of inter-village, inter-regional trade existed.[9] Orchard and vine crops in small quantities could be

1. Stager, 'East Slope', pp. 116-17.
2. Stager, 'East Slope', pp. 111-17.
3. Stager, 'East Slope', p. 116.
4. Cf. Hopkins, 'Dynamics', pp. 182-83; *idem, Highlands*, p. 178.
5. Frick, *Formation*, p. 140; Hopkins, *Highlands*, pp. 227-32.
6. Stager, 'East Slope', p. 116.
7. *Ibid.*
8. Frick, *Formation*, p. 137.
9. *Ibid.*

part of a diversified subsistence agriculture, but in the larger quantities evident in the Israelite hill country more likely were grown for trade as well. Rather substantial trade with the cereal-producing lowlands is implied by the widespread emergence of terrace farming in Iron I. Such trade required social institutions and conventions facilitating regional cooperation and inter-regional agreements.

Additionally, terrace construction and maintenance required a much greater labor force than even the extended family could supply. Hopkins's suggestion[1] has merit that inter-family coordination of the labor supply, particularly in the context of labor-intensive terrace farming, was the primary function of the clan (*mišpāḥah*).[2] Terrace farming required inter-family, inter-village cooperation. That cooperation required corresponding social institutions and conventions.

Finally, horticultural crops require a longer-term investment than annual cereal and legume crops do. Long-term continuity of the production process is necessary. Orchard and vineyard keeping require social institutions and conventions which discourage the transfer of land and encourage longer-term stability of the work-force. In Judah and Israel, long-term continuity of land ownership and stability of the work-force was safeguarded in part by a patrimonial land tenure system by which certain plots, at least, were considered 'ancestral property', not to be sold or otherwise transferred out of the extended family.

To summarize, agricultural strategies in Israel immediately before and during the monarchical era can be characterized as increasingly complex. An uncertain water supply made agriculture highly risky under normal conditions. Disease, pestilence and other natural disasters heightened the vulnerability of Israelite farmers. A diversified crop and cattle strategy gave farmers the best chance of survival. In Israel and Judah, agriculture was diversified in every region. Small cattle herding was common everywhere. However, cereal and grain crops predominated in the lowlands and vine and tree crops were primary in the hill country.

Labor patterns also were complex. Highland terrace farming

---

1. Hopkins, 'Dynamics', p. 183; *idem, Highlands*, pp. 256-61.
2. Hopkins, *Highlands*, pp. 191-92; contra Gottwald (*Tribes*, p. 323), who sees the tribe as providing emergency labor supply; cf. D. Baly, *Geographical Companion to the Bible* (London: Lutterworth, 1963), pp. 67-77.

required occasional large-scale cooperation for construction and maintenance of terraces. Cattle tending and grain and cereal farming were not so labor intensive. They could be accomplished satisfactorally by much smaller labor units.

The growth of highland agriculture through the tribal and monarchical periods indicates that a steadily growing internal trade economy existed in Israel and Judah. The vine and tree crops which constituted the bulk of highland agriculture had to be supplemented by cereals and grains from the valleys and plains. To put it differently, valley dwellers could get by without the vineyards and orchards of the hill country, but highlanders needed the cereal and grain surpluses of the lowlands. This exchange of produce required social and political mechanisms which were sufficiently developed to allow inter-regional cooperation. The birth and development of the monarchy brought a shift in these mechanisms of cooperation.

Such changes never occur with ease.

### Political Economy in Monarchical Judah

Judah's lending system illuminates the character of its productive system in the Davidic period. V.A. Jacobson's comments on lending and production in Assyria[1] are helpful for comparison. He cites 'the very low level of the development of usury'[2] in the neo-Assyrian heartland as evidence that the free-holding of land by peasants was in decline there during this period. Of those whose records survive, most loans were very large, with only a few small grain loans transacted. Pledging oneself or a family member as collateral was increasingly rare and the lengths of loans were short-term, not exceeding a few months. Asserting that usurers flourish primarily at the expense of small proprietors, Jacobson reads the poorly developed lending system as indicating few free-holding small farmers. If he is right, then the converse should be true that a well developed system of usury coincides with a sizeable sector of small proprietors.

Biblical sources, particularly the classical prophets, indicate that monarchical Israel and Judah had well developed usury systems at the

---

1. V.A. Jacobson, 'The Social Structure of the Neo-Assyrian Empire', in *Ancient Mesopotamia: Socio-Economic History* (ed. I.M. Diakonoff; Moscow: Nauka, 1969), pp. 277-95.

2. Jacobson, 'Social Structure', pp. 286-87.

dawn of Assyrian rule in each kingdom.[1] Jacobson's line of reasoning would infer a thriving sector of small proprietors. Economic and other archaeological data[2] confirm that production was organized primarily in small units during this period. Stager's survey, for example, shows that farming and herding was conducted communally and by single households,[3] mostly as very small operations. Regarding local trade, M. Elat concludes that 'sellers of agricultural produce were apparently the producers themselves or the owners of the land on which the produce was grown'.[4] There were few middle people between producers and buyers. Clothing generally was homemade.[5] Some specialized crafts were produced in workshops, often concentrated in certain regions and among particular families,[6] but these were not large operations. Agriculture was the backbone of monarchical Judah's economy[7] and small-scale, family-based production units were the organizational norm.

However, some evidence appears to lead in the opposite direction. A.F. Rainey[8] and M.L. Chaney[9] interpret 2 Chron. 26.10 as evidence of a regional specialization of agriculture under the powerful rule of Uzziah/Jotham. D.C. Hopkins,[10] D.N. Premnath,[11] and Chaney[12]

---

1. See M. Silver, *Prophets and Markets: The Political Economy of Ancient Israel* (Boston: Kluwer–Nijhoff, 1983), pp. 65-70.

2. Cf. L.E. Stager, 'The Archaeology of the Family in Ancient Israel', *BASOR* 260 (1985), pp. 1-35; N.K. Gottwald, 'Israel, Social and Economic Development of', *IDBSup*, pp. 465-68; O. Borowski, *Agriculture in Iron Age Israel* (Winona Lake, IN: Eisenbrauns, 1987). Borowski's book is by far the most in-depth and useful analysis of archaeological data on agriculture in monarchical Israel currently available.

3. Stager, 'Archaeology', pp. 18-23. Note especially his view that archaeology confirms Gottwald's depiction (*Tribes*, pp. 291-92) of the multiple-family compound in the Micah story (Judg. 17–18).

4. M. Elat, 'Trade and Commerce', in *The World History of the Jewish People* (ed. A. Malamat; Jerusalem: Massada, 1979), IV/2, pp. 173-86, 173.

5. *Ibid.*

6. Elat, 'Trade and Commerce', pp. 173-75.

7. Elat, 'Trade and Commerce', pp. 173, 186.

8. A.F. Rainey, 'Wine from the Royal Vineyards', *BASOR* 245 (1982), pp. 57-62, 58.

9. M.L. Chaney, 'Latifundialization and Prophetic Diction in Eighth Century Israel and Judah', paper to the Sociology of the Monarchy Seminar, AAR/SBL Annual Meeting, 1985, p. 5.

10. Hopkins, 'Dynamics', pp. 193, 200 n. 71.

suggest that a form of 'command economy' existed in monarchical Judah and Israel, colliding with and gradually replacing small-scale, village-based agriculture. Chaney draws epigraphic support from the *lmlk* seals,[1] the Samaria ostraca, a Tell Qasileh ostracon, and an eighth-century stone plaque in the city of David perhaps indicating royal stores. He also cites archaeological data on the processing of oil and wine to corroborate the written indications of increased specialization, regionalization and intensification of agriculture under royal impetus.[2]

A degree of support for Chaney's view may be found in Elat's judgment that Judah and Israel's foreign trade 'was initiated by the crown and conducted on its behalf'.[3] At the very least, portions of the economy were dominated by the monarchy which increasingly transformed production to its own benefit. This transformation included consolidation of land ownership and specialization and intensification of agriculture. The extent of this transformation and the precise nature of land ownership remain to be considered.

The question arises whether a royal 'command economy' is consistent with the small-scale units of production indicated by archaeology.

Silver answers negatively, arguing instead that a private free market economy flourished in eighth-century Judah and Israel.[4] He mistakenly characterizes the patrimonial land tenure system described in the biblical sources as 'private ownership'. Nevertheless, he correctly observes that a form of market economy existed, though probably on a smaller scale than Silver envisions.[5] Other factors, such as taxation (tithes) and obligations to military and corvée service, further

---

11. D.N. Premnath, 'The Process of Latifundialization Mirrored in the Oracles Pertaining to Eighth Century B.C.E. in the Books of Amos, Hosea, Isaiah and Micah' (dissertation, Graduate Theological Union, 1984), p. 56.

12. Chaney, 'Latifundialization', pp. 6-18.

1. *Ibid.*; Rainey, 'Wine', p. 58.

2. Chaney, 'Latifundialization'.

3. Elat, 'Trade and Commerce', p. 186.

4. Silver, *Markets*, pp. 94-135, 247-51.

5. Elat's comment better characterizes the commercial reality indicated by archaeology and the biblical texts: 'Commerce, however, seems not to have strongly influenced the patterns of life and thought of [the monarchical] period: the prophetic literature and other literary works of the time, which reflect the various aspects of contemporary life, make little mention of commercial life or of those involved in it' ('Trade and Commerce', p. 175).

complicate his free enterprise model. Whether small producers were able to market some of their products, the crown not only laid claim to a sizeable portion of the annual yield (1 Sam. 8.15), but it also regularly interrupted production itself by impressing able-bodied laborers for royal projects (1 Sam. 8.13, 16) and for war maneuvers (1 Sam. 8.11-12).

Chaney and others who find an increasingly specialized royal command economy account for persistent small production units by viewing them as vestiges of Israel's tribal-era past being rooted out by the monarchy. The small-scale, village-based redistributional land tenure system of the premonarchical period came into conflict with the patrimonial estate-based system of the monarchy. 'From that point on', Chaney says, 'Israel contained two conflicting systems of land tenure which were the material bases of two fundamentally different understandings of society and its proper values'.[1] The monarchy controlled foreign trade, maintained religious, administrative and military bureaucracies and had powers of taxation and compulsory labor; the trabsition from confederation to kingdom must have caused thorough economic, as well as political, metamorphoses. The struggle between conflicting systems of production envisioned by Chaney is probable and consistent with the evidence. Chaney's model does not explain, however, the continued dominance of small-scale production throughout the period of the monarchy.

B. Lang[2] proposes the category 'rent capitalism' to describe Judah and Israel's economy in the monarchical period.[3] Lang's studies of Amos[4] paint a picture of a stagnant economy in which an unproductive, wealthy urban class lived off the exploited labor of rural peasants.[5] In Lang's usage, 'peasant' describes an agrarian laborer who produces primarily for household subsistence rather than for trade and profit. He sees the nuclear family (parents and unmarried

1. Chaney, 'Systemic Study of the Sociology of the Israelite Monarchy', *Semeia* 37 (1986), pp. 53-76.
2. B. Lang, 'The Social Organization of Peasant Poverty in Biblical Israel', *JSOT* 24 (1982), pp. 47-63 (= ch. 4 of his *Monotheism and the Prophetic Minority* (Sheffield: Almond Press, 1983).
3. Cf. O. Loretz, 'Die prophetische Kritik des Renten-Kapitalismus', *UF* 31 (1981), pp. 482-88.
4. Lang, *Monotheism*, and 'Sklaven und Unfreie im Buch Amos', *VT* 31 (1981), pp. 482-88.
5. Lang, *Monotheism*, pp. 116-21.

children) as the basic productive unit in Israel and Judah. Newlyweds built their own houses and farmed their own plots. Extended families may have included three or four generations, but did not constitute meaningful economic units. The chief economic role of extended families was to provide emergency assistance for family members in need.[1]

In addition to the peasant class, Israel and Judah had an urban ruling class. The ruling class was propertied, educated, mercantile and made permanent charges on the agricultural produce of the peasantry. The charges might come through patrimonial land tenure (renting out family or granted lands) or a prebendal system (charges paid by peasants to support a civil or ecclesiastical officer). But in Israel and Judah, surplus was extracted mainly through free market control, whereby the peasant became dependent on a lender or merchant, eventually to the point of share cropping or tenant farming.[2]

Under such a rent-capitalist system, '[t]he urban propertied class skims off the largest possible portion of the agricultural produce as a regular income or 'rent' claimed on the basis of liabilities or full urban ownership of land'.[3]

The highly unstable character of subsistence agriculture motivates the process of 'rent' extraction: crop yields are variable, highly vulnerable to outside factors. Lang estimates that, on average, an Israelite peasant could expect crop failure more often than every fourth harvest.[4] When disaster struck, the peasant turned to a lender. High interest rates (which Lang sees as the norm in ancient Israel) meant 'long-term or even permanent dependence' of the peasant on the lender. With land, tools or other movable property taken as collateral, the wealthy urban lender usually became the actual owner of cultivated lands.[5] The peasant's labor thus became alienated from ownership of the productive means (land).

In Israel and Judah two lending systems coincided.[6] The first was based on kinship: a peasant in financial difficulties borrowed from, or sold a plot to, better-off kin. The borrower could then 'buy back' the

1. Lang, *Monotheism*, p. 167 n. 209.
2. Lang, *Monotheism*, p. 116.
3. Lang, *Monotheism*, p. 117.
4. *Ibid.*
5. Lang, *Monotheism*, p. 118.
6. Lang, *Monotheism*, pp. 119-20.

plot for a regular rent paid to the lender (cf. Jer. 32.6-15). The second lending system was market-based: Transactions operated in much the same way, but, without the additional conventions of kinship, the market-based lending system tended to be merciless toward the debtor.

Lang's analysis of Amos, Isaiah and archaeological data paints a picture of Israel and Judah's usurous elites ruthlessly exploiting an indebted peasantry.[1] Amos (2.8; 3.15; 5.11; 6.4) and Isaiah (3.16–4.1; 5.11-12) describe an urban lifestyle of drunken feasting and shameless luxury. These prophets, according to Lang, present the urban wealthy as unproductive, conspicuous consumers who are parasites on the peasant laboring class.[2] Not only do peasants supply the banquet tables for the wealthy's ostentatious temple parties (Amos 2.8 and 4.1),[3] but overextended debtors trying to work off their liability either sell themselves into bondage or become serfs on their own land.[4] Lang takes Amos's complaint about 'selling the poor for a pair of sandals' as a reference to a legal procedure by which an indebted peasant could be deported and his property seized by the creditor.[5] Finally, Lang interprets Amos 8.4-6 as clear evidence that the urban wealthy hoarded grain and sold it back to peasants at the highest possible price in bad harvest years.[6]

Though of short-term benefit to the unproductive wealthy class, Israel and Judah's 'rent capitalism' was fundamentally stagnant, unable to resolve the deteriorating social conditions it generated.[7]

Lang's portrait of Judah and Israel's economy is helpful in some ways and inadequate in others. 'Rent capitalism' as a descriptive category confuses the issue. Israel and Judah's economy share some characteristics with capitalist economies—labor alienated from the means of production, for example. However, labor alienation in monarchical Israel and Judah (that is, serfdom and debt slavery) also

1. Lang, *Monotheism*, pp. 121-27.
2. Lang, *Monotheism*, p. 123.
3. Cf. J.A. Dearman, 'Prophecy, Property and Politics', *SBLSP* 23 (1984), pp. 385-97 (386-87). Dearman argues that 'wine' here is 'exacted wine'. Also note Dearman's view of the temple's lending function.
4. Lang, 'Sklaven', pp. 482-88.
5. Lang, *Monotheism*, p. 126.
6. Lang, *Monotheism*, p. 127.
7. Lang, *Monotheism*, pp. 120-21.

resembles feudalism and classical slavery. Israel and Judah's economies are pre-capitalist. They are as dissimilar to modern capitalism as they are similar to it. Introducing 'capitalist' terminology to describe these ancient economies too easily leads to serious misconceptions about ownership, labor, distribution of goods and other key economic factors.[1] Lang's rent-capitalist description of the monarchical era economy is also inadequate because it has little to say about the role of the state in the economy's development.

J.A. Dearman[2] builds on Lang's work, but incorporates evidence of the monarchy's role in the economy. Analysing several passages primarily in Amos, Isaiah and Micah, Dearman reconstructs a pre-exilic economic system by which the national government acquired and redistributed goods and services primarily through a wealthy minority, largely comprised of various royal appointees.

Dearman assumes a process existed by which debtors gradually forfeited all their property, until they had only family members or themselves to sell.[3] He also assumes the failure of the judicial-political system to mitigate the harshness of indebtedness.[4] Furthermore, citing Assyrian practice,[5] Dearman argues that Israel's temples had lending and banking functions, as well as religious ones.[6] Money could be deposited at the shrine under the name of the deity and the depositor. The deposit apparently collected no interest, but it could be lent out at

1.    Several other scholars use 'capitalist' terminology to describe Judah's and Israel's economies in the monarchical period: for example, R.B.Y. Scott, *The Relevance of the Prophets* (New York: MacMillan, 1944), p. 30; H.J. Kraus, 'Die prophetische Botschaft gegen der soziale Unrecht Israels', *EvT* 15 (1955), p. 296; H.W. Wolff, *Joel and Amos* (Hermeneia; Philadelphia: Fortress Press, 1977), p. 69.

2.    Dearman, 'Property', pp. 385-97.

3.    Dearman's discussion of Amos 2.7c is convincing: 'a man and his father go into the same girl', refers to a debtor's daughter who becomes the sexual property of the creditor, father and son. Note also his argument that 2.8's 'wine' is exacted from the debtor ('Property', pp. 386-87).

4.    Dearman, 'Property', p. 386; cf. E.W. Davies, *Prophecy and Ethics: Isaiah and the Ethical Traditions of Israel* (JSOTSup, 16; Sheffield: JSOT Press, 1981), pp. 65-82, 93-102; K.W. Whitelam, *The Just King: Monarchical Judicial Authority in Ancient Israel* (JSOTSup, 12; Sheffield: JSOT Press, 1979), pp. 178-80.

5.    Cf. B. Menzel, *Assyrische Tempel*, I/2 (Studia Pohl; Rome: Biblical Institute Press, 1981); reviewed by J.N. Postgate in *JSS* 28 (1983), pp. 155-59; E. Neufeld, 'The Prohibition against Loans at Interest in Ancient Hebrew Laws', *HUCA* 26 (1955), pp. 376-83.

6.    Dearman, 'Property', p. 387.

interest, which was then paid to the depositor. The banking function helps explain Amos's critique of the worship centers of Israel: 'In the case of Amos 2.8, the garment taken in pledge and the wine exacted would be dedicated at the temple and thus removed from profane use. If goods were still technically the property of the debtor, they would no longer be so once deposited in the sacred center by the creditor'.[1] Indeed, '*part* of Amos's critique of worship centers (2.8; 3.14; 4.4-5; 5.4-5, 21-24; 7.17) comes from their involvement in what he sees as social crimes'[2] (emphasis in original).

Dearman offers no direct evidence that Judean cult centers served a banking function like that which Amos identifies in the North. However, Isaiah and Micah share with Amos a condemnation of the judicial-political system, because it expedited rather than hindered the expropriation and consolidation of land.

Amos 5.10-12 elaborates Israel's corrupt judicial system which failed to stop property loss. Isaiah and Micah also condemn the adminstrative-judicial system (Isa. 1.23; 3.14; 10.1-4; Mic. 3.1, 9) for assisting the large-scale accumulation of land, a social crime in its vast dimensions (Isa. 3.14; 5.8-10; Mic. 2.1-2, 9). Against Lang's view of a highly decentralized judicial system in Judah and Israel,[3] Dearman argues the crown appointed judges in regions throughout the realm. The Chronicler's report that Jehoshaphat sent judges to the fortified cities (2 Chron. 19.5) establishes a link between these officials, the military levy and the royal land grant system.[4]

Dearman cites 1 Sam. 8.11-17; 22.7; and Ezek. 46.16-17 as

---

1.  Dearman, 'Property', p. 387. Davies (*Prophecy and Ethics*, p. 68) suggests creditors might have been allowed to take usufruct of land taken in pledge. The pledge (even something other than land) could be used to the creditor's benefit as long as a loan was outstanding. This would provide incentive to lenders when usury was forbidden. Against Davies' reasoning, it should be noted that usury apparently was not forbidden in the monarchical era, if the classical prophets are at all reliable. However, whether Dearman or Davies is right, the point remains that creditors normally had control of the collateral and used it to their own profit. In those cases where debtors were unable to pay back the loan and reclaim the pledged property, ownership passed to the creditor (see Davies, *Prophecy and Ethics*, pp. 66-69).

2.  *Ibid.*

3.  Lang, *Monotheism*, p. 126.

4.  Dearman, 'Property', p. 391; Whitelam, *Just King*, pp. 185-206; Davies, *Prophecy and Ethics*, pp. 90-112; R. Knierim, 'Exod 18 und die Neuordnung der mosäischen Gerichtsbarkeit', *ZAW* 73 (1961), pp. 146-71.

evidence that the king had the right to make prebendal land grants.[1] If
Assyrian practice offers an analogy, several advantages came with
prebendal grants. Recipients were exempted from certain military and
corvée obligations, as well as certain taxes.[2] These perquisites gave
royal appointees 'both the opportunity and the working capital to
accumulate yet more property'.[3] Assyrian practice lends support to
Dearman's portrayal of Judah and Israel's administrative system.
Jakobson finds Assyrian royal appointees heavily involved in
economic transactions: These royal functionaries 'owned large
property and engaged on a big scale in various forms of economic
activity, including the advancement of very considerable sums of
money as loans'.[4]

Dearman calls monarchical Israel and Judah's economy a
'redistribution system'.[5] In such a system, the national government has
a central role in redistributing goods and services. In a pre-industrial
society the redistributional process is heavily dependent on a very
small wealthy class acting both as private citizens and royal
administrators. In Judah and Israel's case, the involvement of this
royal elite in regional affairs within the nations brought about the
deteriorating social conditions decried by the classical prophets.[6]

N.K. Gottwald also takes account of the critical social-economic
role of the crown and its appointees. He proposes a Marxian category,

1.    Cf. M. Weinfeld, 'The Covenant of Grant in the Old Testament and the
Ancient Near East', *JAOS* 90 (1970), pp. 184-203; Z. Ben-Barak, 'Meribaal and the
System of Land Grants in Ancient Israel', *Bib* 62 (1981), pp. 73-91; Davies,
*Prophecy and Ethics*, pp. 76-83; Whitelam, *Just King*, p. 173.

2.    Ben-Barak, 'Meribaal', pp. 73-75.

3.    Dearman, 'Property', p. 391.

4.    Jacobson, 'Empire', p. 281; cf. N.K. Gottwald's argument that Israel and
Judah's lending system was dominated by the crown and its local appointees
('Contemporary Studies of Social Class and Social Stratification and a Hypothesis
about Social Class in Monarchic Israel', Paper to the Sociology of the Monarchy
Seminar, AAR/SBL Annual Meeting, 1985).

5.    Dearman, 'Property', p. 393; Dearman apparently draws this terminology
from the work of economic anthropologist Karl Polanyi (cf. 'The Economy as
Instituted Process', in *Trade and Market in the Early Empires* [ed. K. Polanyi, C.
Arensberg, H.W. Pearson; Glencoe, IL: Free Press, 1957], p. 250).

6.    *Ibid.*

the Asiatic mode of production to describe Judah and Israel during the period of the monarchy.[1]

Three characteristics together distinguish the Asiatic mode of production from other modes of production.[2] First, land is not privately owned. Individual households and extended families operating communally may possess and use land, but ownership is vested in the state. State ownership may not be legally explicit, but is indicated in the state's right to collect taxes on village lands. Second, society is organized primarily around self-sufficient villages devoted to agriculture, herding and craftwork. Village and countryside are largely undifferentiated. Urban areas generally are not well developed. With little productive base of their own, they are heavily dependent upon surplus brought in from outerlying villages. Third, a highly centralized state plays a 'commanding social role'. The state extracts surplus from the villages in the form of (religiously legitimated) taxes. It impresses villagers for military service and state construction projects. A key characteristic of this mode of production is state construction of large public works—irrigation systems, administrative and religious buildings, defense works, central food storage facilities, and so forth.[3]

Gottwald is correct to classify monarchical Israel and Judah as instances of the Asiatic mode of production. The model is not completely satisfactory, however, in its description of land ownership. The crown's ownership of all land may well have been implied in its right to collect taxes and its exercise of authority on behalf of Yahweh, the true owner of all land. However, the crown did not have authority to seize land as it saw fit.[4] The Naboth's vineyard story shows the monarch constrained by customs protecting a patrimonial land tenure system. In the end, the king wins control of the land, but not without overcoming at least nominal impediments. Rather than indicating a single mode of production in which the crown had

1.  Gottwald, 'Hypothesis'.
2.  Gottwald, 'Hypothesis', pp. 12-13.
3.  Gottwald, 'Hypothesis', p. 13.
4.  Ben-Barak overstates the restraint of Israel's monarchs in seizing ancestral land, but his comment is probably accurate as a description of normal practice: 'it was not the practice in Israel to confiscate family estates from their owners, even if the king desired that particular tract of land' ('Meribaal', p. 80). The king did, however, have a great number of resources at his disposal by which to obtain the land by legal, if not ethical, means.

ownership of all land, the Naboth's vineyard story seems to indicate the existence of at least two competing modes: one in which the monarchy owned and controlled land, the other in which land was owned by the family, past, present and future.

The work of French anthropologist E. Terray[1] is illuminating. Terray identifies within any given pre-capitalist social formation 'the combination of at least two distinct modes of production, one of which is dominant and the other subordinate'.[2] The one or more subordinate modes of production exist within the dominant mode, but functionally support the dominant mode. Thus in monarchical Israel and Judah, for example, small-scale agriculture based on a notion of 'ancestral property' continued to exist within a monarchical system in which Yahweh (operating through the king) owned all land. The ancestral property system continued to exist, but was subordinate to the monarchical system. Though nominally protected by custom and statute, patrimonial land tenure could be overridden when it hindered rather than enhanced royal control. Patrimony continued as a 'legal fiction' in the monarchical period.[3]

## Land Ownership: A Clash of Systems

A. Alt[4] first articulated what became the standard scholarly reconstruction of land ownership in Israel and Judah.[5] Comparing Omri's

---

1. E. Terray, *Marxism and 'Primitive' Societies* (London: Monthly Review Press, 1972), pp. 95-186.

2. Terray, 'Marxism', p. 179.

3. Whitelam's comment is insightful in this regard: 'the fact that such a law as Lev. 25.23-28 (cf. Num. 36.7) had to be formulated implies that the legal fiction of the inalienability of Israelite land was, in actual practice, inoperative' (*Just King*, pp. 173-74).

4. A. Alt, 'Der Anteil der Königtum an der sozialen Entwicklung in den Reichen Israel und Juda', in *Kleine Schriften zur Geschichte des Volkes Israel* (ed. M. Noth; Munich: Beck, 1953), III, pp. 348-72.

5. Von Rad, 'The Promised Land and Yahweh's Land in the Hexateuch', in *Problem of the Hexateuch and Other Essays* (New York: McGraw Hill, 1966), pp. 79-93; R. de Vaux, *Ancient Israel* (New York: McGraw Hill, 1965), p. 164; T.N.D. Mettinger, *Solomonic State Officials: A Study of the Civil Government Officials of the Israelite Monarchy* (ConBOT, 5; Lund: Gleerup, 1971), p. 80; G. Buccellati, *Cities and Nations of Ancient Syria: An Essay on Political Institutions with Special Reference to Israelite Kingdoms* (Studi Semitici, 26; Rome: University of Rome, 1967).

purchase of the hill of Samaria from Shemer (1 Kgs 16.24) with Ahab's attempt to buy Naboth's vineyard (1 Kgs 21), Alt drew a distinction between 'Canaanite' and 'Israelite' conceptions of property.

In the tribal era, Alt said, rural Israelites held land as an inalienable trust for posterity. This ancestral property system contrasted with that of the urban Canaanites. The latter, more politically centralized and commerce oriented, understood land as a commodity. Not only was land traded and sold, it was also given as prebendal estates to loyal servants of the king. The 'Israelite' and 'Canaanite' property systems had little overlap in the tribal era since the two cultures remained largely separated.

The emergence of an Israelite monarchy, however, brought rural Israelite and urban Canaanite cultures together. In Davidic Judah, the 'Canaanite' political economy grew as the royal government grew. By the time of the classical prophets the conflict between the two systems of land tenure had reached crisis proportions.

This standard reconstruction rightly has been challenged and modified.[1] It is questionable to distinguish so clearly 'Canaanite' and 'Israelite' ethnic groups in the tribal era. Such a distinction is meaningless in monarchical Judah and Israel.[2] There is no evidence that Shemer (1 Kgs 16.24) was a Canaanite.[3] Additionally, the classical prophets do not question the basic legality of land acquisition by the rich.[4] The biblical writers do not question the legitimacy of land grants (cf. 1 Sam. 22.7; Ezek. 46.16-17).[5] The polemical description of the 'way of the king' in 1 Sam. 8.14 ('he will take the best of your fields...and give them to his servants') and Ezekiel's proscription against the monarch seizing 'the inheritance of the people' for land grants to the royal family (46.18) indicate that the monarchs did, in fact, seize ancestral property and redistribute it (cf. Mephibosheth: 2 Sam. 9; 16.1-4; 19.24-30).[6] The biblical evidence shows different types of land ownership legitimately existed

1. Whitelam, *Just King*, pp. 172-80; Davies, *Prophecy and Ethics*, pp. 65-90; Dearman, 'Property', pp. 389-91.

2. Cf. Dearman, 'Property', p. 390.

3. Whitelam, *Just King*, p. 173.

4. Davies, *Prophecy and Ethics*, p. 69.

5. Davies, *Prophecy and Ethics*, pp. 76-83; Whitelam, *Just King*, p. 173; Dearman, 'Property', pp. 390-91.

6. Whitelam, *Just King*; Dearman, 'Property'.

in monarchical Judah and Israel, but the Bible nowhere characterizes the difference as 'Canaanite' versus 'Israelite'.

The biblical literature does, however, identify a clash between traditional notions of ownership and actual practices of monarchs. The Naboth's vineyard story (1 Kgs 21) is a parable of just such a clash.

Though Welten sees vv. 1-20 as a unity,[1] most scholars identify a break between vv. 19a and 19b[2] and assign vv. 19b-29 to a deuteronomistic editor.[3] Miller notes the exceptionally full development of characters in the story as an indication of narrative embellishment and of a date of authorship considerably later than Ahab's reign.[4] It is difficult to date the final literary composition, but Rofé's suggestion that it has a post-exilic setting[5] is unnecessary and runs counter to most Kings scholarship. An original setting sometime during the monarchy is plausible.

The story likely has anti-monarchical roots,[6] dramatizing the clash between patrimonial land tenure and attempts by the monarchy to rationalize production by consolidating land and intensifying and specializing agriculture. The story could have first appeared in the North or the South and probably floated around both kingdoms in a variety of forms, all making the same general point. By the time the Deuteronomist uses the story, Ahab plays the royal villain's role. The story thus functions literarily in Kings as an anti-Northern rather than more broadly anti-monarchical parable.

The story's details clarify its character as a dramatization of

1. P. Welten, 'Naboths Weinberg (1 Kön. 21)', *EvT* 33 (1973), pp. 18-32; contra O. Steck (*Überlieferung und Zeitgeschichte in den Elia-Erzählungen* [WMANT, 26; Neukirchen–Vluyn: Neukirchener Verlag, 1968], pp. 32-77), who finds this section to be a composite, with Ahab and Jezebel strata.

2. A. Rofé, 'The Vineyard of Naboth: the Origin and Message of the Story', *VT* 38 (1988), pp. 89-104; Whitelam, *Just King*, p. 171; J.M. Miller, 'The Fall of the House of Ahab', *VT* 17 (1967), p. 311; Gray, *I and II Kings*, p. 436.

3. See previous note; note also R. Bohlen's argument (*Der Fall Nabot. Form, Hintergrund und Werdegang einer alttestamentlichen Erzählung (1 Kön. 21)* [Trier: Paulinus, 1978], pp. 304-305 n. 9) that a Chronicles-like appendix appears in vv. 27-29; cf. Rofé, 'Vineyard of Naboth', p. 95.

4. Cf. Welten, 'Naboths Weinberg', p. 30.

5. Rofé, 'Vineyard of Naboth', pp. 97-104.

6. Rofé ('Vineyard of Naboth', p. 91) characterizes the story as a contrast which not only addresses the difference between rich and poor, but also between traditional society and 'a kind of plutocracy'.

conflicting political economies. Its intimate descriptions of Ahab and Naboth's conversation, Ahab's brooding and Jezebel's diabolical maneuvering tell of considerable narrative embellishment, a clue that the story is more typical than factual.[1]

Ahab and Naboth's conversation about the vineyard introduces the tension which motivates the plot. At issue is a vineyard next to the king's residence. Ahab's offer is reasonable and fair. The king wants the vineyard, not because it is high quality land or because he wants to cheat Naboth out of anything. In fact, Ahab offers Naboth a better vineyard elsewhere, at Naboth's choosing. The monarch is willing to pay money if a trade does not suit Naboth. Unlike Nathan's parable (2 Sam. 12), this story does not raise—at least not initially—the problem of royal greed. The king proposes a reasonable land trade, a small-scale rationalization of production which would benefit Naboth and the king. According to the narrative, the vineyard was desirable strictly because it was close to the palace.

From the king's perspective, the land trade made sense. It moved the productive operation closer to the products' final destination.

For Naboth, the issue is not one of fair compensation.[2] He expresses no opinion about the fairness of the king's offer. The very idea of trading ancestral property offends his moral sensibilities. The tension has nothing to do with the king's unfair treatment of a subject. It is rather the result of a conflict between the king's desire for more efficient and personally beneficial production and the vineyard owner's notion that the land could not be transferred.[3]

Ahab's reasoning is sound. Economically, the land swap would benefit the king and Naboth. However, greater economic efficiency could be gained only at the expense of ancestral property. For Naboth, no choice existed. Patrimonial land tenure, at least as it applied to this vineyard, was part of the moral order established by Yahweh.

The Naboth's vineyard story illustrates a clash between different notions of land use and ownership. Naboth defends an ancestral pro-

---

1. Cf. E. Würthwein, 'Naboth-Novelle und Elia-Wort', *ZTK* 75 (1978), pp. 375-97, 385-86 n. 3. Cf. H. Gressmann, *Die älteste Geschichtsschreibung und Prophetie Israels* (Göttingen: Vandenhoeck & Ruprecht, 1921), p. 272.

2. See Jones, *1 and 2 Kings*, p. 353.

3. Contra Whitelam (*Just King*, p. 173), who finds 'no indication in this text that Naboth could not sell the vineyard if he so wished'. See also his comments on p. 175.

perty system which guarantees long-term stability of the productive process. Not surprisingly, the land at issue is a vineyard, requiring long-term investments of capital and labor. Ahab assumes that land can and should be transferred if such a transfer rationalizes production. Probably with a good deal of literary sarcasm,[1] the Deuteronomist reports that the king wants to plant herbs, a crop requiring only short-term investment.

The conflict between differing notions of land use and ownership evident in the Naboth's vineyard story has its roots in the emergence of a monarchy in Israel.

In premonarchical Israel, the 'ancestral property' system offered the chief social control by which long-term stability of land ownership and continuity of the workforce was safeguarded. Kinship ties allowed agricultural production in small-scale units to flourish, supplemented by such farming techniques as terracing, which occasionally required substantial labor cooperation and well developed trade mechanisms. The social mechanisms which allowed this complex agriculture to exist in premonarchical Israel tended to generate greater social integration and centralization of political authority, which in turn further developed the agricultural system. This dialectical growth of Israel's productive system and political institutions eventually led to the establishment of a monarchical state.

The monarchy offered a different set of institutions and customs by which to ensure stability and development of productive processes. A royal theology which identified the monarch as Yahweh's earthly vicar gave a new slant to the probably much older belief that Yahweh was true owner of all Israelite land. The concept of 'ancestral property' continued to exist in North and South throughout the period of the monarchy. Monarchical control meant not the end of ancestral property, but the cooptation of it. 'Ownership' continued to reside nominally in the family, but the monarchy exercised the rights of ownership by exacting an annual tax on the productive yield of the land. The two systems of ownership coexisted, but sometimes came into conflict.

### Summary Remarks

Throughout the period of the monarchy, relatively small-scale, house-

1. Rofé, 'Vineyard of Naboth', p. 90.

hold-unit agriculture was the dominant form of production in Judah. Such a productive base required social institutions and customs which spread risk and discouraged concentration of land ownership. Population pressures alone would have undermined this system.

From the premonarchical era on, small-scale agriculture was supplemented by large-scale operations such as terrace farming. This complex agriculture fueled the development of the monarchy. The monarchy, in turn, contributed to further development of this complex agriculture. The (actually rather typical) irony is that the monarchical system came into conflict with the social institutions out of which it had grown—those mechanisms which had ensured the long-term stability of productive means and labor power. The conflict was expressed in the clash between the patrimonial system which discouraged land consolidation and the monarchy's (probably not always deliberate) tendency to rationalize production by consolidating and specializing agriculture according to principles of regional comparative advantage.

The conflict probably was seldom explicit. Patrimonial claims, as a rule, were respected. Yet the royal house exercised the right of eminent domain on behalf of Yahweh. Its actual ownership of all land was expressed in its right to tax. Its commanding social role was expressed in its right to impress workers for state ventures. As long as the interests of the monarchical class were served by taxes and impressment, the legal fiction of ancestral property was preserved.

In monarchical Judah, state ownership of all land was the practical reality. With the exception of crown lands (of which there is little mention in the Bible), however, land ownership was most often conceived in terms of ancestral property. 'Ancestral property' described a partial reality. Royal theology completed the picture: the king was the vicar of Yahweh, true owner of all Israel's land.

Monarchy- and kinship-based social institutions always made an unstable mix. But several factors made the legal fiction of 'ancestral property' difficult to maintain.

Judah's monarchs may well have tried their hand at large-scale economic planning such as that which Chaney and Rainey see in 2 Chron. 26.10. But even if they had not, pressures introduced by the monarchy would have worked to change the nature of production.

The monarchy transformed production at several points. It interrupted the productive process itself by impressing able-bodied

men and women for royal 'public works' projects. It drafted men for
military service. Royal impressments depleted the labor supply, making production even more difficult. At the same time, the royal house
exacted an annual production tax of at least ten percent. That requirement fueled a fundamental change in production. A diversified,
subsistence oriented agriculture necessarily was shifted toward producing enough surplus to meet royal obligations. Greater surplus
production required greater specialization. The ecology of Palestine
and the level of technological development in the monarchical era,
however, made surplus production through greater specialization a
highly risky strategy. The labor demands of the monarchy only
exacerbated the problem many farmers faced in producing enough
surplus to meet tax obligations.

An increasingly well developed lending system, which included the
option of debt slavery, kept many land holding farmers afloat under
these difficult conditions, but borrowing only delayed the inevitable
for many. The lending system became a chief mechanism by which
land was alienated from small farmers and accumulated by the
wealthy.

Dearman has noted that royal officials were blamed for social dislo-
cations caused by the productive system under the monarchy.[1]
Whitelam, while finding no direct evidence that local officials were
crown employees, has noted that they obviously acceded to the wishes
of the crown in important decisions and actions.[2] Whatever their for-
mal status with the royal house, local officials and wealthy citizens
found their interests closely bound with royal interests. The royal
house benefited from increased production through agricultural
specialization, and wealthy creditors and merchants benefited from
royal pressures on small farmers.[3]

The close identification of upper class and royal interests makes it
difficult to classify monarchical Judah's economy as either a 'royal
command economy' or a 'private free market economy'. Dearman's
description is very close to the mark: the royal government had a

---

1. Dearman, 'Property'.
2. Whitelam, *Just King*, p. 180.
3. Cf. Davies, *Prophecy and Ethics*, p. 80. Alt ('Micha 2,1-5', *KS*, III, pp.
373-81) observes that prophets' threats were not usually leveled directly at the king
but at the upper classes whose elevated position in society was due to their close
association with the king (cf. also 'Der Anteil', *KS*, III, pp. 364-65).

central role in receiving and redistributing goods, but the redistributional process relied heavily on a small wealthy class acting both as private citizens and royal administrators.

What can be said is that land ownership became more and more concentrated as the monarchical era progressed, though production units remained small-scale. Increasing numbers of farmers apparently worked land owned by someone else. The potential existed for widespread social crisis as the process of land consolidation continued. The crisis first came to a head with the division of the unified kingdom into Northern and Southern petty states. It remained largely dormant, however, until the advent of Assyrian imperial rule in Palestine. Imperial obligations would bring the contradictions of supporting a monarchy to the surface, increasing popular discontent with the Davidic house. Out of such conditions deuteronomic theology would arise. For pre-Assyrian Judah, the crisis was yet to come, but the roots of the crisis reached to the very beginning of the monarchical state.

Chapter 2

## THE PRE-ASSYRIAN ERA: CULT REFORM AND ROYAL POWER

The years between the division of the kingdom and Jerusalem's vassalage to Assyria generally were stable ones for Judah. The economic and social tensions which came with the establishment of a monarchical state continued to exist in this period, but they did not come to a head in such a way as to challenge fundamentally the monarchical system. Social institutions continued to grow and adapt, but changes usually were gradual.

Judah's cultic life in the pre-Assyrian era reflected the dynamic but basically stable social environment. Yet, as social factors evolved, religious understandings evolved. Social developments in that relatively stable time prepared the way for the sweeping changes of the Assyrian era, especially cult reforms ignited by the deuteronomic movement. Understanding the official cult in pre-Assyrian Judah is key to understanding deuteronomic reform in the Assyrian era. A clear picture of pre-Assyrian cult practice shows what led to the reform and highlights the radical nature of many of its proposals.

This chapter examines pre-Assyrian reforms of the official Judean cult. It opens with a literary overview of the Deuteronomist's evaluations of Judean kings from Rehoboam to Ahaz. Detailed analysis of Ahaz's reforms follows in the next chapter. The Deuteronomist's formulaic evaluation of Ahaz is discussed in this chapter, because it views Ahaz as the end of an era. Ahaz brought Judah to the crisis which Hezekiah's proto-deuteronomic reform would begin to resolve.

A series of sections on cult reforms and other pertinent royal policies follows the overview of regnal evaluations through Ahaz. The intention of this chapter is to paint a broad picture of the First Temple cult prior to the ascension of the deuteronomists in the Assyrian era. Studies in this chapter will address a few royal policies, such as forced labor, which are not directly related to the cult. It is important to consider these policies, however, because they are key factors in the social world which spawned deuteronomism.

### Evaluations, Rehoboam to Ahaz

The Deuteronomist's evaluations of Judean kings build toward an initial climax in the reign of Hezekiah. The treatments of Manasseh, Amon and Josiah shift in content and vocabulary, indicating that Judah enters a new historical phase after Hezekiah. The evaluations of the final four kings of Judah are patterned on pre-Hezekiah formulations, offering a subtle but important twist meant to explain the disaster of 586.[1] The form and content of the regnal evaluations periodize the history of the Judean monarchy into three major phases: Rehoboam to Hezekiah, Manasseh to Josiah and Jehoahaz to Zedekiah. Although it is not certain that this schema corresponds to redactional layering, it does fix critical moments in the historical self-consciousness of the deuteronomists.

The Deuteronomist's evaluations of Judean kings from Rehoboam through Hezekiah present a mostly positive view of the Davidic dynasty. Judgment of the monarchy in this period is mixed, however. Evaluations of particular kings always are qualified, blunting the force of the initial accusation or praise. Additionally, the history of the monarchy up to Hezekiah is bracketed by accounts of Judah under Rehoboam and Ahaz, each of which draws comparison with the dispossessed Canaanites. Viewed as a whole, regnal evaluations before Hezekiah serve the double purpose of exposing improper cultic practice and affirming Yahweh's eternal election of the Davidic dynasty.

A pattern emerges from the evaluations of the nine kings between Rehoboam and Ahaz. Of these kings, only three are judged negatively (1 Kgs 15.3-4; 2 Kgs 8.18-19, 27). Six are judged positively (1 Kgs 15.11-14; 22.43-44; 2 Kgs 12.3-4; 14.3-4; 15.3-4, 34-35). The Deuteronomist finds a common thread in the reigns of all six good kings: in all of them, 'the high places were not removed'. Maintaining the high places might detract from a king's otherwise solid reputation, but it was not enough to bring condemnation—a Judean king could keep the high places intact and still 'do right in the eyes of Yahweh', according to the Deuteronomist. In fact, among the nine kings

---

1. See the discussion below (Chapter 5) concerning the 'Manasseh alone' explanation of the exile.

between Rehoboam and Ahaz, the Deuteronomist mentions high place worship only in connection with those monarchs who 'did right in the eyes of Yahweh'.

Three kings 'did evil' in this period. Just as the Deuteronomist's good words for the good kings of this era are always qualified by a high place reminder, so bad words for bad kings are buffered by a reference to the eternal election of David's house. Two of the three negative summaries claim Yahweh's promise of an everlasting Davidic 'lamp'[1] or 'yoke'[2] in Jerusalem (1 Kgs 15.4; 2 Kgs 8.19). In the case of the third bad king, Ahaziah (2 Kgs 8.27), history kept the Deuteronomist from using the 'eternal lamp' formula. When the Omride queen Athaliah seized the Jerusalem throne after Ahaziah's murder in the Jehu coup, the flame on the Davidic lamp undeniably sputtered and died for a while.

To summarize, the Deuteronomist finds twice as many good kings as bad kings between Rehoboam and Ahaz. Continuing high place worship is mentioned only and always in connection with good kings. The divinely lit 'lamp in Jerusalem' appears only in connection with bad kings. The historical content of the passage prevents mention of the 'lamp' in the case of the bad king Ahaziah. From these observations, the following pattern emerges:

good king　+　high place worship
evil king　+　eternal lamp

The good kings of this period fail only to abolish high places. The bad kings prove the validity of Davidic election. Both kinds of evaluation highlight Yahweh's commitment to the dynasty and desire to change the cultic status quo, particularly by getting rid of the high places.

Athaliah's rule marks a formulaic shift in the evaluations of these nine kings. First, different verbs introduce the evaluations before and after Athaliah. With one exception, those before Athaliah begin with *wayyēlek*, 'and he walked...' (1 Kgs 15.3; 22.43; 2 Kgs 8.18, 27).[3]

---

1. Noth, *Könige*, p. 261; A.R. Johnson, *Sacral Kingship in Ancient Israel* (Cardiff: University of Wales Press, 1955), p. 1; Jones, *1 and 2 Kings*, p. 245.

2. P.D. Hanson, 'The Song of Heshbon and David's Nir', *HTR* 61 (1968), pp. 297-320.

3. Asa (1 Kgs 15.14) breaks the pattern. Though other kings are judged favorably, Asa joins Hezekiah and Josiah as the truly great reformers in the Deuteronomist's reckoning of history. Unsurprisingly, therefore, his evaluation is distinctive.

Those after Athaliah begin with *wayya'aś*, 'and he did. . . '

Second, the notices about continued high place worship vary in their phrasing. After Athaliah, they are identical to one another and all begin with the restrictive adverb *raq*, 'only', or 'yet' (2 Kgs 12.4; 14.4; 15.4, 35*)*. The two references pre-Athaliah, however, vary in this regard. The Asa summary begins with the waw-adversative, *wᵉhabbāmôt*, 'but the high places. . . ' (1 Kgs 15.14). The reference here is much abbreviated compared to the formula found elsewhere. The normal wording ('yet the high places were not removed, the people continued sacrificing and burning incense in the high places') is shortened to a three-word statement, *wᵉhabbāmôt lōʾ sārû*, 'but the high places were not removed'. The reference to high place worship in Jehoshaphat's reign (1 Kgs 22.43) departs from the post-Athaliah formula by using the restrictive adverb *'ak* in the place of *raq* to introduce the formula.

Third, the evaluations after Athaliah are less flexible than those before. The same kind of stereotypical rigidity Nelson sees in the Jehoahaz through Zedekiah summaries[1] appears also in the evaluations after Athaliah from Joash to Jotham. As noted above, the high place references here are repeated verbatim. In fact, these four evaluations show little structural variation. Evaluations pre-Athaliah show considerable diversity of phrasing and structure in contrast to the relatively tight basic pattern after Athaliah, as follows:

> and he did right in the eyes of Yahweh according to everything his father
> X did; yet the high places were not removed. The people continued
> sacrificing and burning incense in the high places.[2]

Finally, after Athaliah, the status of the monarchy is diminished. Asa (1 Kgs 15.11) and, by implication, Jehoshaphat (22.43) stand in the tradition of David. The four kings who follow Athaliah also do 'right in the eyes of Yahweh; however, not like David' (2 Kgs 14.3). This qualification is stated explicitly only for Amaziah, but the further

---

1. Nelson, *Double Redaction*, pp. 38-42.
2. Since Athaliah immediately preceded Joash on the throne, the adverbial phrase, 'according to everything his father did', does not appear in his evaluation. In its place, the Deuteronomist substitutes, 'all his days while Jehoiada the priest instructed him' (2 Kgs 12.3). The Amaziah story inserts, also following the statement that 'he did right in the eyes of Yahweh', a qualification that this righteousness was 'however not like David' (2 Kgs 14.3). Both Amaziah's and Jotham's comparisons to their fathers add *'āśâ*, 'he did', at the end.

notice that he and his two successors acted, 'according to everything his father X did', implicates all four kings. The Athaliah affair lowers the house of David a notch. The phrasing and structure of the regnal summaries reflect the changed character of the restored monarchy: After Athaliah, Davidic rule exhibited a mediocre sameness, not wicked, but short of the monarchy's earlier glory.

To recapitulate these observations, evaluations of the nine kings between Rehoboam and Ahaz follow a regular pattern by which continued high place worship qualifies good reigns, while divine election, symbolized as an everlasting 'lamp' in Jerusalem, redeems bad reigns. Athaliah's brief interruption of Davidic rule marks a noticeable shift in the form and language of regnal evaluations. This change corresponds to an unelaborated judgment that the four monarchs after Athaliah suffered a diminished capacity for righteousness. Patterns noted in the evaluations of these nine kings assist the reading of the Rehoboam and Ahaz narratives accounts which bracket this period.

Rehoboam's evaluation is disjointed and complicated by the Deuteronomist's larger concern to reflect theologically on the division of the kingdom. Though extremely harsh language describes Judah's behavior under this king (1 Kgs 14.22-24), the Deuteronomist distances Rehoboam from responsibility for the tragic state of affairs. Evaluation of his reign actually begins in 1 Kgs 11.1, as follows: 'Now king Solomon loved many foreign women. . .'. Divine words to Solomon (vv. 11-13) and Jeroboam (vv. 31b-39) explain Rehoboam's greatest political disaster, the secession of the North, as Yahweh's judgment against Solomon. Verse 36 introduces the promise of an eternal 'lamp in Jerusalem', terminology subsequently to be coupled with negative evaluations of kings. Summary remarks on Rehoboam's reign (14.22-24) begin with a variation on the standard negative formula, as follows: 'and Judah did evil in the eyes of Yahweh' (v. 22a). The Septuagint and the Chronicler's corrections to make Rehoboam the subject mistakenly narrow the historical scope of the Deuteronomist's judgment here.[1] Not only is the normal subject of the formula expanded from king to nation, but the formula itself is expanded and

1. Cf. Hoffmann, *Reform*, p. 75; Spieckermann, *Assur*, p. 190 n. 75; H. Gressmann, *Die Anfange Israels* (SAT, 2.1; Göttingen: Vandenhoeck & Ruprecht, 1922), p. 249; Jepsen, *Die Quellen*, p. 6; differently Benzinger, *Könige*, p. 98; Noth, *Könige*, I, p. 323; E. Würthwein, *Das Erste Buch der Könige* (ATD, 11.1; Göttingen: Vandenhoeck & Ruprecht, 1977), p. 181.

the stakes raised with language reserved for the most notorious apostate behavior: 'and they provoked (Yahweh) to jealousy more than everything their ancestors did, by the sins they committed' (v. 22b).

To this point, the disjointed Rehoboam account contains, in slightly varied form, both elements of the negative pattern of evaluation. The Deuteronomist judges the reign 'evil in the eyes of Yahweh', but introduces the promise of an everlasting 'lamp in Jerusalem'. Verse 23 introduces a key element in the subsequent good king pattern, reporting 'they also built high places'. Once again, the normal language is changed and supplemented, its impact heightened by the following elaboration: 'and they built sacred poles and asherahs on every high hill and under every green tree'. Thus Rehoboam's reign contains, in stronger measure, both the evil of the bad kings and the shortcomings of the good kings in the period to follow.

Verse 24a notes the presence of the cult prostitute in the land, setting the stage for the righteous cult reform of Asa (1 Kgs 15.12; see also 22.47).[1] The final assertion that 'they acted according to all the abominations of the nations whom Yahweh dispossessed before the Israelites', characterizes this era as one of Judah's most notorious. Not until the account of Ahaz's rule (2 Kgs 16.3) does this language reappear.

The Ahaz narrative (2 Kgs 16) closes the period opened by the Rehoboam account. As in Rehoboam's case, the Ahaz evaluative summary (vv. 2a-4) mixes elements of the positive/negative pattern. Its phrasing builds to a climax. It begins by contrasting Ahaz's rule with those of his immediate predecessors. It builds by comparing his rule to the period of Omride influence which ended with Athaliah. It climaxes by connecting Ahaz's rule with Rehoboam's, thus comparing the situation under Ahaz to the division of the kingdom. The untypical phrasing of v. 2b,[2] 'and he did not do right in the eyes of Yahweh', makes a direct contrast to Ahaz's four immediate predecessors, all of whom 'did right in the eyes of Yahweh'. Verse 3a, 'and he walked in the way of the kings of Israel', compares Ahaz with the Southern kings Jehoram (2 Kgs 8.18) and Ahaziah (2 Kgs 8.27), whose Northern connections resulted in the temporary cessation of Davidic rule. Verse 3b's comparison of Ahaz's policy with 'the abomination of

---

1.  Cf. Hoffmann, *Reform*, pp. 74, 76.
2.  With the exception of Abijam (1 Kgs 15.3), all bad Judean kings before Ahaz 'did evil in the eyes of Yahweh'. Abijam 'walked in all the sins of his father'.

the nations whom Yahweh drove out before the Israelites' finds its only precedent in the 1 Kgs 14.24 evaluation of Rehoboam's reign. The language used to evaluate Ahaz thus builds a progressively damaging case: he is not like his good though mediocre immediate predecessors; he is like the Omride Judean kings who nearly ended Davidic rule in Judah, and he is *personally* implicated in the worst behavior of the Rehoboam era.

A number of parallels may be drawn between the evaluations of Rehoboam and Ahaz. The statement that Ahaz 'even made his son pass through the fire' (v. 3b) describes personal behavior unprecedented in the Deuteronomistic History for a Judean king. Structurally, however, it mirrors the description in 1 Kgs 14.24a which speaks of Rehoboam's reign as a time when 'even the cult prostitute existed in the land'. In each case, a brief $w^e gam$ clause,[1] describing a particularly loathsome cult practice, introduces a formula comparing Judah to the peoples dispossessed before Israel.

A key difference between these two passages is the latter's emphasis upon the personal involvement of the king. The Ahaz evaluation goes on to describe the king's participation in high place worship, 'and he sacrificed and burned incense in the high places' (v. 4). The Deuteronomist so accuses no other monarch of the First Temple period. The people's sinfulness under Rehoboam becomes the king's personal behavior under Ahaz.

The concluding judgment against Ahaz brings the narrative full circle back to Rehoboam's reign. Verse 4 says Ahaz sacrificed and burned incense 'on the hills and under every green tree'. Such terminology appears in a regnal evaluation only here and in 1 Kgs 14.23, describing high place worship during Rehoboam's reign. In the former case, 'they' built high places and stocked them with pillars and asherahs 'on every high hill and under every green tree'. In the latter case, 'he' worshiped in the high places and 'on the hills and under every green tree'. Again, the very similar, untypical phrasing makes a comparison and a contrast. Ahaz's reign is like Rehoboam's, except Ahaz is personally implicated in the worst cultic abominations.

Finally, in their concluding remarks, the summary evaluations of Rehoboam and Ahaz mirror one another chiastically, as follows:

---

1.    See Hoffmann, *Reform*, pp. 74, 76-77, esp. 76 n. 17.

a   high places. . . every high hill and every green tree
b   and even the cult prostitute. . . like all abominations (1 Kgs 14.23-24)

b′  and even son through fire. . . like the abominations
a′  high places. . . on the hills and every green tree (2 Kgs 16.3-4)

The chiasm functions to bracket the entire history of the divided monarchy through Ahaz, passing a negative overall judgment on the era and displaying a progression in the monarchy's direct accountability for criminal cult practices.

A variety of literary techniques present Judah's history from Rehoboam to Ahaz as a distinct unit in the Deuteronomistic History. The Deuteronomist's judgment of Rehoboam's rule foreshadows much of what follows, while the language describing Ahaz brings the story full circle back to the kingdom's division. Key themes and patterns which characterize the intervening period, such as the eternal lamp in Jerusalem and the good kings who fail to end high place worship, disappear outside this era bracketed by Rehoboam and Ahaz. The unit reveals an unfortunate historical progression, with good kings becoming lackluster in their righteousness and Ahaz personally embodying everything wrong about Davidic monarchs before him. In the Deuteronomist's estimation, Ahaz brought Judah to a crisis comparable only to that which followed the death of Solomon.

For the Deuteronomist, an era ended with Ahaz. The policies of Ahaz brought Judah to the crossroads. In retrospect, the history of Davidic rule since Solomon had been leading in the disastrous direction finally taken by Ahaz. The problem had been present with all the monarchs before Ahaz. Even the good kings failed to be good enough. Even the bad kings could not be bad enough to extinguish the 'eternal lamp' promised David. But something changed with Ahaz. The problem is focused and personalized. A focused and personalized problem requires a focused and personalized solution. An extraordinarily evil monarch calls for an extraordinarily good one. An utterly corrupt era requires a radical break with the past.

Hezekiah and deuteronomic reform offer Judah its only hope.

### Rehoboam

Rehoboam was not a cult reformer. The cultic system he inherited from his father Solomon was essentially the same system he bequeathed to his son Abijam. Rehoboam is important in Judah's cult

history, not so much for what he did, as for where he fits into the
deuteronomistic account of Judah's history under the Davidic kings.
The Deuteronomist telescopes First Temple cult history before
Hezekiah and places the summarized, stereotyped description in the
reign of Rehoboam at beginning of the divided kingdom. The
Chronicler expands, excises and rearranges the Deuteronomist's
Rehoboam narrative in generally predictable ways, adding little reli-
able and significant information about Rehoboam's cult policy.

The Deuteronomist and the Chronicler have different theological
perspectives on Rehoboam, but they share a common goal: their
narratives both begin to set the stage for Hezekiah's reform. The
Rehoboam narratives give the reader information about the First
Temple cult necessary to understand deuteronomic reform under
Hezekiah.

Most importantly, the Deuteronomist introduces the stereotypical
formula by which sanctuaries are condemned in Kings. The
Rehoboam narrative therefore offers a good opportunity to explore
the archaeological and biblical evidence on highplaces.

Besides high place worship, only one other cultic practice is singled
out in the Deuteronomist's Rehoboam narrative: 'and also the cult
prostitute was in the land' (14.24a). Cult prostitution apparently was a
constant feature of First Temple cult practice throughout the monarchy. The Deuteronomist reports a purge of cult prostitutes by Asa
(1 Kgs 15.12), by his son Jehoshaphat (22.47) and finally by Josiah
(2 Kgs 23.7). Further comments on cult prostitution in Judah will
come in my discussion of Asa's reform.

The most important royal institution in Rehoboam's reign had no
direct relationship to the cult. Problems with the royal forced-labor
levy led to the split of the David–Solomon United Kingdom. Forced
labor played an important role in the course of Judah's economic
development during the period of the monarchs. It was an important
symbol of royal authority. In Rehoboam's case, it was the rallying
point for anti-monarchical forces in the North. In the broader history
of monarchical Judah, forced labor helped create the social conditions
which bred classical prophecy and deuteronomic theology. For these
reasons, my comments on Rehoboam include a discussion of state-run
forced labor in Judah.

*1 Kings 14.21-24*

Most commentators have agreed that 1 Kgs 14.21-24 is a deuteronomic rewrite of an earlier annalistic source.[1] Major themes and
language are classic to the Deuteronomist. From Kittel[2] on, however,
commentators have assumed that real historical information appears in
vv. 21, 23 and 24a. Recently, Hoffmann has questioned that assumption, arguing instead that the 'source material' is deuteronomistic
composition describing the overall cult history of the early monarchy.[3] Functionally, the description of the Rehoboam era cult corresponds to 1 Kgs 12.26-33 which describes Jeroboam's cult crimes.[4]
The Rehoboam passage identifies a 'sin of the South' which corresponds to the 'sin of the North'. Spieckermann draws the same conclusion, relating the Rehoboam passage to the treatise on the fall of the
North (2 Kgs 17.9-11).[5]

Hoffmann and Spieckermann are right. The cultic material in the
Deuteronomist's evaluation of Rehoboam is not from annalistic material or from another pre-deuteronomistic source. The Deuteronomist's description of cult practice in Rehoboam's Judah is a general
summary of non-deuteronomic cult practice throughout the history of
the Judean monarchy. The Deuteronomist states it explicitly, deviating
from the normal evaluation formula and identifying 'Judah' rather
than the king as the subject of these cultic violations.[6] The Rehoboam
cult material says a lot about normal First Temple practice, but offers
nothing which is distinctive about Rehoboam's cult policy.

The other important literary-critical issue in the passage is posed by
v. 24. The verse ends with a clearly deuteronomic formulation, 'and
they acted according to all the abominations of the nations whom

---

1.   R. Kittel, *Die Bücher der Könige* (HKAT; Göttingen: Vandenhoeck &
Ruprecht, 1900), pp. 120-21; Spieckermann, *Assur*, pp. 190-92.
2.   *Ibid.*
3.   Hoffmann, *Reform*, p. 77.
4.   'Vielmehr bietet dieser Abschnitt die grundsätzliche Exposition der Kult-
sünden des Südreiches' (Hoffmann, *ibid.*). Cf. Jepsen, *Quellen*, p. 60.
5.   Spieckermann, *Assur*, p. 191: 'Für Leser, die Ohren haben zu hören,
besagen 14.22f: Was beim Nordreich ins Verderben geführt hat, wird im Südreich
kaum andere Konsequenz'.
6.   The Septuagint's substitution of 'Rehoboam' for 'Judah' is a *lectio facilior*.
Cf. Gressmann, *Anfange*, p. 249; Jepsen, *Quellen*, p. 6; Hoffmann, *Reform*, p. 74;
Spieckermann, *Assur*, p. 190 n. 75.

Yahweh dispossessed before the Israelites'.[1] It begins by introducing cult prostitution, a violation the Deuteronomist associates only with Judah (15.12; 22.47; 2 Kgs 23.7). Verse 24a is usually taken as a gloss.[2] The $w^egam$ construction at the beginning of the verse suggests this is additional material.[3] The typical scholarly treatment sees v. 14a as a back-reading of the Asa reform notice (1 Kgs 15.12a) which is taken to be historically reliable.[4] Spieckermann[5] and Hoffmann[6] agree that 14.24a and 15.12a are connected. They argue, however, that neither verse quotes an annalistic source. The Rehoboam account sets up the Asa (and Jehoshaphat) reform, but the Asa reform is itself a deuteronomistic creation. For Spieckermann, the Asa–Jehoshaphat purge of cult prostitutes foreshadows the ultimate deuteronomic reform in the Josianic age.

Whatever the Deuteronomist's reasons were for mentioning cult prostitution, Spieckermann and Hoffmann are right about the historical value of 1 Kgs 14.24a and 15.12a. These passages stand or fall together. Since 14.21-24 generally is a telescoped summary of monarchical era cult history, it is likely that cult prostitution is introduced here because it was a normal feature of the First Temple cult eventually purged by deuteronomic reform. The Deuteronomist's assertion that Asa expelled the cult prostitute is called into question by Jehoshaphat's and finally Josiah's purge of cult prostitutes. It is possible that Asa and Jehoshaphat attempted a purge with limited success, but that cult prostitution remained a constant feature of the non-deuteronomic royal cult throughout the monarchical period.

*2 Chronicles 10.1–12.16*

The Chronicler follows the Deuteronomist in most details of Rehoboam's reign. The Chronicler's account of the kingdom's division (2 Chron. 10.1–11.4) repeats nearly verbatim the Kings *Vorlage*

---

1. Hoffmann (*Reform*, p. 74) notes that v. 24b picks up on v. 22 and rounds out the overall deuteronomic evaluation of Rehoboam. Spieckermann (*Assur*, p. 191) attributes v. 24b to a late deuteronomic redactor who took it verbatim from the description of Manasseh's cult violations in 2 Kgs 21.2b.

2. Noth, *Könige*, p. 330; Würthwein, *Erste Könige*, pp. 182-83; Spieckermann, *Assur*, p. 192.

3. Spieckermann, *Assur*, p. 192; Hoffman, *Reform*, p. 74.

4. Noth, *Könige*, p. 330; Würthwein, *Erste Könige*, pp. 182-83.

5. Spieckermann, *Assur*, p. 192.

6. Hoffmann, *Reform*, p. 77.

(1 Kgs 12.1-24), excising only the reference to Jeroboam's selection as king of the North (1 Kgs 12.20) and rephrasing the opening words of Shemaiah's prophecy (2 Chron. 11.3 = 1 Kgs 12.23). However, the overall literary impact of the kingdom's division is different in Chronicles than in Kings because, unlike the Deuteronomist, the Chronicler puts none of the blame on Solomon.

The deletion of Jeroboam's coronation (1 Kgs 12.20) is consistent with the Chronicler's focus on Judean monarchical history. More importantly, however, the cut allows the Chronicler to avoid confusion later in the narrative. The deleted Kings passage ends with the remark, 'none followed the house of David except the tribe of Judah alone'. 2 Chron. 11.13-17, however, describes a mass exodus of priests and levites from Israel to Judah immediately after the secession of the North. By removing the Kings passage, the Chronicler makes the Rehoboam narrative flow more smoothly.

Besides a couple of insignificant variations from the Kings narrative, the Chronicler also rephrases, to the consternation of modern critics, the opening words of Shemaiah's prophecy. In Kings the prophet is told to address Rehoboam and 'all the house of Judah and Benjamin and the rest of the people' (1 Kgs 12.23). In Chronicles the prophet addresses Rehoboam and 'all Israel in Judah and Benjamin' (2 Chron. 11.3). Von Rad[1] has argued from this verse that the Chronicler now finds 'true Israel' exclusively in the South. Japhet[2] has shown the weakness of von Rad's argument. The problem comes into focus a few verses later (v. 13) when 'all Israel' is used clearly to refer to the Northern tribes (cf. also 10.1, 16; 13.15). Another alternative is that 11.3 refers to a group of Northern émigrés now residing in Judah. This is possible, but the Chronicler elsewhere uses 'Israel', even 'all Israel' (2 Chron. 28.23), to refer to monarchical Judah (2 Chron. 15.17; 19.8; 20.29; 23.2; 24.6, 16).[3] In fact, the Chronicler uses 'all Israel' to refer to Rehoboam's Judah (12.1). So 'all Israel in Judah and Benjamin' in 11.3 could refer to Judah.

The context of the verse makes its meaning vague, however. A few verses before this passage, the Chronicler makes a contrast between

---

1. *Das Geschichtsbild des chronistischen Werkes* (BWANT, 4.3; Leipzig: Kohlhammer, 1932), pp. 18-37.

2. *Ideology*, p. 233.

3. My list of the Chronicler's references to Judah as 'Israel' differs somewhat from Williamson's (*I and II Chronicles*, pp. 97-110).

'all Israel who went to their tents' and 'the Israelites who lived in the cities of Judah' whom Rehoboam ruled (10.17). 'All Israel in Judah and Benjamin' would seem then to refer to these Northerners living in the South. Shemaiah's prophecy, however, cannot be addressed to them alone. In 11.1, Rehoboam assembled 'the house of Judah and Benjamin'. Shemaiah's audience therefore included native Southerners. In its present context, then, 'all Israel in Judah and Benjamin' encompasses both meanings of 'Israel' in Chronicles. It refers to native Southerners and to Northerners now living in the South.

Such a grouping is plausible historically. It is entirely likely some Northerners rejected the decision to secede. Some emigration to both sides of the border probably occurred. It is likely, therefore, that the Chronicler reflects a degree of historical reality here.

The Chronicler keeps the Deuteronomist's basic outline of significant events in Rehoboam's rule, but shifts the chronology to fit the Chronicler's theology of retribution.[1] Thus Rehoboam built and abundantly provisioned fortified cities throughout Judah.[2] Such building projects are a key indicator of successful (and faithful) rule in Chronicles.[3] Rehoboam's kingdom was secure as long as the levites helped him walk in the way of David and Solomon (11.17). Things fell apart only when Rehoboam 'forsook the law of Yahweh' (12.1).[4] The next verse begins the account of Shishak's invasion and attributes it to Judah's unfaithfulness to Yahweh.

The Chronicler's account of Shishak's campaign (2 Chron. 12.2-9) is considerably longer than the Deuteronomist's account (1 Kgs 14.25-26), but supplies little additional information.[5] It is possible the

---

1.  J. Wellhausen, *Prolegomena to the History of Ancient Israel* (Berlin: Reimer, 1883; repr. Gloucester, MA: Peter Smith, 1983), pp. 203-10; von Rad, *Theology*, I, p. 349; Williamson, *Israel*, pp. 67-68; *idem, I and II Chronicles*, pp. 31-33; Braun, 'Chronicles, Ezra, and Nehemiah: Theology and Literary History', *VTS* 30 (1979), pp. 52-64, 53-56.

2.  See Williamson (*I and II Chronicles*, pp. 240-43) for a discussion of the political geography (and archaeological evidence) of Rehoboam's fortified cities.

3.  Welten, *Chronikbüchern*, pp. 9-78.

4.  On the 'satyrs', see Williamson (*I and II Chronicles*, p. 244).

5.  For a full accounting of the extrabiblical and biblical evidence on Shishak's campaign see: Williamson, *I and II Chronicles*, p. 246; K.A. Kitchen, *The Intermediate Period in Egypt (1100–650 B.C.)* (Warminster: Aris & Phillips, 1973), pp. 293-300, 432-47; M. Noth, 'Die Wege der Pharaonenheere in Palästina und

former had access to a better source than the latter had,[1] but all the additional information which the Chronicler provides smacks of narrative embellishment.[2]

The Chronicler's description of a mass influx of Northern priests and levites at the time of the secession (2 Chron. 11.13-17) probably is fictional. The Chronicler had good theological-literary reasons to embellish 1 Kgs 12.31-32 and 13.33, the two passages upon which 11.13-17 is based. The Kings verses describe Jeroboam's appointment of non-levitical priests to the Northern shrines. The Kings passages, however, indicate neither that Jeroboam kept levites from serving alongside the non-levitical priests nor that he expelled the levites as 2 Chron. 11.14 and 13.9 state.[3] The Chronicler's narrative is fiction, loosely based on the Kings *Vorlage*, but the migration of the levites story has a critical function in the Rehoboam narrative. It sets up the condemnation of the North in 13.8-11, and it explains Rehoboam's success after the schism and before Shishak's campaign. In particular, it serves as a theological gloss on Rehoboam's extensive and successful defense buildup, which the Chronicler documents in the verses immediately preceding it.

*The High Places: Archaeology and the Bible*

In the Rehoboam narrative, the Deuteronomist introduces (and the Chronicler excises) the standard deuteronomic formula about the high places. Closing the high places was by far the most far-reaching and radical reform the deuteronomists advocated. It is important, therefore, to find out as much as possible about high place sanctuaries in the First Temple cult system.

Archaeological data on Israelite high places are inconclusive and their interpretation remains controversial.[4] M. Haran's distinction

Syrien. Untersuchungen zu den hieroglyphischen Listen palästinischer und syrischer Stadte, IV: Die Schoschenkliste', *ZDPV* 61 (1938), pp. 277-304; S. Herrmann, 'Operationen Pharo Schoschenks I im östlichen Ephraim', *ZDPV* 80 (1964), pp. 55-79; B. Mazar, 'The Campaign of Pharoah Shishak to Palestine', *VTS* 4 (1957), pp. 57-66; *idem*, 'Ancient Israelite Historiography', *IEJ* 2 (1952), pp. 82-88; W.F. Albright, 'The Date of Sennacherib's Second Campaign against Hezekiah', *BASOR* 130 (1953), pp. 8-9; Jones, *1 and 2 Kings*, p. 278.

1. Williamson, *I and II Chronicles*, p. 245.

2. Kitchen (*Egypt*, pp. 293-300), however, favors the Chronicler's account.

3. Williamson, *I and II Chronicles*, p. 243.

4. Cf. for example, M. Haran, 'Temples and Cultic Open Areas as Reflected in

between temples and open-air altars in the ancient Near East[1] has sparked considerable discussion.[2] The temple (*bêt 'elōhîm*) was a roofed building which housed an altar. Haran thinks relatively few temples existed in Israel,[3] giving them a prestige surpassing that of the more common open-air altars. In keeping with their elevated status, temples accomodated sacrifice and ritual not practiced at the open-air shrines.[4] Israelite high places, 'beyond any doubt', fall within the open-air altar category, Haran says.[5]

The distinction between roofed and open-air altars has some merit for interpretation of archaeological data. The distinction is not as useful for clarifying the biblical terminology.

In the Bible, the deuteronomic literature contains the earliest and most comprehensive treatment of high place sanctuaries. The deuteronomic position heavily influences all other biblical reflections on the high places. Close reading of this material and comparison with archaeology suggest Haran's claim about Israelite high places must be amended: beyond any doubt, the biblical high places included both open-air and roofed altars.

The Northern extension of Josiah's reform provides the clearest examples of roofed altars described as 'high places'. In 2 Kgs 23.15, the Deuteronomist reports that Josiah tore down and burned the altar and high place at Bethel: 'and even the altar at Bethel, the high place Jeroboam ben Nebat made which caused Israel to sin, even that altar and the high place, he tore down and he burned the high place and he pulvarized to dust and burned the Asherah'. At Bethel, the 'high place', was 'built', 'torn down', and 'burned', along with the altar. This is no open-air altar. Of course, Bethel was a temple-type

the Bible', in *Temples and High Places in Biblical Times* (ed. A. Biram; Jerusalem: HUC–Jewish Institute of Religion, 1981), pp. 31-37; M. Dothan, 'Sanctuaries along the Coast of Canaan in the MB Period: Nahariyah', in *Temples and High Places*, pp. 74-81; contra Z. Herzog, 'Israelite Sanctuaries at Arad and Beer-Sheba', in *Temple and High Places*, pp. 121-22.

    1.   M. Haran, *Temples and Temple-Service in Ancient Israel. An Inquiry into the Character of Cult Phenomena and the Historical Setting of the Priestly School* (Oxford: Clarendon Press, 1978).

    2.   See Dothan, 'Coast'; Y. Yadin, 'Beer-sheba: The High Place Destroyed by King Josiah', *BASOR* 222 (1976), pp. 2-17.

    3.   Haran, *Temples*.

    4.   Haran, 'Open Areas'.

    5.   Haran, 'Open Areas', p. 33.

sanctuary. The Deuteronomist's description of Bethel as a roofed altar sanctuary is consistent with other available information, most notably Amos 7.13 where Bethel is called 'a royal sanctuary and temple of the realm (*bêt mamlākâ*)'.

Four verses after Josiah's destruction of Bethel, Haran's theory about Israelite high places runs into more trouble. 2 Kgs 23.19 indicates that several Northern high places had buildings on-site: 'and also all the houses of the high places (*bāttê habbāmôt*) in the cities of Samaria which the kings of Israel made provokingly, Josiah removed and did to them everything he did at Bethel'. The Deuteronomist lays the groundwork for this verse in the narrative about Jeroboam who 'made house(s) of the high places' (1 Kgs 12.31) throughout the cities of Samaria (1 Kgs 13.32). At least in the North, some sanctuaries the Deuteronomist calls 'high places' have buildings on-site.

M. Dothan's excavations at Nahariyah suggest a way to explain the presence of buildings at open-air sanctuaries.[1] Nahariyah has a Middle Bronze Age (MB) Canaanite open-air sanctuary with building attached. Dothan uses 1 Sam. 9.12-19 to illuminate the artifactual data. Comparing MB Canaanite Nahariyah and a Samuel era Israelite high place weakens the argument somewhat, especially since the bulk of the biblical discussion about high places centers on the even later First Temple cultic system. Dothan is appropriately cautious in his claims. Assuming the excavated sanctuary is like the biblical 'high place', Dothan amends Haran's description, arguing instead 'that the sanctuary itself was open to the sky, but that a house was attached to it, where people, for instance the seer Samuel, might stay, receive guests, eat and so on'.[2]

Dothan's correction is useful but inadequate to explain the range of meaning the Deuteronomist attaches to 'high place'. The 'houses of the high places in the cities of Samaria' may well have been set up the way Dothan envisions, but the Bible characterizes Bethel as a temple, not an open-air altar. Yet the Deuteronomist calls Bethel's sanctuary a 'high place'.

Other archaeological data raise further questions. Aharoni's excavations at Arad and Beer-sheba are particularly interesting.[3] Arad has an

1. Dothan, 'Coast', pp. 78-80.
2. Dothan, 'Coast', p. 80.
3. Y. Aharoni, 'The Excavations at Arad and the Centralization of the Cult', in *Reflections on the Bible: Selected Studies of the Biblical Circle in Memory of Yishai*

Iron II roofed altar with a destruction layer Aharoni dates to Hezekiah's reform. Y. Yadin lowers the date of that layer to Josiah's time.[1] Both archaeologists attribute the destruction to deuteronomic reform. This may be true, but it is possible to imagine other causes of the destruction—for example, Sennacherib's invasion, if the destruction layer dates from Hezekiah's reign. The dating and explanation of the destruction at Arad is uncertain. Aharoni theorized that a roofed altar also must exist at Beer-sheba where he found a horned altar,[2] though few now defend his position. What is important for the present discussion, however, is the presence of a temple-type sanctuary at Arad on the southern frontier of Judah during the period of the monarchy.

The archaeological evidence about Israelite high place sanctuaries is scarce and difficult to interpret. However, when compared with biblical references to the high places, archaeology leads to some important conclusions about the First Temple cultic system.

It is clear from the Arad excavations that non-Jerusalem sanctuaries in monarchical Judah included roofed, as well as open-air varieties. It is also clear that the deuteronomic term 'high place' could refer to either type of sanctuary. For the Deuteronomist, there was only one temple, the house of Yahweh at Jerusalem. All other sanctuaries, roofed or open-air, were 'high places'. It is possible that 'high place' originally referred only to open-air altars, distinguishing them from such 'houses of God' as Jerusalem, Bethel and Arad. If 'high place' ever indicated such a distinction, it is now lost because the Deuteronomist used the term pejoratively to describe roofed sanctuaries as well. 'High place' now includes a variety of cult places whose chief common characteristic is that they are not the Jerusalem temple. In deuteronomic literature, 'high place' describes sanctuaries that are illegitimate and inferior, that is, all sanctuaries other than the Jerusalem temple.

Given the range of meaning which the Deuteronomist attaches to 'high place', it helps to keep a few broad distinctions in mind. In Kings, 'high place' refers to Judean royal sanctuaries outside Jerusalem (roofed and open-air), to Northern temples and to Northern rural sanctuaries.

*Ron* (ed. M. Hevav; Tel Aviv: Am Oved, 1974), pp. 13-31 [Hebrew].

1. Yadin, 'Beer-sheba'.
2. Aharoni, 'Arad'; Herzog, 'Israelite Sanctuaries', pp. 121-22.

Until Josiah's invasion of the North, most of the references to 'high places' in Kings are Judean royal sanctuaries outside Jerusalem. The rural cult places were an integral part of the First Temple system. Some, such as Arad, were roofed temples. Others were open-air. The archaeological data is sketchy but sufficient to conclude that the floor plans of the high places varied from place to place.[1] The variety of floor plans is explained by the way the cult places came into the royal system. Monarchs probably built some high places from scratch (2 Kgs 21.3). It is most likely, however, that the majority of royal high places were premonarchical, even pre-Israelite, sanctuaries remodeled to accommodate the royal Yahweh cult.

The range of ritual services offered at these rural sanctuaries also probably varied from site to site. Just as the Jerusalem temple was highly syncretistic (cf. 2 Kgs 23.4-7; Ezek. 8), so the high places were syncretistic. It is likely they offered services for local deities now incorporated into a pantheon headed by Yahweh. Deut. 12.2-4 states the matter as clearly as it can, instructing deuteronomic zealots to destroy in the high places the images of foreign gods, but not to 'do so to Yahweh your God'.

Distance from Jerusalem might have determined what services were offered. Arad, for example, was far from Jerusalem and likely offered a greater variety of services than a sanctuary closer to Jerusalem might offer. Every royal cult center, however, would have performed a core of standard Yahweh services. Whatever non-Yahwistic cult services were offered in addition, the Judean high place remained a Yahweh sanctuary. The high place represented the religious-political authority of the royal house[2] and its God Yahweh.

From deuteronomic literature, minimal high place functions can be inferred. Deut. 14.24-26 gives indirect evidence by addressing a problem caused by shutting down the high places. These verses give citizens of a deuteronomic state instructions on tax payment 'if the way is too long for you, so you are unable to bring the

---

1.  Dothan's comment ('Coast', p. 77) is on the right track: 'a *bamah* is an open cult place whose plan and layout may vary from site to site'. As the Deuteronomist's identification of Bethel as a 'high place' shows, a biblical high place does not have to be an open-air site. Since many of the Israelite high places probably were overhauled cult sites from the pre-Israelite period, it is reasonable to assume the floorplans varied from site to site.

2.  Ahlström, *Administration*, pp. 37-50.

tithe...because the place Yahweh...is too far from you...'
Presumably, the high places were rural collection points for the
annual tithe (cf. also Deut. 12.5-6). A tax-collecting role would be
consistent with their status as royal sanctuaries. The deuteronomic
triennial tithe (Deut. 14.28-29) for the support of levites and other
royal dependants probably reflects the normal method of annual tax
collection in the monarchical period. The tithe was collected and
stored locally, at or near the high places.

Deuteronomy 12 implies the high places were centers of sacrifice
and ritual butchering. Deuteronomy 16 suggests that important
Yahwistic feasts were conducted at the high places. Deut. 12.3 and
16.21-22, as well as stereotypical evaluations in Kings, indicate that
high places typically conducted liturgies utilizing asherahs and sacred
pillars. Since asherahs and sacred pillars are always paired in the
deuteronomic high place formulas, it is likely they were comple-
mentary elements of a single cult—possibly expressing the female and
male aspects of deity (in Judah's case, Yahweh). Unfortunately, the
evidence is scanty. Whatever asherahs and sacred pillars were, they
were doubly problematical for deuteronomic reformers. They were
idolatrous, and they sat in illegitimate cult places.

In Kings, 'high place' usually refers to Judean royal sanctuaries, but
Josiah's invasion of the North gives the Deuteronomist an opportunity
to expand the meaning of the term. In 2 Kgs 23.15, the Deuteronomist calls the temple at Bethel a 'high place'. It is a deliberate slap at
Jeroboam's Yahweh cult, comparable to the Deuteronomist's
reference to Jeroboam's Yahweh bulls as golden 'calves'.

In the Bible, 'high place' has different levels of meaning. At a pre-
deuteronomic level, 'high place' probably referred to open-air altars,
as opposed to roofed temples. It apparently came to mean any altar,
open-air or roofed, which supplemented the religious-political functions of the central temple. In Judah, that meant any royal sanctuary
other than the Jerusalem temple. In the North, it would have referred
to sanctuaries supplementing the 'temples of the realm' at Bethel and
Dan. In deuteronomic literature, 'high place' refers to every Yahweh
shrine other than the Jerusalem temple.

### Statutory Labor in Judah

Rehoboam got into more trouble over his forced labor policy than any
other thing he did. According to the Bible, state-run forced labor was

the flashpoint for the rebellion of the North. The biblical picture is probably accurate, but the factors leading to the rebellion were far beyond Rehoboam's control.

In Kings, the judgment is mixed as to whether the split of the kingdom was a result of Rehoboam's ill-advised forced labor policy or Solomon's dangerous weakness for foreign women. The Chronicler refuses to say anything bad about Solomon, so in Chronicles Rehoboam and Jeroboam bear all the responsibility for the division. The Deuteronomist's sense of the matter is probably closer to the truth. Forced labor was the rallying point for the rebellion. It was the rallying point because it starkly symbolized a larger conflict between centralized monarchical power, on the one hand, and household- and village-based society, on the other.

The revolt came to a head at Rehoboam's accession to the throne, but forced labor had been a breeding ground for revolt at least since Solomon's time. The transition of power after the death of a strong monarch such as Solomon is usually a highly unstable time. The rebels seized the moment. The rebellion was bred by Solomon's forced labor policy. It was successful because Rehoboam had not yet consolidated sufficient power to crush it.

State-run forced labor was a key issue in the secession of the North. It had economic, social and political consequences which helped create the conditions which produced classical prophecy and the deuteronomic movement. For these reasons, it is important to take a closer look at state-run forced labor in Judah.

The House of David, like other ancient Near Eastern monarchies, utilized forced, statutory labor[1] to construct state buildings, defense works and other state projects. It is difficult, however, to determine the precise nature of that forced labor because of apparent inconsistencies in the biblical record. Scholarly discussion has focused on the descriptions of statutory labor given in 1 Kgs 5.27 [Eng. 5.13] and 1 Kgs 9.20-22. The former passage says, 'Solomon raised a levy (*mas*) from all Israel'. The latter identifies people of non-Israelite descent

---

1.   I find the argument of J.A. Soggin ('Compulsory Labor under David and Solomon', in *Studies in the Period of David and Solomon and Other Essays* [ed. T. Ishida; Winona Lake, IN: Eisenbrauns, 1982], pp. 259-67, 261) convincing, that 'statutory labor' is preferable to 'corvée' to describe the labor levy imposed by the Davidic monarchs. Corvée is terminology better confined to medieval European feudalism.

whom Solomon 'raised as a slave levy (*mas 'ōbēd*) until this day'. It goes on to state explicitly, 'but Solomon made none of the Israelites a slave '*ābed* (of).' These passages raise the question who was liable to perform statutory labor: Was it 'all Israel' or only the descendents of Canaanites (cf. Deut. 20.11; 2 Chron. 2.16-17)?

Some see a genuine discrepancy in the two accounts.[1] Others follow I. Mendelsohn[2] and argue the two passages refer to two different kinds of statutory labor.[3] Mendelsohn starts with the Deuteronomist's use of slightly different terminology in the two passages: *mas* (5.27) and *mas 'ōbēd* (9.21).[4] The former was temporary and less degrading. Israelites were subjected to this kind of statutory labor. The latter was a permanent form of serfdom to the state. The surviving Canaanite population was subjected to this state slavery.[5] The apparent contradiction between 1 Kgs 5.27 and 1 Kgs 9.21 thus dissolves.

Rainey[6] and Soggin[7] follow A. Biram[8] who rejected Mendelsohn's distinction as artificial. Parallel passages such as 1 Kgs 9.21 and 2 Chron. 8.8 or Josh. 16.10 and Judg. 1.30, 33 and 35[9] show *mas* and *mas 'ōbēd* are used interchangeably in the Bible. The literature itself thus resists the distinction Mendelsohn proposes. It is also difficult to

---

1.   J.A. Montgomery and H.S. Gehman, *A Critical and Exegetical Commentary on the Books of Kings* (ICC; Edinburgh: T. & T. Clark, 1951), pp. 137, 205; Gray, *I and II Kings*, p. 234; cf. S. Herrmann, *Geschichte Israels in alttestamentlicher Zeit* (Munich: Kaiser, 1973), pp. 224-25; F. Crüsemann, *Die Widerstand gegen das Königtum. Die antiköniglichen Texte des Alten Testaments und der Kampf um den frühen israelitischen Staat* (WMANT, 49; Neukirchen–Vluyn: Neukirchener Verlag, 1978), p. 70; Soggin, 'Compulsory Labor', pp. 265-66.

2.   'State Slavery in Ancient Palestine', *BASOR* 85 (1942), pp. 14-17; idem, 'On Corvée Labor in Ancient Canaan and Israel', *BASOR* 167 (1962), pp. 31-35; idem, *Slavery in the Ancient Near East* (New York: Oxford University Press, 1949), pp. 97-99; Gottwald, *Tribes*, pp. 134, 158, 216, 483.

3.   Cf. Gray, *I and II Kings*, p. 155; Mettinger, *Officials*, p. 134; Jones, *1 and 2 Kings*, p. 158.

4.   Cf. also Noth, *Könige*, I, p. 217; I. Riesner, *Der Stamm 'bd im Alten Testament. Eine Wortuntersuchung unter Berücksichtigung neuerer sprachwissenschaftlicher Methoden* (BZAW, 149; Berlin: de Gruyter, 1979), pp. 138-42.

5.   Cf. Mettinger, *Officials*, p. 137.

6.   'Compulsory Labour Gangs in Ancient Israel', *IEJ* 20 (1970), pp. 191-202.

7.   Soggin, 'Compulsory Labor'.

8.   *'Mas 'obed'*, *Tarbiz* 23 (1952), pp. 137-42 [Hebrew].

9.   I rely on Rainey's summary of Biram's argument ('Labour Gangs', p. 291).

imagine the kind of state slavery Mendelsohn envisions. As Soggin observes,

> It confronts us also with a historical and sociological picture of David's and Solomon's realm which hardly makes any sense: that of entire populations reduced to *perpetual* state slavery. The Davidic–Solomonic kingdom was, further, an extremely complex entity. . ., and the juridical status of its populations can hardly be reduced to elementary categories such as 'free Israelites' and 'enslaved Canaanites'.[1]

Soggin is probably also right to resist giving either term a monolithic meaning. Some texts do seem to indicate some form of permanent statutory labor (Exod. 1.11; Deut. 20.11; Isa. 31.8; Prov. 12.24; Lam. 1.1),[2] though a certain amount of poetic license may be employed in all these cases. 1 Kgs 9.20-22 indicates a permanent form of forced labor different from the temporary levy described in 5.27. The description of the Canaanites' impressment 'until this day' (9.21) expresses the key difference between this kind of state labor and normal statutory labor. Unfortunately for the social historian, the historical reliability of 9.21 is suspect. Several scholars have found a deuteronomistic hand in 9.20-22.[3] The passage seems to be modeled on Deut. 20.11 which mandates enslavement of the defeated Canaanite population. 1 Kgs 9.21, then, presents an idealized picture of Solomonic policy. The historical value of the passage is questionable.[4] Even on the off-chance that 9.21 is historical, it is not *typical* of statutory labor in Davidic Israel and Judah. 1 Kgs 5.27 more closely reflects the situation—all Israel was impressed for temporary state labor.

Arguing against a distinction between *mas* and *mas 'ōbēd*, Rainey nevertheless distinguishes between *mas 'ōbēd* (corvée) and *sēbel* (levy).[5] The levy, Rainey thinks, was made up of 'naturalized' Israelites—former Canaanites who had attained full citizenship. Native-born Israelites may or may not have been included in the

---

1. Soggin, 'Compulsory Labor', p. 262.
2. See Soggin, 'Compulsory Labor', p. 263.
3. E.g. Würthwein, *Erste Könige*, pp. 112-13; A.H.J. Gunneweg, *Geschichte Israels bis Bar Kochba* (Stuttgart: Kohlhammer, 1972), p. 84; Veijola, *Das Königtum*, p. 66 n. 98; Soggin, 'Compulsory Labor', p. 266.
4. Contra Noth, *Könige*, I, pp. 88, 217.
5. 'Labour Gangs', pp. 200-202.

levy.[1] The *mas 'ōbēd*, on the other hand, was taken from resident aliens who were not permitted status as naturalized Israelites. By this distinction Rainey explains why the North rejected Rehoboam ostensibly because of the corvée, and then turned around and appointed Jeroboam, the former administrator of the Davidic labor levy (*sēbel*) as their king.

Rainey's suggestion clears up one of the Bible's greatest ironies, but does so on weak grounds. Rainey's own study of comparative Semitic documents[2] establishes no difference of meaning between *mas* and *sēbel*. Neither does the biblical evidence help his case. Jacob's poetic prediction of Issachar's fate, 'he bowed his shoulder for burden carrying (*lisbōl*) and became a slave laborer (*mas 'ōbēd*)' (Gen. 49.15), treats *sēbel* and *mas 'ōbēd* as parallel terms. Exod. 1.11 describes Egyptian taskmasters (*śārê missîm*) set over Israel to afflict them with forced labor (*beªsiblōtām*). 1 Kgs 5.29 describes one category of *mas* workers as *nōśē' sabbāl*, 'burden bearers'. Biblically, *mas*, *mas 'ōbēd* and *sēbel* are best viewed as synonymous terms.[3] It is possible, though by no means conclusive, that *sēbel* is a special category within *mas*.[4] However, it remains highly unlikely that former Canaanites did all the state labor and native Israelites did none of it.

Another question has important implications for monarchical policy in Judah after the division of the kingdom: were Judeans obligated to perform statutory labor, or did only Northerners have to serve? The issue is raised by two lengthy passages in Kings. The former (1 Kgs 4.7-19) leaves Judah out of a list of Solomon's tax districts. The second (1 Kgs 12) describes the rebellion of the North, ignited by a forced labor riot (v. 18). Soggin argues, on the basis of the tax district list, that Northerners alone performed statutory labor in the United

---

1. 'Labor Gangs', p. 202.
2. 'Labor Gangs', pp. 192-97.
3. Cf. Mettinger, *Officials*, pp. 137-30. He argues that *mas* is of Canaanite origin and that *sēbel* is of Aramaic origin. In Israel they were synonymous, but the former was a Jerusalem dialectal variant and the latter was an Ephraimitic variant.
4. Soggin, 'Compulsory Labor', p. 260. Cf. M. Weinfeld, 'The Counsel of the Elders to Rehoboam and Its Implications', *Maarav* 3 (1982), pp. 27-53, 39. Weinfeld identifies *mas* as state service in general (military and civilian) and *sēbel* as service on civilian building projects in particular.

Monarchy.[1] He considers it likely that no one performed it at all once the North seceded.[2]

Soggin's argument presents a politically implausible picture of the United Monarchy and an incredible picture of Judah after the division of the kingdom. To begin with, Judah surely was taxed during Solomon's time. Albright[3] is more believable on that score than Alt is.[4] Judah is the implied referent at the end of the tax-district list (1 Kgs 4.19): 'and there was one officer in the land'.[5] The Septuagint supplies the word 'Judah' to this verse. Whether the Greek thus preserves or adds to an original text, it presents a more plausible administrative system.[6]

The Bible nowhere states that Judah was exempt from taxes or statutory labor—a substantial oversight, if such were true. By accepting Alt's view that Judah was exempt from taxes and extending that exemption to statutory labor, Soggin proposes a Judean monarchy which continued to build and upgrade defense works (e.g. 1 Kgs 15.22; 2 Chron. 11.5-12), state buildings (e.g. 2 Kgs 16.10-18) and large-scale agricultural works (2 Chron. 26.10) without the benefit of revenue or compulsory labor—a politician's dream to be sure, but hardly possible!

As Soggin himself notes,[7] the universal labor conscription under Asa (1 Kgs 15.22) offers the clearest argument against his view that Judah had no statutory labor obligations. Soggin's dismissal of this case as 'a national emergency caused by the state of war' misses the point of the biblical notice. Asa's levy was exceptional, but not

1. Soggin, 'Compulsory Labor', p. 265.
2. Soggin, 'Compulsory Labor', p. 267.
3. 'The Administrative Divisions of Israel and Judah', *JPOS* 5 (1927), pp. 17-54; *idem, Archaeology and the Religion of Israel* (Baltimore: Johns Hopkins University Press, 3rd edn, 1953), pp. 140-42; *idem, The Biblical Period from Abraham to Ezra* (New York: Harper & Row, 3rd edn, 1963), pp. 56-57.
4. 'Israels Gaue', *KS*, II, pp. 76-89.
5. Cf. Montgomery and Gehman, *Books of Kings*, pp. 122-23; W. Rudolph, 'Zum Text der Königsbücher', *ZAW* 63 (1951), pp. 201-15, 202. For a different view, cf. Mettinger (*Officials*, p. 122).
6. Mettinger (*Officials*, pp. 122-24) does not think Judah is implied in the final verse. Rather, he argues that Azariah ben Nathan (4.5) is chief prefect and prefect over Judah. The net result is the same, however. Either way, Judah is included in the tax list.
7. 'Compulsory Labor', p. 261.

because Judah had no prior labor levy. It was exceptional because of its scope: 'there were no exemptions (*'ên nāqî*)'. Judeans were obligated to perform state labor throughout the monarchical period. It was the only way the government could carry out large-scale state building projects. Asa's emergency proclamation was noteworthy because it removed the normal exemptions from service.

Judah, like other ancient Near Eastern monarchies, utilized statutory labor for large-scale royal projects. How did the levy work?

Statutory labor was compulsory, but extrabiblical literature indicates workers were paid for such service. Rainey lists several Akkadian examples[1] and concludes: 'The corvée men were issued 'wages' like other types of personnel...'[2] Statutory labor was not slave labor offered free of charge to the royal lord. In fact, Jeremiah (22.13-14) criticizes Jehoiakim for building palaces without paying wages to the forced labor.[3]

Wages for statutory labor would have had a couple of important implications. From the standpoint of the citizenry, it made statutory labor an easier pill to swallow than outright enslavement would have been. As the secession of the North shows, the levy was hardly popular. But as the coronation of Jeroboam shows, the levy could be administered in a way which the people found reasonable and tolerable. Wages would have mitigated somewhat popular resentment toward compulsory labor.

From the standpoint of the monarch, wages meant additional expense. Additional expense had to be met by additional revenues. Thus statutory labor and taxation were inseparably bound. They fed on each other. De Vaux's suggestion[4] that statutory labor was offered in lieu of taxes has no biblical or extrabiblical support.[5] It appears that Judeans performed statutory labor in addition to paying annual taxes.

The Bible gives no indication how often or how long at a time

1. 'Labour Gangs', pp. 192-93.
2. 'Labour Gangs', p. 193.
3. Weinfeld, 'The Counsel of Elders to Rehoboam and its Implications', *Maarav* 3 (1982), p. 40.
4. *Les institutions de l'Ancien Testament* (Paris: Editions du Cerf, 1958), I, pp. 125, 138-39, 215. I am unable to find any mention of this in the English translation, *Ancient Israel*. Soggin ('Compulsory Labor', p. 261) cites the French and appears favorable to de Vaux's suggestion.
5. See Weinfeld ('Counsel of Elders', pp. 34-35) for Akkadian examples of tax and corvée exemptions.

statutory laborers were obligated to work for the state. 1 Kgs 5.28 describes what was probably a typical procedure for large projects: labor teams were sent in relays. In this case, the rotation was one month on the project, two months at home. It seems unlikely that Judeans normally gave one third of every year to forced labor for the state. One of the points of 5.28 is that the rotation was extraordinarily demanding. It is logical to assume, however, that statutory labor was an ongoing obligation, an obligation which periodically wreaked havoc with the economic well-being of families.

Samuel's 'way of the king' (1 Sam. 8.11-18) identifies compulsory labor and taxation as the chief reasons a monarchy would lead inevitably to enslavement.[1] The passage emphasizes the disastrous economic impact of the levy and the tithe on Israelite families.[2] Verses 11-12 warn that the king will conscript sons for military service and agricultural labor in royal fields. Compulsory labor will also manufacture weapons and other war implements. According to v. 13, daughters will be drafted to make perfumes and to cook and bake for the royal house. Household servants also will be conscripted for the king's work, v. 16 says.

The 'way of the king' makes several important points. First, Israelites expected to pay taxes and perform compulsory labor under a monarchical state. Apparently those were considered normal obligations. Second, statutory labor affected all citizens. It was all Israel (or all Judah) who would pay the king their due. Forced labor was not something reserved for 'non-Israelite' populations. Third, statutory labor took able-bodied family members ('sons' and 'daughters') and household servants. While every family was affected by statutory labor at some time or another, every individual was not. Thus Asa's emergency conscription 'without exception' (1 Kgs 15.22) meant that no family was exempt, not that every individual Judean was conscripted (which would have been illogical and incredible). Fourth, common sense told at least some people that such a system of taxation and compulsory labor would lead to economic disaster (1 Sam. 8.17). Fifth, the most influential people still thought the benefits of a monarchy outweighed its costs. That reasoning continued to prevail in the North and the South at the time of the division—as indicated by

1. See Crüsemann (*Widerstand*, p. 70) for a discussion of the origins of this passage.
2. This includes Judeans, contra Soggin, 'Compulsory Labor', p. 265.

Judah's unshaken devotion to Rehoboam and Israel's coronation of Jeroboam, the former levy administrator. That pro-monarchical sentiment survived, though not without challenge, through the monarchy's end, into the post-exilic period.

## Asa

As the third Judean king of the divided monarchy, Asa arises as Judah's first great reformer, in the estimation of the biblical historians. Asa's removal of the queen mother and her shocking Asherah cult object is the core of a reform which sought also to purge the First Temple cult of ritual prostitution. In Kings and Chronicles, Asa is presented as a spiritual as well as genetic precursor to Hezekiah and Josiah.

The Asa narratives in Kings and Chronicles reflect broad literary-theological tendencies of the books. For that reason, skepticism about their historical accuracy is warranted. The following discussion of Asa will be devoted largely to sifting through the historical questions about his reform. Brief comments about royal constructions projects and international trade will contribute to a larger picture of Judah's social-political life in the pre-Assyrian period.

### 1 Kings 15.9-24

The Deuteronomist presents Asa as the first great cult reformer.[1] Asa reportedly purged official Yahwism of cult prostitution (v. 12a), removed all the idols his ancestors made (v. 12b) and destroyed a shocking Asherah object made by the queen mother he deposed (v. 13). Compared with the Chronicles version, Kings presents what appears to be a bare-bones account of Asa's reforms. The relative simplicity of the Kings narrative does not necessarily mean it is more reliable, however. In fact, there are good reasons to be skeptical about its historical value.

Just after comparing Asa to David in his deeds of righteousness (v. 11), Kings says Asa removed the cult prostitute.[2] The connection

---

1. Hoffmann, *Reform*, pp. 87-93; Spieckermann, *Assur*, pp. 184-87.

2. The word *qādēš* here is a collective noun referring to male and female prostitutes (C.F. Burney, *Notes on the Hebrew Text of the Books of Kings* [Oxford: Clarendon Press, 1903]; Noth, *Könige*, p. 330; Würthwein, *Erste Könige*, pp. 182-83; Hoffmann, *Reform*, pp. 76-77; Jones, *1 and 2 Kings*, p. 277).

of this verse with 1 Kgs 14.24 is unmistakable. The standard scholarly reading of the relationship between the two passages has been articulated by Noth who holds that 14.24 is a backreading of 15.12a which latter is taken from an annalistic source.[1] The historical implication? Asa's purge of the cult prostitute is historically reliable.[2]

The greatest challenge to the historical reliability of Asa's cult prostitute reform is posed by Kings itself. The Deuteronomist attributes an identical reform to Asa's son Jehoshaphat (1 Kgs 22.47). By Kings' own record then, Asa's reform was not as complete as 15.12 implies. Josiah's destruction of prostitution houses in the Jerusalem temple (2 Kgs 23.7) shows even Jehoshaphat's reform, if historical, to have had limited success. Hoffmann draws a logical conclusion from the biblical passages: 'In any case, one can hardly speak, in a historical sense, about a "drastic reform of Asa". This is only the result of deuteronomistic "idealization".'[3]

The historical question about Asa's reform may be broached by placing it in the larger history of cult reform in Judah. Comparing the Asa–Jehoshaphat purge with Josiah's destruction of the temple prostitution houses raises another interesting question. When did temple prostitution reappear in Judah? The critical issue can be focused further by asking another question. Why did Hezekiah's deuteronomic or proto-deuteronomic reform fail to address cult prostitution? Two possibilities come to mind.

Perhaps the Deuteronomist is telling the story pretty much the way it happened. Asa started and Jehoshaphat finished a purge of cult prostitution. Hezekiah, therefore, did not purge prostitutes because there were no prostitutes to purge. But who built the prostitution houses which Josiah destroyed? If they were not there in Hezekiah's temple, they must have been built by Manasseh or Amon. Amon had insufficient time and power to introduce much of anything to the cult. If he did, the Deuteronomist surely would have noted it. Manasseh had the time, the power and, in the Deuteronomist's view, the wicked inclination to do just such a thing. Yet Kings contains not a word about cult prostitution during Manasseh's reign. This king is charged with just about every other conceivable cult crime. Why would the Deuteronomist keep quiet about it, if Manasseh reintroduced cult

1. Noth, *Könige*, pp. 330-336.
2. Cf. Montgomery and Gehman, *Books of Kings*, p. 268.
3. Hoffmann, *Reform*, pp. 91-92.

prostitution in Judah? It is unlikely that the temple prostitution houses torn down by Josiah were built by Manasseh or Amon.

A more likely possibility is that cultic prostitution was normal fare in First Temple Judah until Josiah's deuteronomic reform (cf. the casual attitude of Gen. 38 toward cult prostitution). The Deuteronomist records no cult prostitution reform for Hezekiah, because Hezekiah did not purge them. Bracketing for a moment the Asa–Jehoshaphat reform, the first recorded critique of cult prostitution by a Yahwist comes in the North from Hosea, shortly before Hezekiah took the throne in the South. Though Hosea was not a deuteronomist, his preaching obviously influenced deuteronomic thought.[1] By the time of Josiah's reform, the abolition of cult prostitution was an established tenet of deuteronomic reform thought (Deut. 23.18-19 [Eng. 17-18]). The rejection of cult prostitution, though already advocated by the Hosea circle in the North, was not yet a concern in the Southern circle which influenced Hezekiah. It became a central deuteronomic tenet sometime between the reform of Hezekiah and the reform of Josiah. Kings' record reflects this historical development in deuteronomic consciousness.

At some point in the redactional development of Kings, however, the failure of Hezekiah to abolish cult prostitution needed to be addressed. Asa's removal of the shocking Asherah object presented a good base from which to build a defense of Hezekiah. The rare terminology used to describe the cult object (*mipleṣet*) was probably not much clearer to late monarchical or early exilic deuteronomists than it is to modern readers. The other biblical occurrences of the root (Job 9.6; 21.6; Isa. 21.4; Ezek. 7.18; Ps. 55.6) seem to indicate trembling or shuddering. Maacah's Asherah object apparently shook up its viewers. It was shocking.[2] Ahlström's suggestion that it was an image of the goddess with exaggerated female characteristics or a phallic symbol standing next to the goddess[3] is conjecture, but very plausible conjecture which also occurred to ancient interpreters of the passage.[4] Given the Deuteronomist's presentation of the Asherah cult as a

---

1. Cf. H.W. Wolff, *Hosea* (Hermeneia; Philadelphia: Fortress Press, 1974), pp. xxxi-xxxii, 4, 177.

2. BDB; Noth, *Könige*, p. 374; cf. Würthwein, *Erste Könige*, p. 187.

3. Ahlström, *Aspects of Syncretism in Israelite Religion* (Lund: Gleerup, 1963), p. 57.

4. Cf. Vulgate's translation of the word as a phallic symbol.

fertility cult, it is likely that late deuteronomistic editors understood the *mipleṣet* as a sexually explicit cult object. It made sense then to expand Asa's removal of the shocking Asherah object to include a purge of cult prostitutes. The problem of Hezekiah's failure to address the issue is thus solved.

Two considerations complicate the above reconstruction. First, Jehoshaphat's cult prostitute reform is difficult to explain if the Deuteronomist made up the Asa reform to take the heat off Hezekiah. Why have a second fictional reform under Jehoshaphat? As I will argue below, it is possible that the report of a prostitute purge under Jehoshaphat is triggered by his characterization as one who 'walked in all the way of Asa his father' (1 Kgs 22.43).

Second, the question remains why the Deuteronomist did not blame Manasseh for cult prostitution. If the Deuteronomist made up the Asa reform to get Hezekiah off the hook for failing to abolish cult prostitution, why then did the author not take the trouble to account for the reappearance of cult prostitution after Hezekiah and before Josiah? This is especially puzzling considering the care the Deuteronomist takes in the Rehoboam summary to set up Asa's reform (1 Kgs 14.24). Such puzzling omission does not rule out the possibility that the Asa reform is fictitious, however, because it would make no more sense if the reform were historical. Whether the Asa–Jehoshaphat reform is history or fiction, it is odd that the Deuteronomist nowhere prepares the reader for Josiah's destruction of the temple prostitution houses.

The Asa–Jehoshaphat cult prostitute reform is questionable historically. Even if they carried out such a reform, it had limited success. Josiah's reform (2 Kgs 23.7) indicates that cult prostitution continued to flourish as an accepted element of orthodox First Temple Yahwism throughout the monarchy.

H.W. Wolff has a thorough discussion of the extrabiblical evidence on cult prostitution.[1] Though it is clear what these cult functionaries basically did, it is not entirely certain what the larger ritual context was. Wolff maintains a distinction between bridal rites and temple prostitution. The first is analogous to Babylonian fertility rites. Brides were required to engage in sexual intercourse with a stranger as a means of ensuring fertility in the marriage. It was a one-time ritual, a temporary sacred prostitution.[2] The second is a permanent form of

1. Wolff, *Hosea*, pp. 86-88.
2. Wolff, *Hosea*, p. 86.

ritual prostitution carried on by priests and priestesses as part of regular fertility rites.[1]

B. Lang argues that temple prostitution had a less holy significance: 'Contrary to widespread assertion, there is no evidence for a religious or magical meaning of copulation, such as the ecstatic experience of the divine in orgasm or the promotion of fertility'.[2] Lang points to Mic. 1.7 and Deut. 23.19 [Eng. 23.18] as evidence that brothels were a chief source of temple income. He allows that temple prostitutes may have been devotees of a love goddess. 'Their actual business, however, is as profane as that of the prostitute who may seek a female innkeeper's protection or keep an inn herself'.[3] What Lang asserts remains plausible, namely, that temple prostitution provided shelter and income for women who were alienated, for a variety of reasons, from their families and clans.

The character of Judean temple prostitution probably lies somewhere between Lang's characterization and the more traditional line articulated by Wolff. It might have been an important source of income for the cult place. Temple prostitutes were women (and men)[4] who were alienated from normal clan support. Contrary to Lang's assertion, however, their behavior clearly was legitimated religiously. The Deuteronomist considered the cultic rationale for temple prostitution illegitimate, not non-existant.

The Judah–Tamar story (Gen. 38) expresses a typical attitude toward cult prostitution in the monarchical period. As the choice of words in the story shows, that attitude was ambivalent. When he first sees the disguised Tamar on the side of the road, Judah thinks she is a 'harlot', zônâ, (v. 15). His request, 'please let me come in to you' (v. 16) appears to have no particular religious significance. Nor does their negotiation over her fee (vv. 16b-18). However, when Judah's friend goes to make payment (vv. 21-22) he tries to find 'the sacred prostitute' (qᵉdēšâ). In v. 24, when Tamar is accused of impropriety, she is charged with being a harlot (zānᵉtâ). Judah's judgment when the whole truth is known is that 'she is more righteous than I' (v. 26). The story shows an ambivalent attitude toward cult prostitution. For

1.  Wolff, *Hosea*, pp. 87-88.
2.  Lang, *Monotheism*, p. 24.
3.  *Ibid.*
4.  B.A. Brooks, 'Fertility Cult Functionaries in the Old Testament', *JBL* 60 (1941), pp. 227-53; Hoffmann, *Reform*, p. 335.

Judah, the whole encounter with Tamar seems to have a thoroughly
profane significance. For his friend, however, the encounter could be
interpreted in a more sacred light.

To summarize, cult prostitution was a normal part of First Temple
Yahwism throughout the period of the monarchy. The first recorded
impetus to outlaw cult prostitution came from the North in the mid-
eighth century. It apparently was not part of the reform consciousness
which motivated Hezekiah's reform. By the time of Josiah's reform,
abolition of cult prostitution was an established tenet of the deuteronomic program. At some point in the redactional history of Kings, a
deuteronomistic author thought it important to explain Hezekiah's
failure to purge cult prostitutes. The Asa–Jehoshaphat cult prostitute
reforms most likely are a fictional device to explain why Hezekiah did
not abolish prostitution in Judah. If, on the other hand, the Asa–
Jehoshaphat reforms are historical, they had very limited success, as
the Josiah reform shows. The larger context of ritual prostitution is
not entirely clear, but temple prostitution was religiously legitimated,
whatever the popular attitude toward it was. Prostitution may well
have been an important source of income for the cult place. Temple
prostitutes were women and men who were alienated from their clans
for whatever reason.

After the prostitution reform account, the Deuteronomist says Asa
'removed all the idols his ancestors made' (v. 12b). The verb which
introduces the reform measure raises questions about its authenticity.
The stereotypical high place formula comes immediately to mind with
the waw-conversive hiphil of *swr*. Hoffmann shows this form of the
verb is typical in the Deuteronomist's cult reform texts.[1] He also
argues that the use of this rather imprecise verb by the Deuteronomist
(and the Chronicler) generally indicates a very thin historical tradition.[2] Equally imprecise is the noun 'idols' (*gillulîm*), which names
the object of Asa's reform. The noun is fairly common the deuteronomic literature (Deut. 29.16 [Eng. v. 17]; 1 Kgs 21.26; 2 Kgs 17.12;
21.11, 21; 23.24; Jer. 50.2) as a generic term for illegitimate cult
objects. The notice ends with the imprecise and stereotypical verbal
modifier, 'which his ancestors made'. Without the vague deuteronomic
clichés, the remaining historical content of the reform account is neg-
ligible and unreliable. The Deuteronomist has reached into the bag of

1.   Hoffmann, *Reform*, pp. 347-48.
2.   Hoffmann, *Reform*, p. 348.

stock terminology to expand the Asa narrative and present this king as the prototypical reformer.

The removal of idols introduces the removal of Maacah and her shocking cult object. It frames that court power struggle as part of a general iconoclastic reform. Asa's removal of idols also balances somewhat his failure to remove high places. In short, Asa's removal of idols is most likely a deuteronomistic creation. Whatever these 'idols' may have been, it is clear that a variety of iconographic cult objects remained an important part of the orthodox royal cult throughout the First Temple period.

Verse 13 contains what is most likely the historical core of the Asa reform account. The deposition of the queen mother Maacah and the removal of her Asherah object from the temple are entirely plausible. The historical question is complicated, however, because the passage is full of stock deuteronomic language. Asa 'cut down' the Asherah object (cf. 2 Kgs 18.4; 23.14) and 'burned' it in the Kidron brook (2 Kgs 23.4, 6). The Deuteronomist narrates the removal of Maacah's Asherah object with words which draw parallels to the deuteronomic reforms of Hezekiah and Josiah. The verse has been thoroughly worked by a deuteronomistic hand.[1] When the deuteronomic formulas are removed, however, a plausible historical core remains. The untypical terminology for the Asherah object indicates it is not a deuteronomistic literary creation.[2] A court power struggle between king and queen mother is certainly plausible, as the Athaliah episode later will show. In fact, the deposing of Athaliah provides the best biblical analogy for the removal of Maacah and her Asherah object. Athaliah's Baal shrine was destroyed to symbolize her removal from power. Likewise, Maacah's favorite cult object was removed to express the 'great lady's' fall from power.[3] This historical core then becomes the basis for an expanded Asa narrative which portrays Asa as the prototypical royal reformer.

One other Asa measure should be mentioned. To relieve Baasha's threatened blockade of Judah at Ramah (v. 17) along the main northern artery out of Jerusalem,[4] Asa maneuvered the dissolution of the

1. Würthwein, *Erste Könige*, pp. 186-87; Hoffmann, *Reform*, p. 89.
2. Noth, *Könige*, p. 336; differently, Würthwein, *Erste König*; Hoffmann, *Reform*.
3. Lang, *Monotheism*, p. 25; Hoffmann, *Reform*, p. 91.
4. See Jones's discussion (*1 and 2 Kings*, p. 285).

Damascus–Israel non-aggression pact (v. 19).[1] Damascus attacked Israel along its northern border (v. 20), causing Baasha to pull back from Ramah and turn attention to the northern front (v. 21). After Baasha abandoned Ramah, Asa proclaimed an extraordinary labor levy, 'without exception',[2] to dismantle the fortifications there (v. 22), presumably rather than risk Israel's reoccupation of the strategic fortress.

Three features of this episode warrent comment. First, Asa's urgent response to the building of Ramah shows how important international trade was to Judah. Judah and Israel were very well situated along key international trade routes from Egypt to Assyria.[3] Presumably both kingdoms collected tolls on the caravans traveling between the great empires. Ramah, located probably some 18 km north of Jerusalem, overlooked the intersection of a key east–west road and the north–south road running out of Jerusalem.[4] Baasha's fortification at Ramah then positioned the Northern king, not only to cut off Judah's trade, but also to control critical east–west and north–south trade which came through Judah. Baasha threatened to deny Judah trade and tax revenues. A drastic response was in order.

Second, Asa's treaty with Damascus apparently was some sort of vassal treaty.[5] Ahaz's later treaty with Tiglath-pileser III (2 Kgs 16.7-9) provides the closest biblical parallel. Both Judean kings seek relief from a Northern military threat against which Judah cannot defend itself. Both kings ask the new treaty partner to attack Israel. Both kings raid the temple and royal treasuries and send ambassadors with a large gift to initiate the treaty. In both cases, the more powerful king 'heard' the request of the Judean king and complied by attacking Israel. The only difference between the two treaties is that Judah remained a vassal to Assyria for at least a century, but there is no record of vassalage to Syria beyond the initial treaty.

Finally, with no recorded qualms or consultation, Asa, like Ahaz (2 Kgs 16.8), cleaned out the temple treasury (1 Kgs 15.18) to make the treaty gift to Syria. The Asa and Ahaz narratives both report the existence of separate temple and royal treasuries. Perhaps under normal circumstances cultic officials had a certain degree of autonomy

1. Jones, *1 and 2 Kings*, p. 286.
2. See my discussion of statutory labor in the section on Rehoboam above.
3. Elat, 'Trade and Commerce', p. 180, 186.
4. Jones, *1 and 2 Kings*, p. 285.
5. Würthwein, *Erste Könige*, p. 189.

from the non-cultic royal administration when it came to collecting and expending temple revenues. The Asa and Ahaz narratives show clearly, however, that the Davidic monarch had final say over temple as well as royal treasuries. The Davidic king was Yahweh's son, the vicar of God on earth. Asa's and Ahaz's ability and willingness to use temple funds for political ends is consistent with the king's role as defined by royal theology.[1] No matter how taxes and other fees were legitimated religiously, temple revenues were at the disposal of the king, the chief representative of Yahweh on earth.

### 2 Chronicles 14–16 [Eng. 14.2–16.14]

Much of the scholarly discussion about the Chronicler's Asa narrative focuses on questions of historicity and chronology.[2] While most scholars see in the Chronicler's arrangement of events a typical and contrived pattern of reward and punishment,[3] others find reason to trust the broad historical outline of the Chronicles narrative here.[4] The chronological issues have no great bearing on the character and impact of Asa's cult policies. Some literary issues should be addressed here, however.

The Chronicler adjusts the Kings *Vorlage* better to fit the Asa reform into the larger history. The reworked Asa reform blunts any implied criticism of Asa's father Abijah, whom the Chronicler presents favorably. To begin with, the Chronicler moves the Maacah account (15.16) to the middle of a much expanded account of Asa's cult measures. The introductory cult reform notice is completely rewritten from the Kings *Vorlage* (1 Kgs 15.12-14). Its meaning is substantially altered. Gone is the reference to the 'idols which his ancestors made'. The Chronicler thus softens negative implications for Abijah and, in the process, probably gives a more accurate picture of

---

1. Cf. T.C.G. Thornton, 'Charismatic Kingship in Israel and Judah', *JTS* ns 14 (1963), pp. 1-11; R.E. Clements, *God and Temple* (Philadelphia: Fortress Press, 1965), p. 60.

2. See Williamson, *I and II Chronicles*, pp. 255-58.

3. Rudolph, *Chronikbücher*; R. North, 'The Chronicler: 1–2 Chronicles, Ezra, Nehemiah', in *The Jerome Biblical Commentary* (Englewood Cliffs, NJ: Prentice-Hall, 1968), pp. 402-38.

4. E.R. Thiele, *The Mysterious Numbers of the Hebrew Kings* (Chicago: University of Chicago Press, 1951); see S.J. De Vries, 'Chronology in the Old Testament', *IDB*, pp. 580-99; *idem, IDBSup*, pp. 161-66; Williamson, *I and II Chronicles*, p. 256.

the Asa period. The Chronicler mentions no cult prostitute reform. This may be another way to protect Abijah's reputation or it may reflect a more reliable source which contained no such reform. Also absent from the introductory verse (14.2) is the power struggle with Maacah. Her shocking Asherah object has become 'the asherahs', turning Asa's reform into a general anti-Asherah measure. By moving the Maacah reference much further down in the narrative, the Chronicler successfully characterizes her fall from power as a small part of Asa's sweeping anti-Asherah reform.

By adding to the Kings *Vorlage* the anti-Asherah reform and the other v. 2 cult measures, the Chronicler presents an Asa who is more deuteronomic than the Deuteronomist's Asa. The Chronicler has Asa removing high places, smashing sacred pillars and getting rid of asherahs.[1] This portrayal coincides with Kings' presentation of Hezekiah, who smashes the pillars and cuts down the asherahs as part of his anti-high place reform (2 Kgs 18.4). More importantly, however, the Chronicler's Asa account has important parallels with 2 Chron. 31.1, where all Israel smashed the pillars, removed the asherahs and got rid of the high places on their way back from the passover extravaganza put on by Hezekiah. For the Chronicler, smashing pillars and pulling down asherahs were part of the normal procedure for destroying high places. Verse 2 then describes a single reform measure, the destruction of the high places. The Chronicler portrays Asa's reform this way to make a further link between Asa and the great reformer Hezekiah.

As shown above, the Deuteronomist also shapes the Asa account to link Asa with Hezekiah and Josiah. The Chronicler's expansion is substantial, but in line with a direction already taken by the Deuteronomist. The biggest problem with the expansion, of course, is the historical problem. The Chronicler takes the next logical step with the Deuteronomist's already inflated Asa reform, but, in so doing, steps on the deuteronomic record. The Chronicler's initial statement of a high place reform in vv. 2 and 4 flatly contradicts 1 Kgs 15.14. The Chronicler's own later statement that the high places 'were not removed from Israel' admits the contradiction and tries to smooth it over. 2 Chron. 14.4 speaks of high place reform in 'all the cities of

---

1. Cf. Exod. 34.13; Deut. 7.5; 2 Chron. 31.1 where *gdʿ* characterizes the action taken against asherahs. Gideon (Judg. 6.25, 28, 30), Hezekiah (2 Kgs 18.4) and Josiah (2 Kgs 23.14) 'cut down' asherahs.

Judah'. In 15.17, the Chronicler takes the Kings *Vorlage* verbatim, 'but the high places were not removed', and changes it by adding 'from Israel' to the end. The Chronicler thus affirms the Kings record but explains it as a reference to Asa's failure to extend the high place reform to the North.

It is safe to say Asa did not shut down Northern or Southern high places. The Chronicler's account of Asa's high place reform is tendentious and most likely unhistorical.

The covenant ceremony reported the Chronicler is also tendentious and historically questionable.[1] It is modeled on similar ceremonies reported for Josiah (2 Kgs 23.1-3) and Nehemiah (Neh. 10). More important, however, is the parallel between Asa's covenant ceremony and Hezekiah's passover celebration (2 Chron. 30.1–31.1). Both ceremonies include Northern worshipers ('all Israel') in a Jerusalem temple-based cultic ceremony, continuing a theme begun with Abijah in 2 Chron. 13.4 whereby Davidic kings reach out to Northerners.[2] However, while Asa's covenant ceremony ends with an admission that 'the high places were not removed', Hezekiah's passover celebration ends with a high place purge that extends throughout all Judah and Benjamin and the North (31.1). Asa's covenant ceremony provides a comparison and contrast with Hezekiah. The Chronicler thus presents Asa as an important but less successful precursor of Hezekiah. It is possible, of course, that an historical event underlies the Chronicler's report here. However, the literary function of the story in Chronicles, along with Kings' failure to mention any such ceremony, throws its historical value into question.

*Summary*
The Deuteronomist and the Chronicler present an idealized picture of Asa. The Chronicler's narrative expands and embellishes the Kings account, but the Deuteronomist's leaner description is also tendentious. In both cases, a very narrow historical core has attracted other reform elements. Both narratives present Asa as the prototypical good reformer. Both connect him with the great reformers Hezekiah and Josiah. Biblically then, Asa is presented as a forerunner of Hezekiah and Josiah, and his reform foreshadows their reforms.

Asa's literary connection with Hezekiah and Josiah is not entirely

1.   Contra Williamson, *I and II Chronicles*, pp. 269-71.
2.   Williamson, *I and II Chronicles*, pp. 251-52.

off base, but his actual 'reform' has little in common with them. Asa's removal and possible destruction of the shocking Asherah object was a symbolic act underlining Maacah's fall from power. It was more likely the result than the cause of her removal from office. Asa's 'reform' then is most like Jehoiada's later destruction of Athaliah's Baal temple. It was a one-time symbolic act underscoring the defeat of an adversary in a domestic power struggle.

Asa's reform does provide a useful contrast with Hezekiah's and Josiah's reforms. Asa's cult reform was a small-scale, internal political act. It has no apparent connection to broader social forces at work in Judah. It was the result of court intrigue rather than social transformation. Both Hezekiah's and Josiah's reforms rested on political considerations, but these reforms reflected the convergence of various social forces in new social-political circumstances.

### Jehoshaphat

Outside of Jehoshaphat's joint ventures with the North, the Deuteronomist has very little to say about this Judean king. The Deuteronomist reports a single cult measure taken by Jehoshaphat. It hardly qualifies as a 'reform', however, because it merely continues a policy started by Asa. As I have argued above, Asa's purge of cult prostitutes is historically questionable. Jehoshaphat's cult prostitution reform also is probably unhistorical.

The Chronicler presents a much expanded version of the life of Jehoshaphat, the centerpiece of which is a sweeping judicial reform. Scholarly opinion is divided on the trustworthiness of the Chronicler's report here. Whatever the final historical verdict, the Chronicler's report yields some important information about royal administration in Judah before the exile.

The bulk of my discussion of Jehoshaphat will focus on the two issues raised by Kings and Chronicles. What is the significance of Jehoshaphat's friendly relations with the North? What can be learned from the judicial reform to clarify the nature of social relations in the Judean monarchical state?

### 1 Kings 22.41-51

Jehoshaphat is viewed favorably by the Deuteronomist. He 'walked in all the way of Asa his father. He did not turn to the right or left,

doing right in Yahweh's view' (1 Kgs 22.43). Characteristically, the
Deuteronomist offers little to substantiate the theological judgment
rendered. Besides noting continued high place worship (v. 44 [Eng.
43b]), only Jehoshaphat's purge of the cult prostitute is cited as noteworthy of the cult under his administration.

As my comments on Asa indicated, cult prostitution apparently was
a constant feature of First Temple practice at least up to Josiah's
destruction of the temple prostitution houses (2 Kgs 23.7). I argued
above that the Deuteronomist extrapolated Asa's prostitution reform
from his removal of the deposed queen mother's favorite Asherah
object from the temple. If the Asa prostitution reform is a deuteronomistic literary creation, then Jehoshaphat's reform is also highly
questionable.

The ten-verse Jehoshaphat summary appears mangled in its present
form, so it is difficult figure exactly how the narrative coheres. The
cult prostitution notice may be triggered by the Deuteronomist's theological evaluation of Jehoshaphat. The summary of this king is very
different from the tight concluding summaries the Deuteronomist
normally writes. The narrative appears to start winding up (v. 46),
only to have a series of unrelated historical notes (vv. 47, 48, 49-50)
inserted before the death and succession notice (v. 51). Whether the
insertions are original or secondary, it is likely the cult prostitution
reform notice (v. 47) was added to elaborate on the statement that
Jehoshaphat 'walked in all the way of Asa his father' (v. 43).

The Deuteronomist's account of Jehoshaphat's rule offers little
useful information about the First Temple cult. The Chronicler, on
the other hand, offers some helpful insights.

### 2 Chronicles 17.1–21.1

If the Deuteronomist's Jehoshaphat account suffers from a dearth of
information, the Chronicler's Jehoshaphat narrative enjoys a glut. The
space the Chronicler devotes to this king is rivaled in the post-
Solomon period only by Hezekiah, whom the Chronicler presents as a
new Solomon, a Davidic king ruling a reunited Israel after the fall of
the North. For the Chronicler, Solomon and Hezekiah bracket the
period of the divided monarchy, a period where Northern kings are
largely ignored and Southern kings struggle to define an appropriate
stance toward the North. In the Chronicler's view, Jehoshaphat defines
the relationship better than any other king of the divided monarchy.

Jehoshaphat represents the Chronicler's ideal Judean king during the time of the divided monarchy. His persistent quest for true prophecy (18.4-7), extensive reorganization of the judiciary (19.4-11) and astonishing faith in battle (20.1-30) provide ample evidence of his unyielding commitment to Yahweh. His achievement of peaceful cooperation with the North without compromising Yahwistic orthodoxy marks the fulfillment of the Chronicler's idea of the ideal relationship between the two kingdoms as long as they had to remain divided. Jehoshaphat alone among the Judean kings of the divided monarchy was able to live up to the standard of reunification by moral example. This path is fraught with danger, as the experience of Jehoshaphat's successors shows. The possibility of domination by the apostate North is ever present, and requires a morally and religiously strong Judean monarch. Only Jehoshaphat possessed that strength.

Jehoshaphat is introduced as one who 'strengthened himself over Israel' (17.1). The surprising reference to Israel is no mistake. It is rather part of the Chronicler's portrayal of him as the model Judean king of the period of the divided monarchy. His strength 'over Israel' was found in his cultic faithfulness and obedience to the protocol of military non-intervention against the North laid earlier in Shemaiah's oracle (2 Chron. 11.2-4 = 1 Kgs 12.22-24). For the Chronicler, the Davidic king was the only legitimate political authority. Jehoshaphat's faithful adherence to Yahweh's prophets, continued cult faithfulness and peaceful relations with the North well expressed the exclusive legitimacy of the Davidic house. Jehoshaphat did the best the Chronicler expected could be done during the period of the divided monarchy. In his faithfulness, he embodied the Solomonic ideal, ruling all Israel, ideally if not actually reunited.

Three verses into the summary introduction of Jehoshaphat's reign, the reader encounters another problematical choice of words: 'and Yahweh was with Jehoshaphat because he walked in the former ways of David his father' (17.3). It is a problem because the Chronicler presents a completely positive picture of David. 'The earlier days of Asa' would have made better sense, since good King Asa reportedly turned bad in his old age. Thus RSV follows some Greek fragments and deletes 'David'. Assuming that 'David' is an accidental gloss has its own problems. The expression, 'in the ways of David his father', or some variation of it does not appear very often in Chronicles. In those few places it does occur, it refers to monarchs who hold a special significance in the Chronicler's schema (cf. 2 Chron. 28.1; 29.2; 34.2). Jehoshaphat certainly has an important place in the Chronicler's history. It would not be surprising for the Chronicler to compare him with David. If there is a scribal gloss, it is the addition of 'former' to qualify 'the ways of David'. The glossator based the addition on the Kings portrayal of David.

Jehoshaphat's description as one who 'sought (*dāraš*) the God of his father and walked according to his commandments and not according to the ways of Israel' (17.4) draws a contrast with Ahaz who 'walked according to the ways of the kings of Israel' (28.2). Thus, the faithful Jehoshaphat who 'strengthened himself over Israel' and 'walked according to the former ways of his father David' attains unique status among the kings of the double monarchy. A series of vignettes demonstrates the reasons for the Chronicler's favorable evaluation.

After the introduction (17.1-6), the Chronicler tells the story of an evangelistic crusade the king carries throughout Judah via 'his princes' and the levites and priests (vv.7-8). Whether by accident or design, the Chronicler characterizes Jehoshaphat here as the reverse of Rehoboam, who was faithful 'for three years' (11.17) before he forsook Yahweh's Torah (12.1). Jehoshaphat, 'in the third year of his reign' (17.7), sends his highest-ranking officers throughout Judah to preach Yahweh's Torah (v. 9). Rehoboam saw his kingdom decimated and the temple treasuries looted by Egypt. Jehoshaphat saw 'the fear of Yahweh' falling on all the kingdoms around Judah (v. 10) and, like Solomon, received tribute from foreigners (v. 11). His construction and supply program supplemented Judah's revitalized and redeployed army (vv. 12-19). The stage is well set for the next major episode. 'Now Jehoshaphat had a lot of wealth and honor, and he made a marriage alliance with Ahab' (18.1).

The Chronicler's account of the Ramoth-gilead incident (18.1–19.3) follows very closely the Kings *Vorlage* (1 Kgs 22.1-36). The theological function of the story is different in the two books, however. In Kings, the Ramoth-gilead incident serves to seal the case against Ahab. Jehoshaphat's faithfulness is a foil for Ahab's faithlessness. The Deuteronomist presents Ahab's demise in gory detail (22.35). The Chronicler is less explicit about Ahab's bitter end. The improbable course of events which leads to Ahab's death is, for the Deuteronomist, confirmation of Yahweh's inescapable judgment. The Chronicler construes those same events to highlight Yahweh's willingness to save: 'Jehoshaphat cried out and Yahweh helped him. God drew them away from him' (18.31). The Chronicler adds a fictitious encounter with the prophet Jehu ben Hanani who rebukes Jehoshaphat for his military venture with Ahab but finally exonerates him because he has 'destroyed the asherahs out of the land' (19.3). There is no reason to believe that the Chronicler reports an actual reform here.

The Chronicler uses the Ramoth-gilead story to make another important point. The story clarifies the nature of Jehoshaphat's dominion 'over Israel' (17.1; 20.29). Jehoshaphat almost lost his life because the Syrians mistook him for 'the king of Israel'. It was only their Yahweh-inspired recognition that he was not the king of Israel (18.32) that saved him. By allowing himself to be 'enticed' (18.2) into a military alliance with the North, Jehoshaphat risked his life and the good favor of Yahweh (19.2). For the Chronicler, military alliance with the North is the flip-side of military intervention against them. During the period of division, Israel cannot be reunited by force of arms.

The Ramoth-gilead incident is followed immediately by the account of Jehoshaphat's sweeping judicial reform.[1] The Chronicler's account of the judicial reform has met with both extreme skepticism and high praise. Not untypically, the bounds of the discussion are set by Wellhausen[2] and Albright.[3] There is some merit to Wellhausen's suggestion that judicial reform came to be associated with Jehoshaphat because of his name, 'Yahweh judges'. Albright collects sufficient evidence from Egyptian sources to cast serious doubt on Wellhausen's assertion that the reform reflects post-exilic reforms back-read into Jehoshaphat's reign. Albright makes a good case that judicial reform could have happened under Jehoshaphat. The Egyptian evidence Albright cites does show that ancient Near Eastern monarchs sometimes did reform their judiciary. However, having rejected the impossibility of such a reform, he does nothing to show its probability. Certainly, he fails to support his claim that the Chronicler

1.   Williamson (*I and II Chronicles*, p. 279) says Jehoshaphat undertakes his judicial reform to avert Yahweh's wrath announced by Jehu ben Hanani. Mosis (*Untersuchungen*, pp. 175-78) denies any thematic link between the two episodes. Mosis is closer to the truth than Williamson is. There is no indication in Chronicles that the judicial reform is the result of Jehu's rebuke.
2.   *Prolegomena*, p. 191.
3.   'The Judicial Reform of Jehoshaphat', in *Alexander Marx Jubilee Volume* (New York: Jewish Publication Society, 1950), pp. 61-82.

presents 'a substantially correct account of the judicial reform of Jehoshaphat, though it does not tell the whole story'.

Neither Wellhausen nor Albright accounts for the judicial reform in a completely satisfactory way. Troubling inconsistencies persist. For example, Williamson argues on stylistic grounds that 19.4 introduces a section of source material in vv. 5-11.[1] If he is right, the Chronicler was not simply making up a story based on post-exilic social realities. Still, it is unlikely the Deuteronomist would have overlooked such a major overhaul of the judicial system. The evidence seems to support both scholarly positions.

Middle ground does exist between the positions of Wellhausen and Albright. It is possible that the reform account is a telescoping of the judicial system as it evolved in monarchical Judah. Wellhausen's instincts are probably right that Jehoshaphat's name was a magnet for judicial traditions. Albright is right, however, to say that such a judicial reform is entirely plausible as early as Jehoshaphat. The close connection of the Chronicler's judicial reform to some of the laws in Deut. 16.18–17.13[2] indicates that the judicial structure and policy outlined in the reform account were familiar in the pre-exilic period. Indeed, some kind of reorganization of the judiciary must have occurred as the monarchical system replaced the decentralized social institutions of the premonarchical era.[3]

Ultimately, it matters little whether the judicial reform occurred over a long period or all at once. Either way, the judicial reform shows the growing and increasingly centralized power of the monarchy over the social life of Judah. Priests serving as royal judicial officers is one more indicator of the close relationship between cult and court. It is also significant that the king had the authority to reorganize the existing system and to appoint priests to serve as he saw fit.

## Summary

The Deuteronomist and the Chronicler share a favorable view of

1. *I and II Chronicles*, pp. 287-89.

2. Cf. E. Junge, *Der Wiederaufbau des Heerwesens des Reiches Juda unter Josia* (Stuttgart: Kohlhammer, 1937), pp. 81-92; A.D.H. Mayes, *Deuteronomy* (NCB; Grand Rapids, MI: Eerdmans, 1979).

3. Cf. Knierim, 'Exod. 18', pp. 146-71; G.C. Macholz, 'Zur Geschichte der Justizorganisation in Juda', *ZAW* 84 (1972), pp. 314-40; Whitelam, *Just King*, pp. 185-206.

Jehoshaphat. The Deuteronomist is more concerned with the wicked behavior of Ahab than with the reign of Jehoshaphat, so Kings offers very little information about the Judean monarch. The cult prostitute reform the Deuteronomist attributes to Jehoshaphat is historically questionable.

The Chronicler has much more to say about Jehoshaphat. Most of it is his own creation, but some useful information is preserved in Chronicles. Most importantly, the Chronicler presents a judicial reform which is plausible for the period of the monarchy, as comparison with judicial laws in Deuteronomy indicates. Wellhausen is right that Jehoshaphat's name attracted judicial traditions over the years. The Chronicler's judicial reform most likely is a telescoped account of a process of change in the judicial system which took place over many years, rather than all at once in the reign of Jehoshaphat. Such an evolution of the judicial system was necessary as Judah moved from the decentralized social system of the premonarchical era to the centralized system of the monarchical state.

### Athaliah

The reign of Athaliah is an anomaly in Judean history. The importance of queen mothers in Judah is underlined throughout Kings by the Deuteronomist's care to name every one.[1] The Asa–Maacah episode shows that the queen mother had some kind of official authority.[2] Ahaziah's death at the hand of Jehu (9.27) gave Judah the chance to see just how powerful a queen mother could be.

Athaliah seized the helm of power and executed all the non-Omride claimants to the Davidic throne. The Deuteronomist and the Chronicler present her as an illegitimate ruler, and thus offer very little information about her reign. What we do know about her cult policy comes in the report of the coup which deposed her. As part of the coup, Jehoiada ordered the destruction of a Baal temple in

---

1. Two cases are exceptions: Jehoram (2 Kgs 8.17) and Ahaz (2 Kgs 16.20).
2. On the role of the queen mother in Judah, see H. Donner, 'Art und Herkunft des Amtes der Königinmutter im Alten Testament', in *Festschrift J. Friedrich* (ed. R. von Kienle; Heidelberg: Carl Winter, 1959), pp. 105-45; G. Molin, 'Die Stellung der Gebira im Staate Juda', *TZ* 10 (1954), pp. 161-75: Ahlström, *Syncretism*, pp. 57-88; de Vaux, *Ancient Israel*, I, pp. 117-19. Molin and Ahlström argue that the queen mother had a specific cultic function.

Jerusalem. My comments on Athaliah will focus on the Baal temple episode.

## 2 Kings 11

Following B. Stade,[1] commentators typically have found two literary sources in the Deuteronomist's Athaliah–Jehoiada coup story.[2] W. Rudolph[3] argues for the unity of the account. Hoffmann[4] builds on Rudolph's argument disputing the two-source theory.

For Hoffmann, the historical kernel of the Baal temple episode lies in the clash between Jehoiada and Mattan, the chief priestly representatives of the two regimes:

> As the confrontation between Athaliah and Joash ended with the death of the queen, so too, Mattan, as the representative of the old regime in the cultic sphere—and, as such, the natural enemy of Jehoiada—must die, when Jehoiada becomes the new high priest.[5]

The replacement of Mattan was a necessary consequence of the coup. Since Athaliah was already connected with the Baal cult by virtue of her ancestry, the Deuteronomist grounds the assassination of Mattan in a religious struggle between Yahwism and Baalism, along the lines of the Jehu rebellion in 2 Kings 9–10.[6]

Hoffmann is close to the mark. The anti-Baal 'reform' of Jehoiada was very limited and obviously related to the political goals of the coup. Whether Mattan was a Yahweh priest or a Baal priest or an overseer of ritual for both gods, he certainly was a high-ranking priest of the official cult in the Athaliah administration. His assassination was probably viewed as a political necessity (cf. Solomon's assassination of Adonijah and and banishment of Abiathar in 1 Kings 2). However, it is also possible that Jehoiada actually ordered the destruction of a Jerusalem-area Baal shrine associated with Athaliah.

Solomon's cult policy toward his marriage-alliance wives is illuminating in this regard. 1 Kgs 11.7-8 reports that Solomon built several

1. 'Anmerkungen zu 2 Ko. 10–14', *ZAW* 5 (1885), pp. 275-97.
2. See Gray's summary of the scholarship (*I and II Kings*, pp. 566-69).
3. 'Die Einheitlichkeit der Erzählung vom Sturz der Atalja (2 Kön 11)', in *Festschrift für Alfred Bertholet zum 80 Geburstag* (ed. W. Baumgartner; Tübingen: Mohr, 1950), pp. 473-78.
4. *Reform*, pp. 106-108, 110-12.
5. Hoffmann, *Reform*, p. 112.
6. Hoffmann, *Reform*.

high places for his foreign wives to burn incense and sacrifice to their gods, including 'a high place to Kemosh, the abominable idol of Moab, on the hill opposite Jerusalem, and one to Molek, the abominable idol of the Amorites' (v. 7). The next time Kings mentions high places in the vicinity of Jerusalem is in Josiah's reform. There, Kings says, Josiah 'put an end to the idolatrous priests appointed by the kings of Judah to burn incense in the high places in the cities of Judah and the surrounding areas of Jerusalem' (2 Kgs 23.5), and 'he defiled the high places opposite Jerusalem south of the Mount of Olives which Solomon King of Israel built to Ashteroth, the abominable idol of the Sidonians, to Kemosh, the abominable idol of Moab and to Milkom, the abomination of the Amorites' (2 Kgs 23.13). According to the Deuteronomist, the cult places Solomon built for his marriage-alliance wives opposite Jerusalem remained intact until Josiah destroyed them. 2 Kgs 23.5 indicates that the priests who burned incense in the high places around Jerusalem, like those in the cities of Judah, had been appointed by the kings of Judah. If the high places of v. 5 include the marriage-alliance cult places of v. 13, then Solomon's policy was continued by other Davidic kings.

It is reasonable to assume such a policy was in place whenever Judah sealed a foreign alliance with a marriage. The wife's cult place, built outside the city limits but in the close vicinity of Jerusalem, may well have served some sort of psychological function for the wife—a taste of home in a foreign land. More importantly, however, the cult center served as a symbol of the alliance.

In the ancient Near East, the national god authorized the political order of the nation. A shrine to the national god on foreign soil represented in that foreign place the political authority of the nation. The foreign cult places just outside Jerusalem then are most comparable to modern embassies. If the Naaman–Elisha episode provides an analogy for how these foreign cult places were conceived, then they may have been very close to the modern conception of an embassy. In 2 Kgs 5.17, Naaman asks Elisha for a two-mule load of Israelite dirt to take back to Syria so Naaman could continue to worship Yahweh. The high places Solomon and other Judean kings built for their marriage-alliance wives may well have been constructed with soil imported from the native land. What is implied in the legal status of modern embassies may have been explicit in the ancient Near East: the foreign cult place literally was the territorial soil of the nation represented.

Assuming the general historical accuracy of the Kings record on this matter, marriage-alliance cult places existed just outside Jerusalem from the time of Solomon until the reform of Josiah. Other Judean kings built them when appropriate. Jehoshaphat probably built a cult-place embassy when he sealed the alliance with the North (1 Kgs 22.45 [Eng. 22.44]) by marrying his heir apparent Jehoram to Athaliah, the daughter of Ahab (2 Kgs 8.18). Representing the house of Ahab and Jezebel, a cult place for the Tyrian Baal would have been built to symbolize the alliance. In that light, Jehoiada's destruction of Athaliah's Baal temple in the Jerusalem area makes sense. By destroying the cult-place embassy, Jehoiada symbolically ended the political influence of the House of Omri in Judah.

*2 Chronicles 22.10–23.21*
The Chronicler's version of the Athaliah story yields no additional social-historical information about the reform. As Williamson notes,[1] the Chronicler alters the Kings *Vorlage* in predictable ways. For example, the Chronicler substitutes priestly terminology and personal names for the military personnel listed in Kings as the shock-troops of the coup. The Chronicler also takes pains to compare this restoration of the Davidic monarchy with the coronation of David (1 Chron. 11).[2] The most important element of the comparison is the enthusiastic participation of the whole people in the overthrow of Athaliah and the coronation of Joash.

*Summary*
Jehoiada's anti-Baal 'reform' was a limited, one-time act, symbolizing the downfall of Athaliah and the end of Omride political influence in Judah. Hoffmann is probably right that the assassination of Mattan was a political necessity of the coup. As the chief religious officer of the ousted regime, Mattan's fate was sealed when Athaliah was deposed. The biblical authors have masked the raw politics of it by identifying Mattan as a Baalist priest. As a key priest of the Athaliah regime, Mattan no doubt oversaw a syncretistic Yahweh cult which included Baal worship. Though the biblical historians skew the picture of Mattan, their report of an assault on a Jerusalem-area Baal shrine is likely. Following Solomon's policy, Jehoshaphat likely built a cult

1.   *I and II Chronicles*, pp. 313-18.
2.   *I and II Chronicles*, p. 313.

place for the Tyrian Baal just outside Jerusalem, as a symbol of Judah's alliance with the house of Omri. By destroying the Baal altar, Jehoiada symbolized the ouster of Athaliah and the end of Omride political influence in Judah. The closest biblical parallel is Asa's destruction of Maacah's Asherah object in connection with her removal from office.

Since Jehoiada was a leading Jerusalem priest, with Yahwistic orthodoxy praised by the Deuteronomist and the Chronicler, it is important to note what he did not do in his coup-related 'reform'. He did not shut down the high places. He did not purge asherahs or smash sacred pillars. He did not close temple prostitution houses or destroy astral cult objects. He pulvarized no bronze serpent and deposed no priest other than Mattan. Either this powerful Jerusalem priest was not a deuteronomist or the above-mentioned cult practices were not part of the Jerusalem cult when Jehoiada had his chance to make a clean sweep. Some of the cult practices later ended by Josiah were introduced while Judah was a vassal of Assyria. I will say more about that later. It is also true that Jehoiada was not a deuteronomist. He showed no interest in centralizing the cult or any of the other deuteronomic concerns. The Deuteronomist's favorable view of Jehoiada, a non-deuteronomic priest, is further evidence that deuteronomism had not yet coalesced in Judah during the time of Jehoiada, and the Deuteronomist knew it. Jehoiada could not have been a deuteronomist, because Judean deuteronomism did not yet exist.

### Joash

Joash was not a cult reformer, but after he was installed on the throne by Jehoiada's coup he undertook extensive repairs of the Jerusalem temple. The episode gives insight into the relationship between the priesthood and the monarchy: priests answered to the king who clearly had final say in important cultic matters. The institution of the user-fee tax for temple repairs (2 Kgs 12.10-17 [Eng. 12.9-16]) raises the issue of taxation in Judah. The discussion in this chapter will focus on the relationship between court and cult, particularly as it concerns regular taxation in Judah.

*2 Kings 12.1-17 [Eng. 11.21–12.16]*
Much of the scholarly discussion of the Deuteronomist's Joash narra-

tive has centered on the author's use of sources. The core of this chapter (vv. 5-17) appears to be source material of some kind, incorporated but not heavily reworked by the Deuteronomist. Opinions vary on the precise nature of the source(s). Noth[1] believes it to be from a literary history of the divided kingdom based on state archives. Wellhausen[2] counts it as part of an independent temple history. Most reject Wellhausen's temple history theory;[3] however, it is widely agreed the material has a priestly origin.[4]

The passage illustrates an important feature of the official cult in Judah. The king was responsible for the upkeep of cultic shrines and had ultimate authority to determine how temple revenues would be spent. Verse 5 is especially interesting. By royal order, priests are commissioned as state tax collectors. When the king becomes dissatisfied with the lack of progress on temple repairs, he calls the priestly hierarchs to task (v. 8), and they stop collecting taxes (v. 9). The new user-fee system (vv. 10-16) was jointly administered by ranking officers in the royal and cultic bureaucracies (v. 11) to ensure proper expenditure of the temple revenues.

The passage, perhaps utilizing source material which pre-dates the Deuteronomist, shows the close connection of cult and court. Priests acted in the service of the king, who had the authority to define priestly roles and expend temple revenues. Here, the royal theology is thus implicitly confirmed: the Davidic king is the anointed one, the vicar of Yahweh on earth. He is protector and chief overseer of Yahweh's cult.

*2 Chronicles 24.1-14*

The Chronicler is heavily dependent on Kings but reworks the *Vorlage* to reflect his own theological interests.[5] The Chronicler includes levites in temple restorations (vv. 5, 6, 11) and draws parallels between the temple and the Mosaic tabernacle (vv. 6, 9; cf.

---

1. M. Noth, *Überlieferungsgeschichtliche Studien: Die sammelnden und bearbeitenden Geschichtswerke im Alten Testament* (Tübingen: Max Niemeyer, 1943), p. 75.

2. *Die Composition des Hexateuchs und der historischen Bücher des Alten Testaments* (Berlin: de Gruyter, 4th edn, 1963), p. 293.

3. Cf. Jones, *1 and 2 Kings*, p. 488.

4. Gray, *I and II Kings*, p. 583; Hoffmann, *Reform*, p. 124; Jones, *ibid.*, pp. 488-89; Šanda (*Könige*, II, p. 148) says that the passage's unfavorable attitude toward priests makes priestly authorship improbable.

5. Williamson, *I and II Chronicles*, pp. 318-26.

Exod. 30.11-16; 38.25-26). Both are consistent with themes elaborated elsewhere in Chronicles. Both are historically improbable.[1]

The Chronicler's comment in v. 7 that Athaliah and her sons had desecrated the house of God is problematical. The syntax of the sentence is difficult, leaving unclear who exactly took part in the desecration. Was it Athaliah and her 'sons', or just her 'sons'? It is also uncertain whether 'sons' is literal or figurative, describing adherents to Athaliah's policies. The violation of the temple and its holy things by the Athalia administration is not mentioned in Kings. Nor does the Chronicler refer to it in the Athaliah–Jehoiada narrative. The Chronicler's assumption that such a desecration occurred is a logical deduction from the Kings portrayal of the Jehoiada coup as an anti-Baal revolt. It is unlikely, however, that the Chronicler had access here to a more reliable historical source. The violation of the temple by Athaliah is the Chronicler's speculation on what must have happened. On the other hand, the Chronicler may be right to assume that some kind of Baalist innovations, probably minor ones, were made. They most likely were made, however, by Jehoshaphat when he forged the marriage alliance with the house of Omri.

The Chronicler's and the Deuteronomist's Joash narratives raise important points about the close relationship between court and cult in Davidic Judah. One of the most important aspects of that relationship is how the monarchy raised revenues to support itself and its cult.

### Taxation in Judah

Joash's institution of a user fee to finance temple repairs in Jerusalem raises the broader issue of taxation in the monarchical period. There is a full history of scholarship on the topic, usually focused on whether the annual tithe mentioned throughout the Bible was a secular tax or a religious duty. The tithe at least eventually came to be considered a cultic tax (Amos 4.4; Gen. 14.20; 28.22; Num. 18; Deut. 12.6, 11, 17; 14.22), but did it start out that way?

W.R. Smith says no.[2] He argues that a state tax was instituted at the dawn of the monarchy. As Amos 4.4 shows, the tithe came to be used for the support of state sanctuaries. This use led to the religious conception of the tithe.

---

1. See Williamson's discussion (*I and II Chronicles*, pp. 319-21).
2. *Lectures on the Religion of the Semites: The Fundamental Institutions* (London: Black, 3rd edn, 1923; repr. 1969), p. 190.

Smith's reconstruction has been rejected by most recent commentators. Eissfeldt[1] pioneered a different line of reasoning on the tithe. He associated it with the offering of the firstlings and placed it in the premonarchical era as a sanctuary payment. The cultic tithe continued through the monarchical period perhaps in addition to a secular tithe.[2] M. Weinfeld[3] and H. Jagersma[4] reject the notion of a double tax, but agree the tithe is rooted in a premonarchical sanctuary payment. It is carried over into the royal system, but remains a cultic obligation.

In his survey of comparative ancient Near Eastern tax systems, F. Crüsemann[5] finds predictable variation, but one constant: tax systems expressed the religious significance of the kingship. In Israel, he argues, a state tax is well documented, but a coexistent state tax and regular temple payment cannot be shown.

Crüsemann pays special attention to evidence unearthed at Arad,[6] a Judaean military garrison in the Negev. Among other things, the fortress contained a roofed Yahweh sanctuary and storage houses where foodstuffs were kept. Archaeologists have found there a bronze serpent altar, apparently of the type purged by Hezekiah (2 Kgs 18.4), as well as several letters and documents.

Crüsemann focuses on letters to Eliashib, commander of the fortress.[7] These letters indicate that the military garrison was supported by in-kind payments from various regions of Judah. According to Aharoni's reading of Ostracon 5, it describes an explicitly men-

1.    *Erstlinge und Zehnten im Alten Testament. Ein Beitrag zur Geschichte des israelitisch-jüdischen Kultus* (BWAT, 22; Leipzig: Hinrichs, 1917).

2.    Eissfeldt, *Erstlinge und Zehnten*, p. 154.

3.    'Tithe', *EncJud*, XV, pp. 1156-62.

4.    'The Tithes in the Old Testament', in *Remembering All the Way... A Collection of Old Testament Studies Published on the Occasion of the Fortieth Anniversary of the Oudtestamentisch Werkgezelschap in Nederland* (OTS, 21; Leiden: Brill, 1981), pp. 116-28.

5.    'State Tax and Temple Tithe in Israel's Monarchical Period', paper presented to the Sociology of the Monarchy Seminar, AAR/SBL Annual Meeting, 1985. Published as 'Der Zehnte in der israelitischen Königszeit', in *Wort und Dienst 1985* (ed. H.-P. Stähli; Bielefeld: Kirchliche Hochschule Bethel, 1985), pp. 21-47.

6.    'State Tax', pp. 7-10; Crüsemann concentrates on the ostraca: Y. Aharoni, *Arad Inscriptions, Judean Desert Studies* (Jerusalem, Israel Exploration Society, 1981).

7.    Ostracon 25: Aharoni, *Inscriptions*, pp. 50-51; Ostracon 5: *ibid.*, p. 20.

tioned 'tithe' under the control of Arad's military commander.[1]
Crüsemann admits that the text is not readable, but observes that these
texts throughout show a very close relationship between the cultic and
military functions at Arad. From the Arad ostraca, Crüsemann concludes that it is highly improbable Judeans would have delivered both
a state tax and a temple tithe to the Arad fortress-sanctuary.

The only unambiguous biblical reference to a royal tithe comes in
'the manner of the king' (1 Sam. 8.11-17). The text, which probably
stems from anti-monarchical circles early in the monarchy,[2] says the
king 'will take a tenth of your seed and your vineyeard' (v. 15) and 'a
tenth of your flock' (v. 17). Crüsemann cites the reference to a regular gift to King Saul (1 Sam. 10.27)[3] and the protection money David
extorted from Nabal (1 Sam. 25)[4] as early examples of a royal tax.
Solomon's tax districts (1 Kgs 4.7-19),[5] set up in part to supply the
Jerusalem court (v. 7), offer further confirmation that a royal tax
system existed. Crüsemann also points to the Joseph narrative[6] as a
short story designed in part to legitimate the royal tax system in
Israel.

Based on Judah's absence from the tax district list, many scholars[7]
have questioned whether Judah had a tax system during the time of the
divided kingdom. Without explicit biblical confirmation, however, the
historian must rely on common sense. Deuteronomy's legislation
assumes the prior existence of a tithe in Judah. Furthermore, the court
and cult continued to function. Kings still went to war, constructed
and maintained state buildings, built defense works and temples. Even
in Bible times, those things took money. A tax system had to exist in
Judah after Solomon.

A state tax existed, but a purely cultic tithe did not. Crüsemann
convincingly assigns a late date to biblical texts, such as Gen. 14.20
and 28.22, which often are used to argue the origin of the tithe in a

1. *Inscriptions*, p. 20.
2. Crüsemann, *Widerstand*, pp. 66-73.
3. Crüsemann, *Widerstand*, pp. 54-60.
4. Crüsemann, *Widerstand*, pp. 138-42.
5. See my comments on the tax districts above in the discussion of statutory
labor in Judah.
6. *Widerstand*, p. 143.
7. Soggin, 'Compulsory Labor', pp. 265-67; Noth, 'Gaue', pp. 76-89; differently, Albright, 'Administrative Divisions', pp. 17-54; *idem, Archaeology*, pp. 140-
42; *idem, Biblical Period*, pp. 56-57; Mettinger, *Officials*, pp. 122-24.

premonarchical sanctuary payment. Additionally, he notes that monarchical era cultic texts, other than Deuteronomy, fail to mention a cultic tithe. Even the Holiness Code and Ezekiel are silent on this matter. Such omissions are evidence that no exclusively cultic tithe existed in the monarchical era.[1]

Deuteronomy's tithe legislation is a special case which raises a number of interesting questions. Deuteronomy names two kinds of tithe: an annual tithe paid 'at the place Yahweh chooses' (12.6-7, 17-19; 14.22-27), and a triennial tithe stored 'within your gates' (14.28-29; 26.12). On close examination, Deuteronomy's tithe legislation has some strange characteristics.

Deut. 14.22-23 indicates the tithe is required every year (v. 22). It is connected here with offering the first-born from the flock and herd (v. 23), but is characterized as strictly an agricultural tax. The annual tax obligations, then, consisted of first-born livestock and a tenth of all field produce—grain, wine and oil (v. 22; 12.17).

The tithe was collected at the religious sanctuary. Deut. 14.24-27 assumes the tithe payment normally was in-kind. The passage makes provision, however, for people some distance from Jerusalem who might not be able to transport their tithe produce to the central sanctuary there. Such farmers could convert the tithe to cash at home and reconvert the cash to produce in Jerusalem.

Deuteronomy's relatively elaborate discussion of tithe payment in a deuteronomic state without high places implies that, before the deuteronomic reform, people paid their tithes at the local high place. Echoes of this pre-deuteronomic system may be discerned in Deuteronomy's instruction to store the triennial tithe 'within your gates'.

Collecting the tithe at the high place made sense, given the political function of the royal religion. J.S. Holladay, in his illuminating archaeological reconstruction of monarchical religion, has recently found the rural sanctuaries to be part of 'an officially established hierarchically organized state religion..., operative in close co-ordination with the state's political apparatus'.[2] As G. Ahlström

---

1.   Crüsemann, 'Der Zehnte'.

2.   J.S. Holladay, 'Religion in Israel and Judah under the Monarchy: An Explicitly Archaeological Approach', in *Ancient Israelite Religion: Essays in Honor of Frank Moore Cross* (ed. P.D. Miller, P.D. Hanson, S.D. McBride; Philadelphia: Fortress Press, 1987), pp. 249-99.

argues,[1] the Israelite high place represented the religious-political authority of the royal house and its God Yahweh. It made sense to collect the religiously legitimated state tax at high places.

The deuteronomists had to make some provision for collecting the tithe once the king shut down the high places. Their solution that tithes should be paid in Jerusalem was probably burdensome for most people, but it made sense, given the decommissioning of the royal high place shrines. What is difficult to understand, however, is the deuteronomic approach to tithe payment, summarized as follows in Deut. 14.22-27 (cf. 12.6-7):

> You must tithe a tenth of all the yield of your seed, the output of your field annually. And in front of Yahweh your God in the place where he chooses to make his name dwell, you will eat the tithe of your grain, your wine, your oil and the firstborn of your herds and flocks, so that you will learn to fear Yahweh your God all your days. But if the distance is too great for you, if you are not able to bear it because the place where Yahweh chooses to set his name is too far for you, then, when Yahweh your God blesses you, convert it into money, take money in hand, carry it to the place Yahweh your God chooses and spend the money for whatever you want—for cattle, sheep, wine, strong drink, anything your heart desires—and eat there in front of Yahweh your God. Be happy, you and your household. Just do not neglect the levite within your gates, because he has no portion, no inheritance with you.

Under deuteronomic law, Israelite families are required to set aside ten per cent of their annual income, and, at an appointed time, throw a party for themselves with it. The only catch to this taxpayer's dream is that the party must be thrown in Jerusalem, with the hometown levite on the guest list. In effect, the tithe is abolished.[2]

The triennial tithe is the only thing which qualifies this practical abolishment of the tithe in the deuteronomic legislation. Once every three years, the tithe payment stays 'within your gates' for the exclusive support of royal cult officials (levites) and royal dependents (resident aliens, widows and orphans). Even in the annual tithe consumed by the tither, Deuteronomy warns not to exclude levites from the party (12.19). The triennial tithe, however, apparently is completely reserved for these government functionaries and other dependents. Actual tax obligations, therefore, continue under deuteronomic

---

1. Ahlström, *Royal Administration*, pp. 37-50.
2. In Crüsemann's words, Deuteronomy 'factually abolishes' the tithe.

reform. The deuteronomists were not completely impractical about the necessities of government. They made provision for the support of the cultic-bureaucratic apparatus, but cut taxes by two-thirds. The deuteronomists' bizarre tax policy makes sense in an extraordinary social-political context which I will explore in the next chapter, in my comments on Hezekiah and the rise of deuteronomism.

To summarize, several points arise from the discussion of taxation in Judah. It is safe to say the tithe was an agricultural production tax. It most likely originated with the advent of a monarchical state, though premonarchical prototypes are conceivable. Tithes were normally paid in-kind at local religious shrines, the high places. The deuteronomic reform, which shut down those high places, created problems for tithe payment. Cult centralization made it necessary to allow cash conversions so people could transport their tithe to the central sanctuary. Other taxes besides the tithe were collected, of which the most germane to the present discussion is the temple user fee instituted by Joash.

The tithe was religiously legitimated, but it was a state tax. Arguing about whether the tithe had a 'cultic' or 'secular' function in monarchical Judah starts from the faulty premise that such a distinction would have made sense in the First Temple period. To the contrary, as Yahweh's adopted son, the Davidic king had power of attorney over Yahweh's estate, including Yahweh's treasuries (2 Kgs 12.1-17; 16.8; 18.15-16). Examining First Temple Judah, it is inappropriate to draw a distinction between support for the royal cult and support for the royal house. Supporting the Davidic king was the practical expression of devotion to Yahweh, and worshiping Yahweh was the Judean's patriotic duty. Just as the Davidic monarchs exercised practical authority over Yahweh's land, so the kings had ultimate say over Yahweh's treasuries. Attempts to distinguish 'cultic' and 'secular' functions of the tithe are misleading and render the biblical evidence unintelligible. The cultic tithe was the religiously legitimated state tax.

### *Amaziah (2 Chronicles 25.14-16)*

Amaziah was not a cult reformer, but a brief note by the Chronicler deserves comment.

After describing Amaziah's gruesome campaign against Edom (2 Chron. 25.11-13 = 2 Kgs 14.7), the Chronicler makes the surprising statement that Amaziah 'brought the gods of the Seirites and set them up for himself as gods, bowing before them and burning incense to them' (v. 14). For this shocking transgression, Yahweh becomes angry with Amaziah and sends an unnamed prophet to scold him for seeking the advice of other gods (v. 15). The king's rejection of the prophet's warning (v. 16), leads to a disastrous battle against the Israelite king Joash at Bethshemesh (vv. 17-28; cf. 2 Kgs 14.8-14).

The episode clearly fits the Chronicler's pattern of reward and punishment. Williamson's comment well expresses the scholarly consensus: 'It can all be explained on the basis of the theological constraints which the Chronicler will have felt, so there is no need to look further for the origins of the material'.[1] With no Kings parallel and a solid fit with the Chronicler's overall theology of retribution, this report of Amaziah's inexplicable behavior appears clearly to be fictional.

The story may have an historical core, however. Spieckermann's textual reconstruction of the Gaza episode in Tiglath-pileser III's Palestinian campaign (c. 734 BCE)[2] gives a plausible analogy for Amaziah's transportation of the Seirite gods.

In the passage cited, Tiglath-pileser describes the replacement of Hananu's Gazan gods (ilānī [DINGIR.MEŠ-ni] -šú) with 'images of the great (i.e. imperial) gods' (ṣa-lam ilāni [DINGIR.MEŠ] rabûti [GAL.MEŠ]). Tiglath-pileser also boasts of putting a golden image of his majesty (ṣa-lam šarrū-ti-a ša ḫurāṣi [KU.SI$_{22}$]) in the palace of Gaza.[3] Spieckermann views this as the most drastic measure the Assyrian imperialists took against a rebellious vassal, effectively ending the cultic veneration of the state gods and, thus, the protection those gods afforded the nation.[4]

The deportation of the national gods and their replacement with the imperial gods effectively ended the rebellion. It meant the loss of divine support for independence.

This kind of imperial deportation of a vassal's gods may well underlie the Seirite gods episode in the Chronicler's account of Amaziah's reign. The clear impression of vv. 5-10 is that Amaziah

1.  Williamson, *I and II Chronicles*, p. 330.
2.  Spieckermann, *Assur*, pp. 325-30. Spieckermann compares three texts to arrive at his translation. See p. 327 n. 47 for full references.
3.  See Spieckermann, *Assur*, p. 326.
4.  Spieckermann, *Assur*, p. 329.

initiated the action against the Edomites. Judah was not defending itself against attack. Amaziah apparently intended to re-establish Judah's suzerainty over Edom (and partial control over the southern leg of the Kings' Highway) lost during the reign of Jehoram (2 Kgs 8.20-22). While Amaziah may well have been partially successful,[1] he did not make Edom a permanent vassal of Judah.[2] Amaziah's brutal treatment of these Edomites (2 Kgs 14.7) shows that he was willing to take drastic measures against them.

In light of roughly contemporary Assyrian imperial practice, Amaziah's capture and transportation of the Seirite gods to Jerusalem makes sense. It symbolized the re-establishment of Edom, albeit partial and short-lived, as a vassal of Judah. Such a practice was known to Israel at least in the monarchical period, as I Samuel 5 shows. In that story, of course, the Philistines capture the ark of the covenant in battle at Ebenezer and transport it to Ashdod where they set it up in the temple of Dagon. The irony of the story, that Dagon's idol falls face-forward before Yahweh's ark, plays on the unstated assumption that the Philistine action was supposed to symbolize Israel's defeat. Far from being implausible and unintelligible, Amaziah's transportation of the Seirite gods to Jerusalem fits well attested contemporary imperial practice familiar to Judeans.

Amaziah's action is somewhat mystifying because of the Chronicler's embellishment. The Chronicler inherited a plausible historical reference to Amaziah's deportation of the Seirite gods. The Chronicler embellished it to fit the reward–punishment pattern, thereby explaining the disastrous military campaign against the North which followed the Edomite expedition. In the present form of the narrative, Amaziah's perfectly intelligible imperial act of deporting the vassal's gods becomes an illogical act of personal apostasy. Rather than symbolizing the defeat of the Edomites, Amaziah inexplicably starts to worship the gods of the people he has defeated. The Chronicler's theology of retribution is thus salvaged at the expense of the historically plausible imperial action.

---

1.   Jones, *1 and 2 Kings*, p. 509.

2.   J.R. Bartlett, 'The Moabites and the Edomites', in *Peoples of Old Testament Times* (ed. D.J. Wiseman; Oxford: Clarendon Press, 1973), pp. 229-58 (237).

## Summary: Pre-Assyrian Cult Reform

The biblical historians offer a skewed picture of cult reform in the pre-Assyrian period. While the accuracy of their reports is questionable, however, the broad social picture they paint of cult and court under the Davidic kings is enlightening.

Most importantly, the cult and the court were inextricably bound together. Yahweh authorized the social-political power of the Davidic monarchy, and the monarchy became the chief representative of Yahweh on earth. The king built sanctuaries, instituted and ultimately controlled religiously legitimated taxes, used the temple treasuries as political events dictated, appointed and deposed priests, erected and demolished cult objects, and defined priestly roles. Though he probably held no cultic office, the king was the single most important figure in the cultic life of Judah.

The pre-Assyrian reforms show that the First Temple cult was a syncretistic cult. Yahweh indisputably headed the national pantheon, but other gods sat in that heavenly court. These Judean gods had cultic rituals performed for them as part of the official royal cult (Asherah is the most prominently mentioned by the biblical authors, but others surely existed). Additionally, in accordance with international agreements, non-Judean gods were worshiped in the capital city's 'embassy row', along the Mount of Olives opposite Jerusalem.

The pre-Assyrian reforms also show an increasingly centralized and powerful monarchical intrusion into Judah's social life. Taxation, statutory labor and an evolving state judiciary indicate that the monarchy exerted ever greater control over the lives of families, clans and villages. An increasingly centralized state no doubt brought some benefits to ordinary citizens. Perhaps its military and defense works afforded a certain degree of security. A more highly organized production and trade system may have benefited some. For most people, however, the costs outweighed the benefits. State tax and labor requirements disrupted the productive cycle and caused farmers to move away from diversified subsistence-oriented agriculture toward cash crops. That move will have made them much more vulnerable to natural disaster.

Social crisis was built into the situation evolving under an increasingly powerful monarchy. The crisis, however, did not erupt with full force in the South or the North until the Assyrian emperors brought Palestine into their orbit. Imperialism would heighten tensions already

built into Judah's monarchy-dominated society, creating popular discontent with the royal status quo. The impending social crisis, however, would generate a new way of conceiving Judah's national
identity—deuteronomic theology.

## Chapter 3

### AHAZ: REFORM AND IMPERIALISM

Cult and society underwent a gradual but steady transformation in Judah's pre-Assyrian period. The religious life of Judeans, like other aspects of life, came increasingly under the control of the monarchy. Power became more centralized. Centralization of power no doubt had social benefits, but the social burdens of supporting the state left Judean farmers even more vulnerable. Though a social crisis was brewing, it had not yet reached the boiling point. Assyria turned up the heat.

The economic, political and cultural demands of subservience to Assyria put an additional strain on Judah (and Israel) which led to increasing dissatisfaction with the monarchical status quo. By the mid-eighth century, even royal insiders like Isaiah were offering a stiff critique of the increasingly polarised economy. The poor were getting poorer and larger in numbers. Under Assyrian pressure, the detrimental effects of the monarchy were exacerbated. Whatever benefits imperialism might have brought surely were hard to see from the ground floor of Judean society.

The social turbulence of the era is reflected in a turbulent cultic life. Official cult reforms came fast and furious in the century from Ahaz to Josiah. The Assyrian period was a costly one for Judah. Much blood was shed as rebellions were attempted and squashed and reforms were instituted and undone. Out of this tragic period, however, grew one of Judah's most influential and lasting contributions to Western culture. Assyrian imperialism brought together the various traditions and class interests which form deuteronomic theology. As we study cult reform in the Assyrian period, we watch the birth of deuteronomism.

The Davidic king Ahaz ushered in the age of Judah's subjugation to Assyria. In so doing, Ahaz became the most important Judean king since Solomon. His submission to Assyria permanently changed the course of Judean history. The political, economic and religious implications of Assyrian imperialism for Judah were far-reaching and long-lasting. This chapter examines the biblical histories and takes a look at the economic and religious impact of imperialism on Judah.

## *2 Kings 16.1-19*

For a king so significant in Judah's history, Ahaz gets little attention from the Deuteronomist. The commentaries typically distinguish three blocks of material in chapter 16. The chapter consists of the deuteronomic framework (vv. 1-4, 19-20), a poorly detailed report about the Syro-Epraimitic war and Judah's appeal to Assyria for help (vv. 5-9), and an account of Ahaz's temple renovations, possibly based on archival material from the temple (vv. 10-18).[1] I will consider the three blocks in reverse order, starting with the temple narrative.

R. Rendtorff[2] finds two sources which have been woven together in the temple material, vv. 10-18. He sees a tension between vv. 12-14 and vv. 15-16. In the former, the king himself performs the various offerings on the altar. In the latter section, the priest is instructed by the king to perform the same sacrifices. Rendtorff also notes that v. 12, the only verse in vv. 12-14 where Ahaz is mentioned, refers to him as simply 'the king'. This contrasts with vv. 15-16 which refer to him as 'King Ahaz'.[3] Hoffmann correctly dismisses the significance of the short title for the king in v. 12. It is simply a stylistic variation prompted by the use of the longer 'King Ahaz' twice in the previous two verses.[4] Hoffmann also rejects Rendtorff's assertion of a contradiction between Ahaz performing sacrifice in v. 13 and his instructions to the priests in v. 15. The two verses refer to two different events. In the former, the king is dedicating the new altar.[5] Solomon's

---

1. Cf. Jones, *1 and 2 Kings*, p. 532; Šanda, *Die Bücher*, pp. 207-208. Spieckermann (*Assur*, p. 365) divides the sources between house annals (vv. 7-9) and a temple document (vv. 10-16). He further connects vv. 7-9 with the references to stripping the temple 'on account of the king of Assyria' (vv. 17-18), drawing a parallel with 2 Kgs 18.13-16.

2. *Studien zur Geschichte des Opfers im alten Israel* (WMANT, 24; Neukirchen–Vluyn: Neukirchener Verlag, 1967), pp. 46-47.

3. Rendtorff, *Geschichte des Opfers*, p. 46.

4. *Reform*, p. 142.

5. *Reform*, pp. 142-43.

role in the original temple dedication (1 Kgs 8.62-64) is the model for Ahaz's action here.[1] In v. 15, the king gives the priests instructions for ongoing sacrifice on the altar.[2] The tension between the verses thus disappears. The temple innovation narrative is best viewed as a unity.

Scholarly opinion has varied widely on the nature and purpose of the temple narrative. The depiction of Ahaz's unrestricted power over the cult, as well as the specific cultic concerns of the passage, point clearly to a pre-exilic setting, Spieckermann says.[3] He also cites the completely unpolemical character of the narrative which 'would be impossible in later times', as evidence of a pre-exilic setting.[4] The pre-exilic temple archive theory has many adherents[5] and some detractors.[6]

Hoffmann forwards the most radical proposal, however, arguing that the whole section is post-exilic.[7] The passage's vocabulary and cultic system is closely related to the P-literature (Num. 28; Lev. 23). It does not reflect the Deuteronomist's concern about how cult reform relates to the rejection of pagan practices. It does not question the introduction of a new altar. Its only concern is with the proper consecration and execution of sacrifice. Ahaz is not condemned, Hoffmann says, because the reported changes are wholly consistent with post-exilic priestly norms.[8]

Hoffmann's proposal of a post-exilic setting for the passage is interesting, but finally unconvincing. It depends upon his questionable assumption that the Deuteronomist freely composed just about everything in Kings. When older sources were used, Hoffmann believes, the Deuteronomist so reworked them as to leave them no longer identifiable as pre-Deuteronomist material. When confronted with a clearly

---

1.   Jones, *1 and 2 Kings*, p. 539.
2.   Hoffmann, *Reform*, pp. 142-43; Jones, *1 and 2 Kings*, p. 540.
3.   *Assur*, p. 365.
4.   *Assur*, p. 366.
5.   Benzinger, *Könige*, p. 170; Rendtorff, *Geschichte des Opfers*, p. 50. Gray (*I and II Kings*, p. 631) attributes it to a deuteronomistic compiler who was probably part of a priestly family.
6.   R. Kittel, *Handkommentar zum Alten Testament* (ed. E. Kautzsch; Tübingen: Mohr, 4th edn, 1922–23), p. 270; Noth, *ÜS*, p. 76; Jepsen, *Quellen*, p. 54; Šanda, *Könige*, II, p. 207; Jones, *1 and 2 Kings*, p. 533.
7.   *Reform*, pp. 143-45.
8.   *Reform*, p. 144.

identifiable non-deuteronomic source right in the middle of an important deuteronomic passage, Hoffmann has no choice but to consider it a post-Deuteronomist addition. He is locked in by his conviction (shared, of course, with Noth) of the Deuteronomist's all-encompassing creative genius. Hoffmann does not present sufficient cause to reject the weight of scholarly opinion that the temple narrative (vv. 10-18) has a pre-exilic origin.

Jones[1] follows Šanda[2] in rejecting the priestly origin of the material. The 'objective, non-moralizing narrative of the exotic innovation', as Montgomery characterizes it,[3] is the basis of this rejection. The absence of 'forthright criticism of Ahaz',[4] expected from priestly quarters, makes a priestly origin unlikely.

The flaw in this reasoning is its romanticized view of the royal priesthood. The royal priesthood served the king. Kings periodically introduced cult changes, minor and major. Such was their prerogative as chosen sons of Yahweh. More importantly, the king had the power to appoint and depose priests. Those priests who did not like the king's cult policies ordinarily either kept their mouths shut or were removed. It is conceivable that a discontented group within the priesthood secretly kept documents critical of royal policy. The discovery of the lawbook in Josiah's time shows that just such a thing happened in Judah. It is difficult to imagine, however, that an official temple archive from the time of Ahaz would contain criticism of Ahaz's innovations. The absence of priestly judgment against Ahaz in the report of his temple renovations (vv. 10-18) is not only unsurprising; it is exactly what should be expected from official archival material.

The temple narrative appears to have a pre-exilic, non-deuteronomic origin. The basic information is historically plausible. The content of the passage suggests it originated in the temple or among people with a keen interest in temple matters. Its neutral tone does not argue against a priestly origin, but it does argue against a deuteronomic origin. If this narrative is from temple archives, then the people writing official temple archives during Ahaz's reign were not deuteronomists.

The other block in the Ahaz chapter usually considered 'source

1. Jones, *1 and 2 Kings*, p. 533.
2. *Könige*, II, p. 207.
3. Montgomery and Gehman, *Book of Kings*, pp. 459-60.
4. Jones, *1 and 2 Kings*, p. 533.

material' is the account of the Syro-Ephraimitic war (vv. 5-9). The account is exceedingly brief and appears to telescope the actual course of events.[1] Šanda argues that the form of Ahaz's request to Tiglath-pileser III is stylized and clearly not from the annalistic source.[2] Hoffmann argues that the section holds together as a unity with the temple narrative (vv. 10-18) through the *Leitmotiv* of the king of Assyria's role in Judean affairs.[3] Spieckermann says that vv. 7-9 contain information from 'house annals', but that they are rendered tendentious by deuteronomic formulation.[4] He connects these verses with vv. 17-18 and compares them with 2 Kgs 18.13-16 (Hezekiah's payment to Sennacherib), since both passages describe tribute payments to Assyria from the palace and temple treasuries.[5]

The historical details of the Syro-Ephraimitic war and Ahaz's appeal to Tiglath-pileser III are sketchy in Kings. Isa. 7.1-9 offers additional historical background.[6] Hos. 5.8–6.6 is delivered in the context of the Syro-Ephraimitic war. 2 Chron. 28.5-7 contains an alternate version which portrays the campaign against Judah as two distinct events. In effect, the Chronicler describes no alliance between Damascus and Israel. To punish Judah, Yahweh first brings the Syrians against them, then brings the Israelites. Furthermore, the Chronicler characterizes Ahaz's plea to Tiglath-pileser III as the result of an Edomite–Philistine invasion of Judah (vv. 16-18). Finding no literary-theological explanation for the divergence from Kings here, Williamson regards the Chronicler's account of the Syro-Ephraimitic war as derived from 'a separate and valuable alternative source'.[7] He finds it likely that Israel in fact decimated Judah. He views an attack by Edomites and Philistines as historically plausible in light of conclusions in recent scholarship[8] that the Edomites were growing in

1.  Gray, *I and II Kings*, pp. 630-31.
2.  *Könige*, II, pp. 207-208.
3.  *Reform*, p. 142.
4.  *Assur*, p. 364 n. 130.
5.  *Assur*, p. 364.
6.  Cf. M.E.W. Thompson, *Situation and Theology. Old Testament Interpretations of the Syro-Ephraimite War* (Sheffield: Almond Press, 1982), p. 85.
7.  *I and II Chronicles*, p. 345.
8.  Bartlett, 'Moabites', pp. 229-58; 'An Adversary against Solomon, Hadad the Edomite', *ZAW* 88 (1976), pp. 205-26.

strength and interested in the Negev, and that Edom and Philistia were 'natural allies against Judah'.[1]

Whether or not the Edomites and Philistines were natural allies against Judah at this time, the Chronicler's explanation of Ahaz's plea to Tiglath-pileser III is less plausible than the Deuteronomist's explanation (2 Kgs 16.7). Rezin of Damascus and Pekah of Israel, vassals of Assyria since 738,[2] began pressuring Judah before Jotham died (2 Kgs 15.37). It is entirely likely from the description in Kings (16.6c) that the Syro-Ephraimitic league did not prosecute their war to conquer Judah, but rather undertook a limited action to depose Ahaz and replace him with a Judean king more favorable to their plans—a picture of events supported by Isa. 7.6.[3] Ahaz's response leaves no doubt that the motive of the allies was to enlist Judah's assistance in a regional revolt against Assyria.

Ahaz's message to Tiglath-pileser III (v. 7) suggests two possible motives for his offer to become Assyria's vassal, 'I am your servant and your son'.[4] Ahaz may have sent the message to the Great King to assure Assyria that Judah had no part in the Western uprising. Ahaz read the handwriting on the wall and took action to pre-empt reprisals against Judah when Assyria would finally crush the rebel league.[5] On the other hand, Ahaz may have sent the message to meet a more pressing need: 'come up and save me from the power of the king of Syria and the king of Israel who are set against me' (v. 7b). The former motive for Ahaz's message is usually preferred,[6] but ultimately the matter remains unresolved.

Whatever Ahaz's motives, the result was the same. Whether Ahaz

1. Williamson, *I and II Chronicles*, p. 348.

2. Jones, *1 and 2 Kings*, p. 535.

3. Jones, *1 and 2 Kings*, p. 535; Donner, 'The Separate States of Israel and Judah', in *Israelite and Judaean History* (ed. J.H. Hayes and J.M. Miller; OTL; Philadelphia: Westminster Press, 1977), pp. 381-434 (426); S. Herrmann, *A History of Israel in Old Testament Times* (Philadelphia: Fortress Press, 1973), p. 247; B. Oded, 'The Historical Background of the Syro-Ephraimite War Reconsidered', *CBQ* 34 (1972), pp. 153-65.

4. On the treaty significance of 'servant', see Montgomery and Gehman, *Book of Kings*, p. 348). On the significance of 'son', see D.J. McCarthy ('Notes on the Love of God in Deuteronomy and the Father–Son Relationship between Yahweh and Israel', *CBQ* 27 [1965], pp. 144-47).

5. Jones, *1 and 2 Kings*, p. 536.

6. Jones, *1 and 2 Kings*, pp. 536-37.

submitted to Assyria to relieve the short-term threat of Assyrian reprisal or the even shorter-term threat of destruction by the Syro-Ephraimitic league, he submitted because he perceived submission as a way to avert immediate danger. As long as the danger was perceived as pressing, the costs of submission would appear well worth the benefits of being in the imperial system and under imperial protection. As the perceived threat waned, however, the costs would appear less and less worthwhile.

The introductory deuteronomic evaluation of Ahaz (vv. 1-4) contains all of the standard elements, except, inexplicably, for the name of his mother, which surely even the wicked Ahaz had. I have already commented on the significance of the Deuteronomist's characterization within the larger framework of the regnal evaluations. Most importantly for the larger structure of Kings, the Ahaz evaluation portrays his reign as a return to the utterly chaotic days of Rehoboam. Its comparison of Ahaz's cult policy with 'the ways of the kings of Israel' and 'the abominations' of the dispossessed peoples peoples of Canaan (v. 3) combine with its very specific language about high place worship ('on the hills and under every green tree') to point forward, as well, to the treatise on the fall of the North (especially 2 Kgs 17.8-11). Judah's monarchy had come full circle back to the chaos following Solomon's demise. Only now, it stood on the brink of total disaster, like that which was about to strike the North. After Ahaz, only a new Solomon could save Judah from destruction and exile.

The Deuteronomist's impassioned rhetoric notwithstanding, the regnal summary offers virtually no information about cult reform under Ahaz. Later descriptions of Manasseh's (2 Kgs 21) and Josiah's reforms (2 Kgs 23; especially v. 12 which speaks of the rooftop altars built by Ahaz) probably address some of the cultic elements introduced by Ahaz. The Ahaz chapter itself, however, mentions only high place worship (v. 4) and making children pass through the fire (v. 3b) as cult offenses of Ahaz. As already established, high place worship was part of First Temple orthodoxy from the very beginning.

This is the first time, however, a Judean king is accused of 'making his child pass through the fire', a reference to child sacrifice.[1] Only Manasseh (2 Kgs 21.6) is similarly charged (though Solomon may be implicated through his devotion to the Sidonian Milkom in 1 Kgs

---

1. D. Plataroti, 'Zum Gebrauch des Wortes *mlk* im Alten Testament', *VT* 28 (1978), pp. 286-300.

11.5). The treatise on the fall of the North (2 Kgs 17.17) lists the immolation of children as one of the reasons for Israel's destruction.

Albright[1] makes a connection between the Molek child sacrifice cult and the Mesopotamian god Malik and notes that child sacrifice is mentioned in Israel and Judah only during the period of Assyrian domination. The recent scholarly consensus, however, places this fiery child-sacrifice cult in a West Semitic milieu.[2] A suggestion is frequently made, based on the Moabite king's sacrifice of his son during a disastrous battle with Israel (2 Kgs 3.27), that Ahaz may have sacrificed his own child as a response to the Syro-Ephraimitic crisis.[3] The Kings text itself, however, indicates the allies were unable to achieve more than a stalemate with Ahaz (v. 5b, contra 2 Chron. 28.5).[4] Furthermore, Manasseh's evaluation (2 Kgs 21.6) and Josiah's reform (2 Kgs 23.10) indicate that child sacrifice was an ongoing cult practice, not a one-time emergency measure.

The child sacrifice cult in nor near Jerusalem probably pre-dated Ahaz (1 Kgs 11.5), and it certainly survived him. It is possible that Ahaz himself participated in it. However, the tone of the whole deuteronomic evaluation of Ahaz indicates that his personal involvement in child sacrifice is like his personal involvement in high place rituals. It is a literary device to bring to a climax the indictment of Davidic cult policy before Hezekiah. By focusing cult aberrations in the person of Ahaz, the Deuteronomist prepares the way for a new royal character who personally will overturn two centuries of practice in the official cult of Judah. The apostasies of Ahaz make the reforms of Hezekiah possible and necessary.

## 2 Chronicles 28.1-27

The Chronicler shares the Deuteronomist's view that Ahaz brought an era to a close. In Chronicles, the Ahaz reign brings Judah to its

---

1. *Archaeology*, pp. 162-64.

2. H.W.F. Saggs, *Assyriology and the Study of thge Old Testament* (Cardiff: University of Wales Press, 1969), p. 22; McKay, *Religion*, pp. 39-41; Cogan, *Imperialism*, pp. 77-83; Jones, *1 and 2 Kings*, pp. 77-83.

3. E.g. Šanda, *Könige*, II, pp. 24, 195; Montgomery and Gehman, *Book of Kings*, p. 363.

4. McKay (*Religion*, p. 78) takes Isa. 7.2, 4 as evidence of a massive military defeat in the making. See also Williamson, *I and II Chronicles*, p. 345.

darkest hour. But it is there that Yahweh offers Judah its brightest hope, removing the final barrier to a reunited Israel. It is in spite of Ahaz that Israel, by the time of his death, has begun the process of reunification, lacking only the Davidic leadership necessary to seal its unity in a restored, purified cult. The way has been made straight for the coming of Hezekiah.

Most striking about the Chronicler's Ahaz account is the nearly exact role reversal of the South and the North. As Williamson has shown,[1] the Chronicler so construes the Ahaz rule as to equalize North and South. The depiction of Ahaz's apostasy later in 2 Chron. 29.7 in terms diametrically opposed to Abijah's portrayal of faithful worship (2 Chron. 13.11) highlights the reversal in Judah's cult practices. The curious account of Judah's defeat and capture by the North (28.8-15) puts the North in the situation of Abijah (2 Chron. 13), complete with prophetic instruction and faithful response (28.9-15). The v. 13 acknowledgment by the chiefs of the Ephraimites[2] that Israel has sinned carries a double significance in the Chronicler's story here. It contrasts the North's faithful behavior with Ahaz's apostasy. It also clears the way for the North's reunification with Judah under Yahweh's chosen Davidic line.

The new situation brought about by the repentance of the North and the apostasy of the South explains the Chronicler's surprising designation of Ahaz as 'king of Israel' (v. 19). Though the North's fall in fact removes the last political barrier to reunification, Ahaz's title, 'king of Israel', has its chief significance as a religious, not a political, reality. The Chronicler makes no mention of Samaria's fall. The literature does, however, bring North and South into alignment religiously. Under Ahaz, Judah has sunk to an all-time low cultically, while Ephraim has moved up a notch because of its confession of past sin. Ahaz thus rules over an Israel reunited—united in apostasy and in the hope that Yahweh's anger may be appeased by true repentance.

Ahaz and reunited Israel stand as the photographic negative of the Chronicler's Davidic–Solomonic ideal. Where David and Solomon had established true cult organization and worship, Ahaz introduced the worship of foreign gods (vv. 2-3, 23, 25).[3] Solomon faithfully over-

1.   *Israel*, pp. 97-118; *I and II Chronicles*, pp. 343-50.

2.   The term 'chiefs of the Ephraimites' appears to indicate the Northern monarchy had already fallen (Williamson, *I and II Chronicles*, p. 347).

3.   Williamson (*I and II Chronicles*, p. 344) thinks Isa. 2.8 and 20 prove that the

saw the construction, furnishing and opening of God's house whose blueprint had been hand-delivered from Yahweh by David. Ahaz, by contrast, cut down the temple's cultic vessels and shut up its doors (v. 24). David and Solomon's imperial splendor was replaced by an Ahaz-ruled Judah decimated in succession by Syria, Israel, Edom and Philistia (vv. 5-18). Instead of receiving tribute from the nations, Ahaz frantically stripped the temple and handed over Jerusalem's cultic and royal treasuries in a disastrous attempt to enlist Assyria's assistance (vv. 16-21). Ahaz, 'king of Israel', rules a formerly divided kingdom now reunited in spiritual and political decay.

The stage is set. From the depths of humiliation and faithlessness, Hezekiah rises to rebuild and restore the imperial glory of united Israel. Ahaz is the anti-type of David and Solomon. Hezekiah is their reincarnation.

### Judah's Economic and Political Obligations to Assyria

Ahaz's submission to Tiglath-pileser III came at a high price to Judah. His initial payment to the Great King depleted the temple and royal treasuries (2 Kgs 16.8). This was not the last contribution Judah would make to the imperial lord. Virtually without interruption, Judah paid imperial tribute at least once a year for the next century. Judah also supplied troop and forced-labor quotas to the empire. In the new alliance with Assyria, Ahaz may have found the security he needed to survive in the short run (2 Kgs 16.9), but over the long run the vassal relationship drained the life from Judah. The economic pressure of meeting obligations to the empire sent Judah headlong into social crisis.

The Assyrian imperial system, as imperial systems do, served the chief purpose of siphoning wealth from the peripheries of the empire (vassals and provinces) to its center (the Mesopotamian heartland). In his excellent book, *Taxation and Conscription in the Assyrian Empire*, J.N. Postgate concludes the following: 'There is no doubt that tribute was a most important element in the empire's economy, and it certainly was one of the major sources of precious metals and other

Chronicler is accurate in charging Ahaz with making 'molten images for Baal' (28.2). The Isaiah verses indeed provide further evidence of idolatry in 'the house of Jacob' (Isa. 2.7). That may even refer to Judah, but it does not indicate that Ahaz is the one who introduced such idolatry.

luxury goods in which the empire itself was poor.'[1] Elsewhere he observes that 'the royal reserves in gold and silver surely constituted a significant component of the economy as a whole'.[2] The royal gold and silver reserves came primarily from gifts (*nāmurtu*), booty and tribute (*maddatu*.).[3] By the time of Tiglath-pileser III, Assyria's chief means of extracating wealth had shifted. No longer relying primarily on plunder from military campaigns to fill the imperial coffers, the Assyrians now had the bureaucratic machinery in place to extract tribute systematically from all parts of the empire.[4]

Vassal treaty texts recovered so far contain no references to tribute obligations.[5] It is clear from the annals, however, that tribute was expected annually and that withholding tribute was considered an act of rebellion.

Annual tribute (*maddatu*,[6] *pirru*[7] and *biltu*[8]) was normally paired with special gifts (*nāmurtu*[9]) and levies (*bitqu*[10]) delivered annually to the Great King. Typical tribute payments included gold and silver,[11] precious stones and prized substances,[12] wine, oil and textiles,[13] grain,

---

1. *Taxation and Conscription in the Assyrian Empire* (Rome: Pontifical Biblical Institute), p. 217. Postgate summarizes and updates W.D. Martin's *Tribut und Tributleistungen bei den Assyrern* (Studia Orientalia, 8; Helsinki, 1936).

2. 'The Economic Structure of the Assyrian Empire', in *Power and Propaganda: A Symposium on Ancient Empires* (ed. M.T. Larsen; Mesopotamia, 7; Copenhagen: Akademisk, 1979), pp. 193-221 (202).

3. *Ibid.*

4. N.B. Jankowska, 'Some Problems of the Economy of the Assyrian Empire', in *Ancient Mesopotamia*, pp. 253-76 (255-56); cf. Postgate, 'Economic Structure', p. 194; H. Donner, *Israel unter den Völkern* (VTS, 11; Leiden: Brill, 1964), p. 1.

5. Postgate, *Taxation*, pp. 120-22.

6. *Taxation*, pp. 111-30; H. Tadmor, 'Assyria and the West', p. 37; I.M. Diakonoff, 'Main Features of the Economy in the Monarchies of Ancient Western Asia', in *Proceedings of the Third International Conference of Economic History, Munich, 1965* (Congrés et Colloques, 10.3; Paris, 1969), pp. 28-29.

7. Postgate, *ibid.*, pp. 163-66.

8. Spieckermann, *Assur*, p. 312; Cogan, *Imperialism*, p. 55.

9. Postgate, *Taxation*, pp. 146-62; Spieckermann, *ibid.*

10. Postgate, *Taxation*, pp. 57-62.

11. Jankowska, 'Some Problems', p. 254; cf. texts cited by Postgate, *Taxation*, pp. 306, 308, 311-14, 316-21, 337-42, 387-89.

12. Jankowska, 'Some Problems', p. 260 n. 43.

13. Jankowska, 'Some Problems', p. 256; Postgate, *Taxation*, pp. 328-32, 387-89.

flour, sheep, oxen, donkeys, carts,[1] exotic fruits and nuts,[2] fish and papyrus.[3]

Horses were an especially prized item of tribute,[4] as the very high price of horses at that time indicates.[5] Horses were key to the military operations of the empire.[6] Postgate says they were used as draft horses and 'must have been used almost exclusively for wars'.[7] Indeed, as Jankowska notes, '[w]henever the Assyrian army was reinforced by troops of the subjugated regions, or whenever a country sent auxiliary forces to the Assyrians on march, the reinforcements are always reported to include horses'.[8]

Another important obligation of vassals and provinces was the supply of soldiers (*ṣābē šarri*)[9] for imperial military maneuvers.[10] They supplied labor power for imperial building projects (*dullu ša šarri*).[11] Postgate argues the term *bitqu*, one of the normal tribute terms, refers specifically to the requisition of people, horses and materials for the military and forced labor requirements of the empire.[12] The *bitqu*

---

1. Postgate, *Taxation*, pp. 122, 308, 328-32, 376-79, 387-89, 391-92; cf. R.McC. Adams ('Common Concerns but Different Standpoints: A Commentary', in *Power and Propaganda*, pp. 393-404) on the delivery of such bulky raw materials and animal shipments.

2. Postgate, *Taxation*, pp. 328-32.

3. Postgate, *Taxation*, p. 155.

4. Postgate, *Taxation*, pp. 16-18, 57-62, 117-18; Y. Ikeda, 'Solomon's Trade in Horses and Chariots', in *Studies in the Period of David and Solomon*, pp. 215-38, 229; Cogan, *Imperialism*, p. 118; and especially, M. Elat, *Economic Relations in the Lands of the Bible c. 1000–539 BC* (Jerusalem: Mosad Bialik, 1977), pp. 69-82 [Hebrew].

5. Elat, *Economic Relations*, p. 69. He cites a bill of sale which shows one horse exchanged for six servant boys.

6. *Ibid.*

7. *Taxation*, p. 18.

8. Jankowska, 'Some Problems', p. 273. For textual references, see her n. 117.

9. Spieckermann, *Assur*, p. 315; Postgate, *Taxation*, p. 218; Saggs, 'The Nimrud Letters: Part VI', *Iraq* 25 (1963), p. 145; Cogan, *Imperialism*, p. 55.

10. Cogan, *Imperialism*, p. 93.

11. Spieckermann, *Assur*, p. 314; Postgate, *Taxation*, pp. 57-62.

12. Postgate, *Taxation*, p. 62: 'it seems that from the time of Slm III [Shalmaneser] onwards, the word *bitqu* (+ *kasaru*) was used to describe the state's levy on men and animals, intended to supply the standing army and labor force of the empire'.

seems to have been a regular, possibly annual requirement.[1]

The burden of supporting the imperial army and forced labor was not borne by the conscripts alone. Supplying imperial troops and labor gangs was a substantial economic burden on provinces and vassals.[2] The rural areas typically were able to supply adequate food for the troops, but it was very difficult to keep the mules and horses in straw.[3] Troop and labor obligations created a double burden for the subjugated peoples: the empire took able-bodied labor from the subject nations at the same time that it demanded increased production for the support of its armies and labor gangs.

The structure of Assyrian imperialism guaranteed the economic security of Assyria, at least in the short term, by increasing the economic insecurity of the nations and provinces on the empire's periphery. Assyrian imperial policy could only result in the economic starvation of the countries united under the empire.

It is possible that international trade was stimulated by Assyria's exploitation of subjugated peoples.[4] But the establishment and protection of trade between the peripheries and the Assyrian heartland was inherently exploitative. Whatever Assyria bought from its vassals was paid for with wealth extracted from them as tribute.[5] In the vassal states, those groups well situated to supply the trade goods demanded by the empire's royal and private[6] traders were the most likely to profit from the imperial trading relationship. Though some surely found a way to profit from imperial subjugation of their land, the long-term overall impact of imperial trade on the vassal's economy

1.  Postgate, *Taxation*, p. 59.
2.  Postgate, 'Economic Structure', p. 203.
3.  Postgate, 'Economic Structure', also *Taxation*, p. 397.
4.  Jankowska, 'Some Problems', p. 256.
5.  Jankowska, 'Some Problems', p. 275.
6.  The existence of private trade in the Assyrian empire remains a point of controversy in the scholarly literature (Postgate, 'Economic Structure', p. 206; *idem*, *Taxation*, p. 391). It is clear, however, that private enterprise 'was surely too solidly established [in Assyria] to have been superseded by state control of trade' (Postgate, 'Economic Structure', pp. 206-207). It seems likely that private trade was allowed alongside state-controlled trade. In any case, the inherently exploitative nature of the trading relationship between vassal and Assyria is constant whether Assyrian trade is conducted as a private or state enterprise or some combination of the two.

was disastrous.[1] The imperial system created international economic disparity, with the heartland's economy growing at the expense of the vassal states. In the process, the imperial system reproduced that disparity on a smaller scale in each of the vassal states. As is typically the case in such circumstances, a few managed to profit from stimulated trade, while the economy generally strangled in the grip of imperialism.

Under this kind of system, one would expect to find in a vassal economy a greater push toward surplus and trade-oriented production, greater consolidation of land, and greater disparity of wealth. Trade-generated economic activity in the overall context of an unhealthy economy would have made the vassal state ripe for social protest and even rebellion, as rising expectations from the trading boom clashed with the actual experience of the laboring majority whose circumstances were deteriorating under the imperial strain.

In Judah's case, as doubtless in the case of other vassal states as well, the social impact of the imperial economy was nothing new. The nature of the economic burden, as well as its practical result for the laboring majority, was not qualitatively different from the prior economic burden of supporting the domestic monarchy. Judeans were still expected to produce more with fewer people and resources in order to support a royal upper class which made little if any contribution to material production. What changed with Assyrian imperialism was the magnitude of the burden. As the classical prophets testify, the material conditions of the laboring majority deteriorated substantially in the Assyrian period.

## Assyrian Cult Introductions

The Deuteronomist's Ahaz narrative raises the issue of Assyrian interference in Judah's cult. The coincidence between Ahaz's submission to Assyria (2 Kgs 16.7-9) and his adoption of horribly apostate cult practices (vv. 3-4) implies a possible linkage. The verse which concludes the account of Ahaz's temple remodeling (v. 18) makes the point explicitly: Ahaz made the changes 'on account of the king of Assyria' (*mipp<sup>e</sup>nê melek 'aš šûr*). The author thus makes a direct link between Ahaz's temple renovation and his vassal treaty with Assyria.

---

1.   Spieckermann, *Assur*, pp. 312-13.

The question is whether Ahaz did it voluntarily or whether he was forced to do it by Assyria.

Scholarly discussion has focused considerable attention on the matter of imperial cult impositions. A brief review is in order.

Oestreicher[1] argued that Assyria did impose ritual obligations on its vassals, a view also held by A.T. Olmstead,[2] one of the leading Assyriologists of the early 20th century. The Damascene altar Ahaz put in the Jerusalem temple was in fact an Ashur altar. Gressmann[3] supported Oestreicher's thesis by appealing to various Assyrian texts. Gressmann concluded that more than half the recorded reforms of Josiah were directed against Assyrian deities (2 Kgs 23.4-7, 11-12).[4] The Oestreicher–Gressman thesis went unchallenged until the late 1960s.

From different directions, McKay[5] and Cogan[6] challenged the scholarly consensus. McKay argued primarily from the biblical evidence[7] that the cult practices condemned by deuteronomic reform theology are to a large degree indigenous West Semitic cults. He rejects Gressmann's argument that Baal, Asherah and the host of heaven were really Assyrian gods.[8] McKay hedges somewhat on exactly when the astral deities entered Judah's pantheon. On the one hand, he argues that they are West Semitic cults which pre-date Assyrian influence in Palestine.[9] On the other hand, he argues that they entered Judah's cult during the Assyrian period in 'the age of license which started about 734 BC' as a result of Yahweh's perceived impotence against the imperial power of Ashur's Assyria.[10] After briefly assessing some Assyrian texts, McKay concludes that the 'various deities worshipped during the period of Assyrian domination lack the definitive aspects of the Assyrian gods and generally exhibit

1.  *Grundsatz.*
2.  *History of Assyria.*
3.  'Josia', pp. 313-35.
4.  *Ibid.*
5.  *Religion.*
6.  *Imperialism.*
7.  He does spend some time looking at Assyrian evidence (*Religion*, pp. 60-70).
8.  McKay, *Religion*, p. 30.
9.  *Religion*, p. 58.
10.  *Religion*, p. 59.

the characteristics of popular Palestinian paganism'.[1] He does not dispute that Mesopotamian gods were worshiped in Judah after 734. Such worship, however, was the result of a general Assyrian cultural hegemony in Judah, not something required by the terms of Judah's vassalage.

Cogan reached similar conclusions with the Assyrian evidence as his starting point. After an excellent survey of relevant texts,[2] Cogan draws the following picture of neo-Assyrian policy toward the cults of vanquished nations: At times, the imperial army captured divine images and held them hostage until the enemy capitulated and offered a loyalty oath to the emperor. Once the vanquished publicly submitted, the gods were returned and their cults restored with no further interference from Assyria. Inscriptions, however, were placed on the idols to signify the vassal relationship. Otherwise, no substantive demands were made on the vassal's cult. In fact, the emperor frequently acted as a benefactor to the native cult, buying the favor of the local gods and their devotees.[3]

Cogan further argues that Assyria had different policies for different categories of international relationship. He distinguishes three categories of imperial domination. The vanquished could be incorporated as vassal states, as provinces, or they could be assigned an intermediate status in which they were nominally vassals but were actually ruled by Assyrian-installed puppets.[4] Vassals paid tribute, supplied troop quotas and generally defended the interests of Assyria in their region,[5] but they otherwise were free to run their own affairs. Most importantly, they had no religious obligations to Assyria. No sacrificial dues were required nor religious symbols erected.[6] Provinces, on the other hand, were incorporated directly into Assyria. They were administered by Assyrian-appointed governors. Local populations were considered Assyrian. The cult of Ashur, symbolized by the 'weapon of Ashur',[7] was installed as the chief national cult.

---

1. *Religion*, p. 67.
2. *Imperialism*, pp. 21-36.
3. *Imperialism*, pp. 37-40.
4. *Imperialism*, p. 42.
5. *Imperialism*, p. 55.
6. *Imperialism*, p. 56.
7. *Imperialism*, pp. 55, 60.

Local cults continued to operate,[1] though in some cases local deities were not accorded an official position in the newly established imperial pantheon.[2]

Like McKay, Cogan traces the cult apostasies of Ahaz and Manasseh to Canaanite paganism.[3] Those Mesopotamian elements which are discernible in the First Temple cult (for example the horses of Shemesh) appear to have entered through Aramaic acculturation after first merging with local pagan traditions.[4] Cogan envisions a thoroughgoing process of acculturation, particularly during the reign of Manasseh, by means of which Judah's distinctive Yahwistic traditions were weakened and syncretism based in national despair ran rampant. Trade with Assyria, joint military ventures with Assyria, the settlement of foreigners in Assyrian provinces to the west and north and the mingling of languages contributed to the process of acculturation. Judah was surrounded by Assyrian culture and dominated politically and economically by Assyria. Disenchanted with Yahwistic tradition after Hezekiah's rebellion failed, Judeans turned elsewhere for help. Religious syncretism in the Assyrian period was the result of 'the voluntary adoption by Judah's ruling classes of the prevailing Assyro-Aramaean culture'.[5] Confidence in Yahweh was at an all-time low. 'This unprecedented demoralization threatened Judah's unique cultural and religious identity; only with the return of national self-confidence, which was to follow upon the decline of Assyria, could the assimilation of Manasseh's age be halted.'[6]

With the publication of Cogan's book, the half-century scholarly consensus came crashing down. Under the rubble lay decades of assumptions about the nature and purpose of deuteronomic reform. Nearly everyone embraced Cogan's revision (and ignored McKay's similar contribution). H. Spieckermann did not.

Spieckermann re-examined texts cited by Cogan and introduced other Assyrian texts[7] to show that 'the religious-political measures which the Assyrians enforced against conquered peoples were an

---

1. *Imperialism*, pp. 55, 60.
2. *Imperialism*, p. 47.
3. *Imperialism*, p. 88.
4. *Imperialism*, p. 88.
5. *Imperialism*, p. 113.
6. *Imperialism*, p. 96.
7. *Assur*, pp. 307-62.

integnal part of their imperial policy'.[1] He rejects Cogan's thesis that
vassals were treated differently from provinces with regard to cultic
obligation.[2] The degree of imperial repression indeed varied from
state to state, but the variation was related to the attitude of the subject
people. Harsh religious-political measures were taken against rebellious vassals. Since Judah, with the brief exception of Hezekiah, was a
very faithful vassal, harsh impositions were unnecessary.[3] The
Davidic kings willingly adopted Assyrian cult practices without formally being forced to do so.[4] The problem for Judah then became
how exactly to assimilate the Assyrian gods to the fiercely intolerant
exclusively Yahwistic Judean cult.[5]

Ahaz found a clever compromise.[6] He gave Yahweh a new,
improved Damascene altar[7] and took the less impressive old
Solomonic altar for the king's personal use (2 Kgs 16.14).[8] On the old
altar, now moved off to the side, the king performed the imperial
rituals required by Judah's vassal status. The brilliant double altar
solution secured Ahaz's reputation as a loyal Yahweh worshiper and
simultaneously showed him to be a loyal vassal to Assyria. Ahaz's
cultic compromise held through the reigns of Hezekiah and Manasseh
until the eighteenth year of Josiah.[9]

Spieckermann makes a compelling case. His argument appears to

1.  *Assur*, p. 369.
2.  *Assur*, p. 370.
3.  *Assur*, p. 371.
4.  *Ibid.*
5.  *Assur*, p. 363.
6.  *Assur*, pp. 367-69.
7.  K. Galling's study (*Der Altar in den Kulturen des alten Orients. Eine archäologische Studie* [Berlin: Curtius, 1925], pp. 43, 45, 54) shows clearly that the altar Ahaz copied was Syrian, not Assyrian (cf. also de Vaux, *Ancient Israel*, p. 410). Jones (*1 and 2 Kings*, p. 538) has a convenient summary of the possible reasons mentioned in the scholarly literature for Ahaz's adoption of this model (see also Gray, *I and II Kings*, p. 635). The unambiguous implication of the Kings nar-rative is also the most likely reason for setting up the new altar: Ahaz did it because he had to, under the terms of his vassalage. 'Because the treaty sealing the vassalage agreement between Tiglath-pileser and Ahaz was accompanied by the offering of sacrifice on a Syro-Phoenician altar in Damascus, this altar became the model for the Jerusalem Temple, where it served as a reminder of the people's new status as vassals of Assyria' (Jones, *1 and 2 Kings, ibid.*).
8.  Jones, *1 and 2 Kings*, p. 368.
9.  Jones, *1 and 2 Kings*, p. 369.

strike at the heart of Cogan's and McKay's conclusions. On key issues, however, these seemingly opposite positions overlap. For example, all three scholars assume that the official cult became syncretistic for the first time in the Assyrian period. Thus, all three assume the probability of a serious backlash from characteristically intolerant Yahweh loyalists. My study of the pre-Assyrian period, however, shows that syncretism was the norm in the First Temple cult from the very beginning. The assumption of an exclusively Yahwistic official cult does not even square with the biblical picture. M. Smith is closer to the mark in his claim that '[s]yncretism was dominant in the cult of Yahweh at Jerusalem to the very last days of the First Temple'.[1] It is unnecessary to seek such extraordinary circumstances as the advent of Assyrian imperialism to explain the introduction of non-Yahwistic practices in the official cult. Syncretism was very ordinary. What was different about syncretism in the Assyrian period, however, was what the syncretism represented. Assyrian rituals in the Judean cult represented imperial domination of Judah.

Spieckermann clearly disagrees with Cogan about Assyria's cult policy toward vassals. His view of what actually happened in Judah, however, is not all that different from what Cogan and McKay think happened. For Spieckermann, Assyria did not have to impose harsh religious obligations on Judah, because Ahaz voluntarily adopted Assyrian rituals. For Cogan and McKay, Judah's rulers must have adopted Assyrian rituals voluntarily, because Assyria, as a matter of policy, did not impose religious obligations on vassals. Either way, Judah voluntarily adopted Assyrian rituals. Cogan and McKay do argue that most of the cults purged by deuteronomic reform are indigenous Palestinian cults, but both scholars say some of these indigenous cults exhibit Mesopotamian influence. Both scholars attribute the rise of these cults to social-psychological conditions in Judah under Assyrian imperialism. All three scholars then agree that some of the cult elements purged by deuteronomic reform entered the official cult under the pressure of Assyrian imperialism. All three also agree that, in Judah's case, these cultic innovations were voluntarily adopted.

This surprising agreement between Spieckermann, Cogan and McKay illustrates the important point that the debate about imperial

---

1. *Palestinian Parties and Politics That Shaped the Old Testament* (New York: Columbia University Press, 1971), p. 25.

religious policy toward vassals is moot in the case of Judah. Whether something is 'imposed' or 'voluntarily adopted' is a matter of perspective. To cite a modern illustration, an American visitor and an African national might have opposite views about the significance of an African bride wearing a very Western-looking white lace wedding gown. What the American might view as voluntary imitation, the African might consider cultural imperialism. There is an element of truth in both views. In lopsided social-political relationships, the line between force and persuasion is very thin. In such cases, 'imitation' is very difficult to distinguish from 'imposition'. Judah and Assyria had that kind of lopsided relationship.

The texts cited by Cogan and Spieckermann do not settle definitively the issue of imperial religious policy toward vassals. They do show, however, that subject peoples, whether by 'force' or by 'persuasion', typically incorporated into their own cults some of the religious rituals and symbols of the imperial lord. Judah was no different.

The house of David adapted its cult to accommodate the imperial gods. Whether voluntary or imposed, the presence of Assyrian rituals in the official cult of Judah would have had pretty much the same impact on the local population. It would have been a constant reminder of Judah's subjection to Assyria. That relationship would have irked some Judeans, pleased some others, and probably made little difference to most. What is certain, however, is that resistance to Assyrian rituals—even when joined with a broader rejection of all 'foreign' gods—was not 'purely religious'. As is always the case with religious controversy, a whole range of social, economic and political factors came into play. Purging Assyrian rituals from the Judean cult, regardless of the larger scope of the reform, was also a rejection of the political, economic and cultural hegemony of the empire.

## Summary

For the biblical historians, the reign of Ahaz closed a chapter in Judean history. Ahaz brought Judah to the brink of disaster religiously and politically. He created a dangerous situation which could be addressed only by a courageous leader, one who was willing and able to make a break with the policies of the past.

In Kings and Chronicles, the depiction of Ahaz is heavily stylized. For the Deuteronomist, he represents a return to the chaotic days of

Rehoboam, when Solomon's kingdom fell apart. Thus Rehoboam and Ahaz introduce and close the history of the divided kingdom. For the Chronicler, Ahaz represents an exact reversal of the pristine days of cult faithfulness (and political strength and prosperity) in Judah, exemplified by Abijah's military-evangelical crusade in the hills of Ephraim (2 Chron. 13). More importantly, Ahaz is an exact reversal of the Davidic–Solomonic ideal.

Finally, Ahaz's submission to Assyria brought with it a heavy economic burden. Lopsided trading relationships with the Assyrian heartland further fueled the centralization of production and the unequal distribution of wealth already institutionalized in Judah by the formation and ongoing support of a monarchical state. Social conditions for the laboring majority continued to deteriorate, eventually to the point of a full-blown social crisis, the details of which are outlined in the declarations of the classical prophets.

For all his strategic importance in the biblical histories, Ahaz's actual cult policies are described with astonishing lack of detail. Even where detail is provided, as in the case of his major renovation of the temple, it is described with mystifying dispassion. As the biblical sources strongly imply, Ahaz surely changed the First Temple cult 'on account of the king of Assyria'. It is probably also true that imperial beliefs and practices entered the Judean cult over time (even after Ahaz) through acculturation, as Cogan and McKay argue. Whether by political policy or cultural hegemony, Judah's cultic life changed because Ahaz submitted Judah to Assyria.

The Deuteronomist acknowledges imperial influence on the First Temple cult but does not spell out which 'foreign' practices are Assyrian and which are from indigenous non-Yahwistic cults. Educated guesses can be made. Ultimately, however, it is unnecessary to distinguish Assyrian practices from 'Canaanite' ones. Imperial religion influenced the Judean cult after Judah's submission to Assyria. Whichever specific practices happen to have been Assyrian, it remains the case that the coming deuteronomic campaign to purge the cult of non-Yahwistic practices was also to be a campaign to purge Assyrian cultic elements. The deuteronomic reform would express the nationalistic aspirations of some Judeans ready to discard the yoke of Assyria for the mantle of Yahweh.

Chapter 4

## HEZEKIAH: REFORM AND REBELLION

When Hezekiah took the the throne, Judah was squarely in the imperial camp, a good place to be, given Assyria's iron grip on the West and iron-handed treatment of rebellious vassals. The first shift in the geopolitical equation came, ironically, after the failed Philistian uprising against Assyria. Sargon's subjugation of Ashdod in 712 not only nailed the coffin shut on the revolt in Philistia, it also left Judah the ascendant power in the West.[1] With the cities of Philistia in decline and the Transjordan states already decimated by Tiglath-pileser III's earlier expeditions, Judah became 'the main political and military power in the region, depicted as comparatively large, strong, and prosperous', as Reviv says.[2]

This happy state of affairs for Judah was made even happier by Sargon's distraction in the East with rebellious Babylonians. Things got better and better for the anti-imperialist element in Judah. Sargon's death on the battlefield in 705 brought political instability to the imperial heartland and signaled the Western vassals that the time was ripe for rebellion.[3] Luli, king of Tyre and Sidon, rebelled against Assyria, cutting off the imperial army's main route to Palestine. Marduk-apal-idinna posed a new, more serious threat to the empire on

1. Reviv, 'The History of Judah from Hezekiah to Josiah', *WHJP*, pp. 193-204; A. Jenkins ('Hezekiah's Fourteenth Year. A New Interpretation of 2 Kgs xviii 13–xix 37', *VT* 26 [1976], pp. 284-98) is unconvincing in his claim that Hezekiah actually joined the Philistian revolt in 712.

2. Reviv, 'History of Judah', pp. 193-204.

3. Reviv, *ibid.*; B. Oded, 'Judah and the Exile', in *Israelite and Judaean History* (ed. J.H. Hayes and J.M. Miller; OTL; Philadelphia: Westminster Press, 1977), pp. 436-88, 447; N. Na'aman, 'Sennacherib's "Letter to God" on his Campaign to Judah', *BASOR* 214 (1974), pp. 25-39, 33-35; *idem*,'Sennacherib's Campaign to Judah and the Date of the *lmlk* Stamps', *VT* 29 (1979), pp. 61-86.

the eastern, Babylonian front. Hezekiah strengthened his control over the Philistian cities[1] and formed an alliance with Ṣidqa of Ashkelon.[2] He apparently established diplomatic relations with Egypt sometime between 705 and 701 (cf. Isa. 31.1), as Reviv says, 'to ensure military support from Shebitku the second king of the XXVth (Nubian) Dynasty'.[3] As the probably misplaced account of 2 Kgs 20.12-13 shows,[4] Hezekiah may well have established diplomatic contact with the Babylonian rebel Marduk-apal-idinna during this time. By the time Sennacherib was able to regain control, Hezekiah had successfully forged a formidable regional alliance against Assyria, with himself at the head,[5] as Sennacherib's own account indicates.[6]

Sennacherib did regain control of the situation in the West. In 701, he marched against Jerusalem, stripping Hezekiah of Judah's outlying towns and shutting him up in his own capital city 'like a bird in a cage'. Sennacherib's account of the siege of Jerusalem presents its own historical problems,[7] but the broad picture, consistent with 2 Kgs 18.13-16, is probably accurate.

The political and economic cost of Hezekiah's failed rebellion was high (vv. 14-15). In one sense, however, Sennacherib treated Hezekiah with curious leniency. Unlike his ally Ṣidqa,[8] Hezekiah was allowed to remain on the throne, and Jerusalem was spared. But why?

Zion theology had a clear answer: Jerusalem, the home of Yahweh and God's chosen dynasty, was inviolable.[9] The Deuteronomist has access to three explanations of Jerusalem's deliverance: the most straightforward, annal-like report of 18.13-16 that Hezekiah surren-

1. Oded, 'Judah', pp. 444-46; Reviv, 'History of Judah', pp. 193-204; Jones, *1 and 2 Kings*, p. 560; *ANET*, p. 287; Na'aman, 'Letter to God', p. 27; H. Tadmor, 'Philistia under Assyrian Rule', *BA* 29 (1966), pp. 86-102.

2. Reviv, *ibid.*; *ANET*, p. 287; Jones, *1 and 2 Kings*, p. 560.

3. Reviv, 'History of Judah', p. 196.

4. Reviv, *ibid.*; Gray, *I and II Kings*, p. 668; Jones, *1 and 2 Kings*, p. 589.

5. Reviv, 'History of Judah', pp. 193-99.

6. *ANET*, p. 287.

7. B.S. Childs, *Isaiah and the Assyrian Crisis* (Studies in Biblical Theology, 2.3; London: SCM Press, 1967), pp. 69-103.

8. *ANET*, p. 287.

9. Cf. de Vaux, *Ancient Israel*, p. 327; E.W. Nicholson, 'The Centralisation of the Cult in Deuteronomy', *VT* 13 (1963), p. 386.

dered at Lachish,[1] a tradition that Sennacherib pulled back to Ninevah because of a rumor about military moves by Tirkahah of Ethiopia (2 Kgs 19.9a, 36-37) and a tradition that the siege ended because of a sudden plague in the Assyrian camp (2 Kgs 19.35).

The latter two traditions, as they appear in Kings, are more clearly 'narrative theology',[2] than the annal-like explanation of 18.13-16. The military-rumor tradition offers a non-supernatural explanation preferred by some.[3] As Clements notes, it does not contradict the annal-like report in Kings or the Assyrian records.[4] S. Herrmann prefers the plague-in-the-camp tradition, though he admits 'we cannot exclude the possibility that Hezekiah sent his tribute and ostentatiously reasserted his allegiance'.[5] It seems most likely that Jerusalem and Hezekiah were spared because Assyria wanted to retain political stability without keeping a substantial Assyrian force in Judah[6]—it was a cheaper strategy and politically plausible given Hezekiah's clear repentance. However, Millard has made a compelling case that the plague-in-the-camp tradition reflects a common imperial literary style to explain natural disasters, a style contemporary with Hezekiah.[7] Millard suggests the plague story 'could easily be a contemporary report written by a Judean historian trained in the traditional outlook of orthodox Israelite faith'.[8]

The 'rumor' and 'plague' explanations of Jerusalem's deliverance appear in Kings in the middle of a narrative illustrating a central tenet of royal theology: the inviolability of Zion. They appear to contradict one another and the annal-like material of 18.13-16. It is entirely possible, however, that the three explanations reflect actual historical factors which together caused Sennacherib to withdraw and leave a

---

1. Cf. *ANEP*, pp. 371-74; R. Barnett, 'The Siege of Lachish', *IEJ* 8 (1958), pp. 161-64; R.E. Clements, *Isaiah and the Deliverance of Jerusalem* (JSOTSup, 13; Sheffield: JSOT Press, 1980), p. 19; Jones, *1 and 2 Kings*, p. 565; but contrast A.R. Millard, 'Sennacherib's Attack on Hezekiah', *TynBul* 36 (1985), pp. 61-77.

2. Clements, *Deliverance*, pp. 21, 59, 95.

3. Cf. W. von Soden, 'Sanherib vor Jerusalem', in *Antike und Universalgeschichte* (FS H.E. Stier; Münster: Aschendorff, 1972), pp. 43-51.

4. *Deliverance*, p. 55; Jones, *1 and 2 Kings*, pp. 568-69.

5. *History*, p. 259.

6. Clements, *Deliverance*, pp. 19, 62.

7. 'Sennacherib's Attack', pp. 74-76.

8. *Ibid.*; Clements, however (*Deliverance*, p. 59), dates it to Josiah's reign.

properly chastened Hezekiah on the throne. It is not at all unusual for important military-political decisions to rest on a combination of factors, no single factor alone being sufficient to explain the course of action finally taken. Such may have been the case with the deliverance of Jerusalem.

Before leaving the historical discussion about Sennacherib's campaign, it is necessary to note another important debate. Some have found in the multiple explanations of Jerusalem's deliverance an indication that Sennacherib mounted two campaigns against Jerusalem. The two-campaign theory takes two forms. H.H. Rowley[1] argues that Hezekiah surrendered along the lines of 18.13-16 and was allowed to stay on the throne. A few months later, however, Sennacherib learned a powerful Egyptian army was approaching. He decided to take Jerusalem after all, as a strategic buffer against the advancing Egyptians. He dispatched a small contingent led by the Rabshaqeh. When the Assyrians arrived at Jerusalem, however, they found a defiant Hezekiah, encouraged by Isaiah and bolstered by the original terms of surrender—terms which did not include the occupation of Jerusalem. The Assyrian troops failed to occupy Jerusalem in the face of Hezekiah's resistance. The second campaign was the occasion of the miraculous deliverance of Jerusalem and the historical source of the rumor and plague traditions. The Assyrian annals, as one might expect, mention only the first campaign.[2] Rowley's suggestion is theoretically possible, but lacks sufficient evidence to suggest a failed second campaign.

The second form of the two-campaign theory has more to support it. The key is the obviously anachronistic reference in 19.9 to Tirkahah 'king of Ethiopia'. Tirkahah became king of Ethiopia in 689.[3] L. Macadam's suggestion, based on epigraphic evidence from Kawa,[4] that Tirkahah would have been too young to have conducted a

---

1.  H.H. Rowley, 'Hezekiah's Reform and Rebellion', *BJRL* 43 (1960–61), pp. 395-461 (= *Men of God. Studies in Old Testament History and Prophecy* [London: Nelson, 1963], pp. 98-132).

2.  *I and II Kings*, pp. 420-23.

3.  Jones, *1 and 2 Kings*, p. 375; Gray, Rowley, 'Reform', p. 661; Rowley ('Reform', p. 420) and Noth (*History*, p. 268) take the mention of Tirkahah as an inaccuracy. He was simply the best-known of the Ethiopian dynasty.

4.  M.F.L. Macadam, *The Temples of Kawa I: The Inscriptions* (London: Oxford University Press, 1949).

military campaign in 701 has led Albright[1] and Bright[2] to suggest that Sennacherib led a second campaign at the end of Hezekiah's reign. Macadam's claim about Tirkahah's age has been challenged.[3] K.A. Kitchen,[4] however, has sealed the case against the two-campaign theory, leaving no doubt that Tirkahah, though certainly not yet 'king', was indeed old enough to command an army in 701.[5]

The date of Sennacherib's campaign against Hezekiah raises a question about Hezekiah's cult reform. At issue is whether the reform occurred before or after the rebellion was crushed in 701. It is an important question, because the timing of the reform *vis-à-vis* the rebellion may determine the primary character and purpose of the reform.

The weight of scholarly opinion has fallen on the side of a pre-701 date for the centralization reform.[6] If that date is correct, Hezekiah's religious reform probably had an important political dimension to it. It was part of a general move to consolidate Davidic power in Judah,[7] a thorough battening down of the hatches in preparation for the rebellion against Assyria.[8] If the reform occurred after 701, however, the

---

1. 'The Date of Sennacherib's Second Campaign against Hezekiah', *BASOR* 130 (1953), pp. 8-9; 'Further Light on Synchronisms between Egypt and Asia in the Period 935–685 BC', *BASOR* 141 (1956), pp. 23-27.

2. *History* (3rd edn), pp. 298-309; Nicholson ('Centralisation', pp. 386-89) agrees with Bright's two-campaign theory.

3. J. Leclant and J. Yoyotte, 'Notes d'histoire et de civilisation éthiopiennes', *Bulletin de l'Institut français d'archéologie orientale* 51 (1952), pp. 17-27. They retranslate the texts and argue Tirkahah was 20 years old at the time.

4. *Intermediate Period*, pp. 158-59, 383; 'Late Egyptian Chronology and the Hebrew Monarchy', *JANESCU* 5 (1973), pp. 225-33; and especially, 'Egypt, the Levant, and Assyria in 701 BC', in *Fontes atque Pontes. Eine Festgabe für Hellmut Brunner* (Wiesbaden: Otto Harrassowitz, 1983), pp. 243-53.

5. Cf. Gray, *I and II Kings*, pp. 660-61; Millard, 'Sennacherib's Attack', p. 63; and Jones, *I and 2 Kings*, p. 567 for summaries.

6. Montgomery and Gehman, *Book of Kings*, p. 488; Gray, *I and II Kings*, p. 682; E.W. Todd, 'The Reforms of Hezekiah and Josiah', *SJT* 4 (1956), pp. 288-93; Weinfeld, 'Neo-Babylonian Analogy', pp. 202-12; J. Rosenbaum, 'Hezekiah's Reform and Deuteronomistic Tradition', *HTR* 72 (1979) pp. 23-44; Reviv, 'History of Judah', p. 194; Jones, *I and 2 Kings*, p. 559.

7. Cf. Oded, 'Judah and Exile', p. 443; Reviv, *ibid.*; Nicholson, 'Centralisation', pp. 383-89.

8. Jones, *I and 2 Kings*, p. 562. Note M. Haran's suggestion (*Temple*

anti-Assyrian political dimension of the reform evaporates. The post-701 dating has fewer adherents.[1] Even Nicholson, who dates the reform post-701, does so because he believes Sennacherib mounted a second invasion of Judah toward the end of Hezekiah's reign. The anti-imperialist thrust of centralization is thus left intact.[2] As I shall argue below, cult centralization, particularly when it is considered in the light of Deuteronomy's peculiar tithe legislation, has a host of implications which make it a fitting strategy for rebellion. Having already rejected the idea that Sennacherib made a second march on Jerusalem late in Hezekiah's reign, I find Hezekiah's centralization reform to be more plausiby dated shortly before 701.

Some scholars think the whole business of dating the centralization reform is moot, because they consider it fictional. Since Wellhausen, a number of scholars have questioned the historical value of the brief reform account in 2 Kgs 18.4.[3] In this scholarly reconstruction, the removal of the bronze serpent cult object, Nehushtan, is the historical core of an expanded reform account modeled on Josiah's later deuteronomic reform.[4] The Nehushtan removal fits no larger theological-literary tendency of Kings and therefore should be considered historically reliable. The high place, Asherah and sacred pillar reform, however, show clear deuteronomic tendencies and should be rejected as fictional.[5] These Josianic reforms in miniature are meant

*Service*, p. 140) that Hezekiah's reform reflects a priestly ideology.

  1. V. Maag, 'Erwägungen zur deuteronomischen Kultzentralisation', *VT* 6 (1956), pp. 10-18 (10-11).

  2. 'Centralisation', pp. 384-86. Nicholson says cult centralization rose 'out of the conditions brought about by Sennacherib's first invasion of Judah in 701 BC'. The decimation of the kingdom in the wake of the 701 campaign and rising religious syncretism afterward led to 'a dampening of nationalistic fervor' (p. 386) in Judah. Hezekiah decided to shut down the high places 'where, we may presume, these foreign cults were gaining ground'. Centralization, even though it occurred after 701, remained 'largely a political move', Nicholson says (p. 386).

  3. Wellhausen, *Prolegomena*, pp. 25, 47-48; Gressmann, 'Josia und das Deuteronomium', *ZAW* 42 (1924), pp. 313-27; Hoffmann, *Reform*, p. 154; Spieckermann, *Assur*, pp. 170-75; see, however, A. Bentzen, *Die josianische Reform und ihre Voraussetzungen* (Copenhagen: Gad, 1926), pp. 73-74; Noth, *ÜS*, p. 85; Gray, *I and II Kings*, pp. 670-71; Todd, 'Reforms', pp. 289-91; Rowley, 'Reform'; McKay, *Religion*, p. 13.

  4. Burney, *Notes*, p. 337.

  5. Hoffmann, *Reform*, pp. 151-55; Spieckermann, *Assur*, pp. 172-73.

either to foreshadow Josiah's reform (so it appears to have a precedent) or to enhance Josiah's reputation by making Manasseh look even worse than he already would have.

The Nehushtan reform, probably from a reliable annalistic source, becomes the 'historical model',[1] the 'crystallization point'[2] around which the Deuteronomist builds a broader, fictional reform. As Spieckermann argues, this literarily expanded reform introduces a necessary historical break between Manasseh and his predecessors. Manasseh is not merely continuing the cultic policy of his Davidic forebears, he is reversing the righteous reform of his father. Thus, the Deuteronomist draws even more starkly the contrast between faithless Manasseh and faithful Josiah.[3]

The arguments against a Hezekian centralization reform are not compelling. The reports of cult centralization and Asherah and sacred pillar reforms indeed show clear deuteronomic tendencies. That alone, however, is insufficient reason to reject the reform as fictional. Deuteronomic theology did not spring out of nowhere in Josiah's time. It grew out of historical experience. The Arad excavations,[4] though inconclusive, raise the possibility of high place reform during Hezekiah's reign. In light of this and other considerations to be discussed below, the points of contact between Hezekiah's reform and deuteronomic theology are best viewed as the result of historical dependency. Perhaps Hezekiah was influenced by some kind of 'proto-deuteronomic' theology, but certainly subsequent deuteronomic theology was influenced by Hezekiah's reform.

The brief report of Hezekiah's reform in 18.4 is not meant to detract from Manasseh and thus elevate the reputation of Josiah. Hezekiah's high place reform does not set up Manasseh for criticism like other cult measures might have. As I have shown in the chapter on pre-Assyrian cult reforms, the continued functioning of the high places is not considered a serious cult crime in Kings. It is a shortcoming easily forgiven. In fact, continued high place worship (except in the cases of Ahaz and Manasseh) is mentioned among Judean kings only and always in connection with those who 'did right

---

1.   Hoffmann, *Reform*, p. 154.
2.   Spieckermann, *Assur*, p. 173.
3.   *Assur*, p. 173.
4.   Aharoni, 'Arad', *BAR* 31 (1968), p. 26.

in Yahweh's view'. If in 18.4 the Deuteronomist were fictionally building a case against Manasseh to enhance the reputation of Josiah, it is strange that the author should ignore astral worship, augury, Baalism and child sacrifice. These, after all, are the especially abominable cult practices purged by Josiah which the Deuteronomist attributes to Manasseh. Instead, the Deuteronomist reports four cult measures, two of which are not even mentioned in the Manasseh chapter. Of Hezekiah's cult measures—removing the high places, smashing the sacred pillars, cutting down the Asherah and cutting out Nehushtan—only rebuilding the high places and making an Asherah are mentioned as corresponding cult measures of Manasseh. Sacred pillars appear nowhere in the Manasseh chapter. So it is safe to say their mention in the Hezekiah reform is not an attempt to smear Manasseh. Though Manasseh does make an Asherah, the Deuteronomist compares it to an Asherah made by Ahab. It is not contrasted with Hezekiah's anti-Asherah reform.

Cult centralization may well have been the most drastic and far-reaching reform Hezekiah could have accomplished. It may even have been the most important reforms he tried, in the opinion of deuteronomists. But its mention in 2 Kgs 18.4 does little to damage Manasseh's reputation. Hezekiah's reform mentions cult measures not picked up in the Manasseh chapter and ignores some of Manasseh's juiciest crimes. The Hezekian reform, as it is reported in Kings, is more plausible as history than as fiction.

Hezekiah actually centralized the cult, and he did it before 701. As part of Judah's rebellion against Assyria, it had religious, political, military, economic and social dimensions which made it very smart strategy. It almost worked.

If the speeches of the Rabshaqeh (2 Kgs 18.19-35) reflect actual arguments at the time of Jerusalem's siege, then Assyria noticed Hezekiah's centralization reform. They took note for good reason.

It is hard to know just where the Rabshaqeh speeches originated, though in their present context they are related to the Isaiah stories[1] and are designed to highlight the inviolability of Zion motif which runs through the larger narrative.[2] B. Childs[3] has confirmed form-

---

1.  Gray, *I and II Kings*, p. 659; Clements, *Isaiah*, p. 281.
2.  Gray, *I and II Kings*, p. 661; Clements, *Isaiah*, p. 282.
3.  *Assyrian Crisis*.

critically the scholarly consensus that the passage 18.17–19.37 contains two parallel versions of the deliverance of Jerusalem from Sennacherib's siege.[1] Childs finds an actual historical situation reflected in the speeches of the Rabshaqeh which constitute the bulk of the first version of the lifting of the siege (18.17–19.7, 36).[2] Certainly, it was the kind of diplomatic argument Assyrian envoys sometimes made to rebellious subjects.[3] A speech at the wall of Jerusalem is historically plausible.

The Rabshaqeh's claims that Assyria now marched against Judah as the historical agent of Yahweh (v. 25) is consistent with imperial ideology, as it is described in the Assyrian annals.[4] It is entirely likely that the Assyrians and Judeans opposed to Hezekiah's rebellion mounted just such an argument (cf. Isa. 10.5-11). The Judean request that the Rabshaqeh continue his monologue in Aramaic (v. 26) plausibly indicates that the speech had its intended effect. It made sense to the people of the city. Hezekiah had taken a great risk domestically, closing down the high places, reversing more than 200 years of cult policy in Judah.[5] An argument like the one the Deuteronomist attributes to the Rabshaqeh would have rattled the rebels. Whether it was actually made by an Assyrian official or not, the Rabshaqeh's speech reflects an actual argument of the day.

Montgomery[6] and Gray[7] see v. 22 ('is it not [Yahweh's] altars Hezekiah has removed...?') as confirmation that Assyria took notice of Hezekiah's high place reform. Centralizing the cult was odd domes-

---

1.  B. Stade, 'Anmerkungen zu 2 Kö. 15–21', *ZAW* 6 (1986), pp. 156-89 (173); cf. Gray, *I and II Kings,* p. 659; Jones, *1 and 2 Kings*, p. 568; differently, Šanda, *Die Bücher,* II, p. 289.

2.  Childs, *Assyrian Crisis*, pp. 69-103.

3.  *Ibid.*; Gray, *I and II Kings*, p. 664; M. Weinfeld, 'Neo-Babylonian Analogy'; Herrmann, *History*, p. 259; von Soden, 'Sanherib', pp. 43-51 (46-48); Saggs, 'The Nimrud Letters, Part I', *Iraq* 17 (1955), p. 23.

4.  Gray, *I and II Kings*, pp. 664-65; Jones, *1 and 2 Kings*, p. 571; cf. Cogan, *Imperialism*, pp. 21-40.

5.  Cf. Gray, *I and II Kings.*, p. 665. I agree with Gray that the Rabs'aqeh speech 'is a cunning appeal to popular misgiving, since the local sanctuaries were undoubtedly in favour...'. I disagree that the high places were tombs of the ancestors.

6.  *Book of Kings*, p. 488.

7.  *I and II Kings*, p. 682.

tic policy, but might it have had political consequences for Judah's vassal relationship with Assyria?

The political consequences of centralization come into clearer focus when its economic consequences are considered. If indeed the high places were collection points for the annual tithe, then closing them would be something like revenue suicide. Assyria, a chief beneficiary of Judah's revenue collection, might well take notice of Hezekiah's move to close down the high places.

Deuteronomy's peculiar tithe legislation draws out some of the implications for Judah's internal revenue system. Though written down after Hezekiah's revolt had been crushed, the deuteronomic legislation suggests how cult centralization and rebellion might have been related. A comparison of tithe legislation and the deuteronomic 'law of the king' brings that relationship into clearer focus.

Deuteronomy identifies two different kinds of tithe, an annual tithe (12.6-7, 11-12, 17-18; 14.22-27) to be consumed at the central sanctuary and a triennial tithe (14.28-29) to be stored 'within your gates', that is, in the local villages. Deuteronomy appears to view the triennial tithe as an obligation in lieu of the annual tithe every third year, rather as an additional payment that year. In any case, the triennial tithe was to be collected and processed differently from the annual tithe. Stored 'within your gates', the triennial tithe is set aside for the direct support of cult officials and other royal dependents. It is not consumed by the tither, in contrast to the annual tithe. The triennial practice outlined by Deuteronomy likely reflects the normal annual tithe practice when high place abolitionists were not making the rules.

The strangest thing about the annual tithe in Deuteronomy is how it was to be paid. The faithful are told to consume their own tithes (12.7, 17-18; 14.23, 26). This innovative approach to taxation has a single condition: the tithe must be consumed at the central sanctuary.

In this comprehensive survey of ancient Near Eastern tax systems, including that of Israel,[1] Crüsemann does not try to explain why Deuteronomy 'factually abolishes' the tithe, but he mentions three reasons deuteronomists would have disliked the tithe. First, the tithe supported high places. Second, a portion of the tithe was transferred to Assyria as imperial tribute. Third, the tithe supported the monarchy, which the deuteronomists believed should be weak.

---

1.  'Der Zehnte'.

Crüsemann's last point is debatable. Did the deuteronomists really favor a hamstrung monarchy?

Although deuteronomic literature has incorporated clearly anti-monarchical material in places, the overall portrait of the Davidic monarchy is flattering. The book of Kings is strongly pro-Davidic, as is shown by the Davidic promise theme and the generally glowing portrayals of David, Solomon, Asa, Hezekiah and, certainly, Josiah.

It is hardly surprising that a group of people who wanted to centralize all worship in the Davidic capital city whould be pro-Davidic. Whatever its historical accuracy, Kings plausibly portrays Rehoboam I as being afraid of the political ramifications of regular pilgrimages by Northerners to the Jerusalem temple: 'if these people go up to offer sacrifices in the house of Yahweh at Jerusalem, then the heart of this people will turn again to their lord, to Rehoboam king of Judah, and they will kill me and return to Rehoboam...' (1 Kgs 12.26-27). Exclusive worship at Solomon's temple would bind the people more closely to the Davidic house. Cult centralization in Jerusalem was a pro-Davidic move.

The unambiguously anti-monarchical material in the Deuteronomistic History is a more complicated matter. 1 Samuel 8–12 provides a fascinating case study of the Deuteronomist's editorial skill.[1] This portion of the history describes the selection of Saul to be United Israel's first king. In this section, anti- and pro-monarchical material are interspersed, with the anti-monarchical material opening and closing the section. While it is true that this literary structure offers overall a negative judgment on the monarchy, the narrative placement of this generic anti-monarchical material gives it an interesting twist. By putting Samuel's 'manner of the king' at the beginning of Saul's reign, the Deuteronmist passes a negative judgment on Saul's kingship, coopting anti-monarchical literature and turning it into a polemic against Saul. This literary sleight-of-hand serves the Deuteronomist's pro-Davidic purposes nicely.[2]

Deuteronomy itself says very little about the monarchy. However,

---

1. G.E. Gerbrandt, *Kingship according to the Deuteronomistic Historian* (SBLDS, 87; Atlanta: Scholars Press, 1986). Gerbrandt has an excellent review of the scholarship on these chapters (pp. 18-38).

2. R.E. Clements, 'The Deuteronmistic Interpretation of the Founding of the Monarchy in I Sam. 8', *VT* 24 (1974), pp. 398-410.

from its call for cult centralization to its list of abominable cult practices, Deuteronomy assumes that royal cultic-political structures are
already in place. Though the law code contains some ancient, perhaps
even premonarchical traditions, the society it seeks to reform is a
monarchical one. In keeping with its literary fiction of Mosaic authorship, however, Deuteronomy ordinarily says nothing explicit about
the royal system. The 'law of the king' in Deut. 17.14-20 is the
exception.

The law of the king is usually viewed as an anti-monarchical mani-
festo, revealing a deep distrust of the monarchy and a strong commitment to curtail the powers of the king. There is no doubt that the law
of the king intends to limit what a king can do in a deuteronomic state.
The unanswered, usually unasked, question is why the deuteronomists
wanted to constrain the king. The assumption seems to be that the
deuteronomists' reasons are self-evident: they dislike kings, because
kings divert people's attention from Yahweh. The law of the king
itself, however, offers a very different explanation for its curtailment
of royal power.

What bothers the deuteronomistic authors about a king is the danger
of getting into bad international alliances. They are worried about
losing national sovereignty to a foreign power. Verses 14-17 describe
the limitations on a deuteronomic king.

Grist for the anti-monarchical mill comes immediately in v. 14. It is
the first part of an awkward complex sentence which is completed in
v. 14. Verse 14 reads as follows: 'When you come into the land which
Yahweh your God gives you and you possess it and settle down in it
and then say, "let me have a king over me like all the nations around
me..." '. Perhaps this offers an allusion to 1 Sam. 8.5. In that passage, the elders of Israel urge Samuel to 'appoint us a king to judge us
like all the nations'. The request sets up Samuel's searing indictment
of the monarchy, the 'manner of the king'.

Deut. 17.14 may well draw its words from Samuel's 'manner of the
king', but in its present literary context in Deuteronomy, having a
king 'like all the nations' has a different implication. In the Samuel
passage, the threat is inherent to the monarchy itself. Israelites are
encouraged to look around at 'all the nations'. Monarchs invariably
exploit the people. In Deuteronomy, by contrast, the threat of having
a king 'like all the nations' lies in the people's temptation to allow a
'foreigner' to rule them. Verse 15 completes the sentence begun in

v. 14: 'When you come into the land. . . and say, "Let me have a king like all the nations around me".' Then v. 15 says, 'you certainly must appoint yourself a king whom Yahweh your god chooses. From among your kin you must appoint yourself a king. You may not set over yourself a foreigner who is not your kin.'

The commentaries have a tendency to read this as an egalitarian statement: the king should think himself no better than anyone else, because he is 'from among your kin'. Some support for this reading might be found in v. 20 which explains that the king should study the deuteronomic lawbook, 'so that he will not have a haughty attitude toward his kin'. Verse 15, however, says nothing about the king's attitude. Rather, it warns against submission to a 'foreign' king.

There is some merit in recent treatments of v. 15 which see 'kin' as a reference to 'covenant kinship'. 'Foreigner', therefore, refers to someone outside the covenant. Gerbrandt expresses this view when he says that 'the motivation for this requirement was religious. If Israel was to have a king, then the king should be a brother, someone who was also under the covenant.'[1] In the context of Deuteronomy, the 'kin' is the one who lives within the deuteronomic covenant.

The problem with this reading, however, is that deuteronomic literature hardly ever uses 'foreign/foreigner' (*nēkār/nokrî*) terminology to distinguish non-deuteronomic things from deuteronomic ones. Rather than railing against 'foreign' influences, deuteronomic literature typically contrasts faithful covenant behavior with the (usually 'abominable') practices of 'the nations' (*haggôyîm*; Deut. 9.4, 5; 12.2, 30; 18.9, 14; 19.1; 20.18; Judg. 2.21, 23; 3.1; 1 Kgs 11.2; 14.24; 2 Kgs 16.3; 17.8, 11, 15; 21.2, 9). Correspondingly, there is little deuteronomic complaint about 'foreign' gods (Deut. 32.12; Josh. 24.20, 23; Judg. 10.16; 1 Sam. 7.3), but there is much concern about serving 'other gods' (*'elōhîm 'ªhērîm*; Deut. 5.7; 6.14; 7.4; 8.19; 11.16, 28; 13.2, 6, 13; 17.3; 18.20; 28.14, 36, 64; 29.26; 30.17; 31.18, 20; Josh. 23.16; 24.2, 16; Judg. 2.12, 17, 19; 10.13; 1 Sam. 8.8; 26.19; 1 Kgs 9.6, 9; 11.4, 10; 14.9; 2 Kgs 17.7, 35, 37, 38; 22.17). The term *îš nokrî* used here in v. 15 is unique, so direct comparison with other passages is not possible. However, deuteronomic literature does occasionally use *nakrî* or *nēkār* to describe people (*nakrî*: Deut. 14.21; 15.3; 23.20; 29.22; Judg. 19.12; 2 Sam. 15.19;

1. Gerbrandt, *Kingship*, p. 111.

1 Kgs 8.41, 43; *nēkār*: 1 Kgs 11.1, 8; *ben nēkār*: 2 Sam. 22.45, 46). In all these cases, the people thus designated literally are foreigners, non-Israelites. In deuteronomic literature, then, 'foreigner' appears to describe a social-political reality. The term is not as theologically loaded in deuteronomic literature as the 'covenant kinship' explanation of v. 15 would suggest.

Deut. 17.15 is straightforward. It warns against the actual domination of the Israelite throne by a foreign power. The law of the king thus starts on an anti-imperialist, not an anti-monarchical, note.

This anti-imperialist concern helps explain vv. 16-17. It clarifies the otherwise obscure connection between horses, wives, taxes and Egyptian bondage.

Verse 16 constrains the king from leading the people back to Egypt as a result of horse trading: 'he must not multiply horses for himself lest he return the people to Egypt on account of multiplying horse(s)...'.[1] Although the author possibly has Egypt literally in mind, the more generalized warning against foreign rule in v. 15 suggests that Egypt here symbolizes all foreign threats to Israel and Judah's sovereignty. It is a veiled reference to Assyrian imperialism.[2]

Assyrian records shed some light on how horse trading might pose a threat to Judah's national sovereignty. Horse tribute and cavalry support for the empire were expected obligations of vassals.[3] Judean kings are on record as having met those obligations.[4] Viewed in the

---

1. Cf. the jussive + non-converted imperfect construction in T.O. Lambdin, *Introduction to Biblical Hebrew* (New York: Scribner's, 1971), pp. 119, 107.

2. A superb modern example of this kind of coded reference to an imperial oppressor is found in a recent article by Carlos Fuentes (*The Nation*, February 12 [1990], p. 200), which reflects on a trip he made with fellow Latin American authors Gabriel Garcia Marquez and Julio Cortazar to Czechoslovakia in 1968, during the ill-fated 'Prague Spring'. He writes as follows: 'When Garcia Marquez, Cartazar and I reached Prague in the cold winter of 1968, the operative fiction—Kafka-cum-Schweik—was that the Russians were not there at all, and that the "Spring" could continue right into winter. While we couldn't refer directly to the Brezhnev Doctrine, we could talk about the Monroe Doctrine, so that when we mentioned U.S. intervention in Latin America, everyone understood that we were talking about Soviet intervention in Eastern Europe.'

3. Postgate, *Taxation*, pp. 16-18, 57-62, 117-18; Jankowska, 'Some Problems', p. 273; Ikeda, 'Solomon's Trade', pp. 215-38 (229); Cogan, *Imperialism*, p. 118; especially Elat, *Economic Relations*, pp. 69-82.

4. *ANET*, p. 287.

light of Judah's obligations as an Assyrian vassal, the law of the king's restriction on horse collecting serves as a further warning against foreign entanglements which threaten national sovereignty. It is a rejection of crippling vassal obligations. Thus it raises the spectre of a reverse exodus, of Israel and Judah's total loss of national identity under the domination of a foreign empire.

This striking theme is continued in v. 17b, which warns about multiple marriages. The multiplication of wives will lead to the king's apostasy (v. 17b). Solomon, as described in 1 Kgs 11.2-4, 9, is the obvious anti-type of this legislation, but the terminology is different here in Deuteronomy.

1 Kings 11 says that Solomon's foreign wives 'caused him to incline his heart' (*yātû 'et-libbô*), an idiom used elsewhere in deuteronomic literature to denote affirmation of loyalty by a human subject to a human monarch (Judg. 9.3; 2 Sam. 19.15 [Eng. 19.14]; see also 1 Kgs 2.28). 1 Kings 11 is the only time in deuteronomic usage that this expression refers to a relationship between a human and God.

Solomon has been disloyal to Yahweh, but Yahweh's anger is focused on Solomon, not the whole people—though, of course, Solomon's son Rehoboam ultimately must pay for his father's sin (v. 12). The punishment, though severe, fundamentally threatens neither Israel's right to the land nor the Davidics' right to the Jerusalem throne.

The idiom used in Deut. 17.17, however, 'to turn aside his heart' (*yāsûr lᵉ bābô*), suggests a greater apostasy and more severe punishment. In deuteronomic use, this expression refers only to apostate worship. Furthermore, in deuteronomic literature, 'turning aside the heart' consistently results in a radical threat to the people's promise of the land (Deut. 9.12, 16; 11.16; Judg. 2.17). The apostasy imagined in the law of the king is a more radical threat than Solomon's apostasy in 1 Kings 11 is. Solomon's misplaced loyalty threatened his own ability to govern. In the law of the king, however, apostasy introduced through marriage alliances cuts to the very core of the people's promise to possess the land. This idiom is appropriate within the context of the reverse exodus theme raised in v. 16.

The primary concern of vv. 16-17, then, is the threatened annihilation of the nation through unfavorable foreign alliances. The danger of imperial domination is expressed as the loss of the promised land and a reverse exodus.

The final clause of v. 17 provides the strongest argument that the law of the king envisions a weak monarchy: 'he must not greatly multiply silver and gold for himself'. The immediate concern of this clause is to limit the taxing authority of the king. Such a limitation surely confronts the excesses of the monarchy in its domestic policy. However, the law of the king's overarching concern about foreign domination suggests that, here too, the deuteronomists are concerned about imperialism. Limiting the Davidic king's tax revenues would choke the flow of wealth to the foreign suzerain, a flow which ran through the conduit of the royal treasuries.

Thus the law of the king leads back to Crüsemann's second reason the deuteronomists would have disliked the tithe. Deuteronomy 'factually abolishes' the tithe, because tithes were siphoned off by Assyria.

Cult centralization was revenue suicide. Hezekiah shut off the tax flow from the outlying areas to the royal treasuries and from the royal treasuries to Ninevah. The strategy made sense in the context of rebellion, but it probably would not work as permanent policy. Shutting off the profit source might discourage the imperial raiders, but it would also deplete the resources required to support Judah's monarchical bureaucracy.

Deuteronomy's peculiar tithe consumption may describe the plan of survival during the period of centralization. By requiring Judean tithers to consume their own tithes in the capital city, the deuteronomic legislation would produce an economic boom for Jerusalem, chiefly inhabited by courtiers and cult officials who would most benefit by the economic activity. It would also provide an income for local levites and other royal dependants who must be brought along for the tithe feast (12.12, 18-19; 14.27). A third-year tithe for these royal dependants, stored in the villages, would supplement whatever they received through the consumption of annual tithes. Royal administrators and others ordinarily dependent on tax revenues could thus be supported in a way which completely bypassed the normal tax system. Centralization and the tither's consumption of the tithe in Jerusalem together dried up the domestic coffers, regularly raided by the empire, while providing for the continued support of royal bureaucrats and other dependents.

In addition to its economic and its social-political benefits for the consolidation of Davidic power, cult centralization had strategic benefits in the face of an Assyrian campaign. As Cogan[1] and Spieckermann[2] have shown, Assyria on the march typically captured the idols of the invaded nations and marched, idols in tow, into battle. The presence of the idols with the Assyrian army showed the invaded people that their gods had abandoned them and submitted to Assur.[3] By closing the high places, Hezekiah guaranteed that Yahweh's cult objects could not be captured unless Jerusalem fell. Cult centralization thus ensured Yahweh's continued support of Judah's rebellion, even if the imperial army marched all the way to the gates of Jerusalem. Furthermore, the closed-up rural sanctuaries would offer little in the way of stored-up taxes for the imperial army as it marched toward Jerusalem. Cult centralization thus had practical benefits as a military strategy in the context of rebellion.

Cult centralization under Hezekiah was an emergency measure with multiple benefits during the period of rebellion. Centralization in the deuteronomic program, however, is not an emergency measure. It is a permanent restructuring of the cultic-political system. The Josianic reform had every appearance of permanence—at least that was the king's intention. How does this permanence square with a temporary centralization by Hezekiah?

The tendency to assume that Hezekiah's and Josiah's centralization reforms were essentially identical in form and intent has led archaeologically-minded biblical scholars in one of two directions. Some search for material confirmation that Hezekiah, too, destroyed outlying cult centers.[4] Not finding indisputable evidence of such destruction in the archaeological record, others question or reject the historicity of cult centralization under Hezekiah.[5] Either position assumes centralization under Hezekiah must have left a record of destruction. Both treat Hezekiah's and Josiah's high place reforms as essentially identical. If Hezekiah's reform was temporary, however, then no destruction layer from the reform should exist.

Hezekiah's centralization is the historical model for Josiah's reform, but the two acts of cult centralization are different in character and

---

1. *Imperialism*, pp. 21-40.
2. *Assur*, pp. 325-30.
3. Cogan, *Imperialism*, p. 21.
4. Aharoni, 'Arad'.
5. Yadin, 'Beer-sheba'.

function. Kings describes cult centralization under Josiah differently from the way that it describes centralization under Hezekiah. According to Kings, Josiah's reform included the defilement and physical destruction of high place sanctuaries. Hezekiah is said to have 'removed' the high places, but the Deuteronomist makes no mention of 'defilement' and 'destruction'.

The brief account of Hezekiah's reform (2 Kgs 18.4) begins, 'he removed the high places'. The verb *hēsîr*, 'he removed', needs closer scrutiny.

In basic stem, *swr* bears the root meaning, 'to turn aside'. Often it is used metaphorically, indicating a change of course, whether moral, legal, political or otherwise. Ordinarily, it is a change for the worse, the verb conveying a sense of rebellion or apostasy. The causative stem yields the primary meaning, 'to remove, take away'. In deuteronomic literature, the causative refers to such diverse activities as shedding a garment (Deut. 21.13), deposing royal officers (1 Kgs 15.13; 20.24) and 'removing' the head of a seditious prophet (2 Kgs 6.32). In four cases in Kings, however, the causative of *swr* describes a cult purge: Asa removed the idols his ancestors had made (1 Kgs 15.12), the Northern king Jehoram removed the Baal pillar (2 Kgs 3.2), Hezekiah removed the high places (2 Kgs 18.4, 22) and Josiah removed and destroyed Samaria's high place buildings (2 Kgs 23.19).[1] The first two passages use *waw*-consecutive constructions which formally could be either basic or causative stem. The last two use perfect forms and are unambiguously causative. Besides these causative forms of the verb, the basic form acquires an unusual causative-passive meaning in Kings in the stereotypical criticism of good monarchs who fail to centralize the cult: 'the high places were not removed' (1 Kgs 15.14; 22.44; 2 Kgs 12.4; 14.4; 15.4, 35; cf. 2 Chron. 15.17; 20.33).[2] This meaning of the basic stem is best explored by examining the use of the causative form in describing the four cult purges.

1.    Other cult purges using this verb and showing a deutronomic editorial hand are Josh. 24.14, 23; Judg. 10.16; 1 Sam. 7.3, 4; 28.3. The last passage (1 Sam. 28.3) records Saul's purge of 'mediums' and 'knowers' from the land.

2.    Beyond these high place references, the basic stem has the sense 'to be removed', in Isa. 10.27 and 14.25. With the preposition, the verb here means 'to turn from upon' = 'to be removed'. In Exod. 25.15, the verb also takes a preposition, yielding, 'to turn from', warning against removing the staves from the ark.

Closer examination of these passages raises questions. First, what exactly did Hezekiah do when he 'removed' the high places? The other three purges removed physical objects, presumably human-made: Asa removed idols, Jehoram removed the Baal pillar and Josiah removed the destroyed high place buildings. Hezekiah, however, 'removed' high places. How is a sacred site removed? Is it dug up or plowed under? Perhaps the Deuteronomist uses shorthand here: when he 'removed the high places', Hezekiah actually removed artifacts from the sacred shrines—the buildings, altars and cult objects. In that case, the Rabshaqeh merely repeats himself when he says that 'Hezekiah removed (Yahweh's) high places and altars', (2 Kgs 18.22). Here, 'high places' and 'altars' must just be two ways of saying the same thing. 'Altars' amplifies 'high places', both terms referring to sacred objects on the site rather than the high place site itself. Thus, the removal of high places involves transporting (and possibly destroying) hand-fashioned objects or architectural structures. Such a reading is consistent with the statement that high places were 'built' (1 Kgs 14.23; 2 Kgs 17.9; 21.3).

Another possibility exists, however. The removal of high places by Hezekiah could be less concrete. It may refer simply to the removal of high places from the royal cultic system. To remove high places was to decommission them as royal sanctuaries. Such decommissioning would entail at least the suspension of official Yahweh cult functions. The authorities may have shut the high place doors, closed the sanctuaries altogether. This could have been done, however, without physically destroying the cult objects or architecture of the high places.

Comparing Josiah's reform with other cultic 'removals' lends support to this reading of high place removal in Hezekiah's time. Of the four purges in Kings where cult objects are 'removed', only Josiah's removal of the Samarian high place buildings records the physical destruction of the thing removed. The defilement and destruction of the high place buildings is presented as additional information: Josiah not only 'removed' them, he defiled and destroyed them. Throughout ch. 23, Josiah's purge of the high places also involves defilement (*ṭm'*) and destruction (*ntṣ*).

Hezekiah's centralization reform provided the historical model for deuteronomic and Josianic centralization, but it differed from the later Josianic reform. Centralization under Hezekiah was temporary, an expediency of rebellion. By taking this radical step, Hezekiah prepared the nation for its coming battle against Judah's imperial lord, Assyria. Under Josiah, however, just as it is codified in Deuteronomy, cult centralization was meant to be permanent. The reasons for this evolution in the idea of centralization will be explored further in my discussion of Josiah.

## 2 Chronicles 29–32

The Chronicler reworked Kings' Hezekiah narrative in mostly predictable ways. For the Chronicler, Hezekiah is David and Solomon rolled into one. He 'did right in Yahweh's eyes, just like everything David his father did' (29.2). Like a second Solomon, he reopened the doors of the temple, as soon as he took the throne (29.3). With all the instruments of David (29.27) and 'according to the commandment of David and of Gad the king's seer and Nathan the prophet' (29.35), Hezekiah cleansed and rededicated God's house. He reunited the Davidic–Solomonic kingdom in a massive cult festival (ch. 30) and made provision for ongoing orthodox worship in Israel reunited (ch. 31). Fittingly, the tale of the new David–Solomon is punctuated with levites, cymbals, harps, lyres, offerings, prayers, rejoicing, prosperity and prestige for the Davidic king. Hezekiah marks a return to the glory days of the Davidic kingdom before Solomon died and the kingdom split. Not 'since the time of Solomon' had there been such great joy in Jerusalem (30.26).

The Chronicler does not mention the political intrigues of Hezekiah's rebellion against Assyria. There is no vassal treaty, no revolt. Sennacherib marches against Jerusalem for no good reason, at least in human political terms. His unexplained behavior served a divine purpose, however. Sennacherib's campaign is yet another opportunity for Yahweh to demonstrate his power, putting the Assyrian emperor down in short order and elevating his chosen Davidic king to his rightful place as chief among kings. The Chronicler's abbreviated account of Jerusalem's siege ends not only with a miraculous deliverance but also with a new imperial status for Hezekiah to whom many nations now bring tribute (32.23). Yahweh 'gave Judah rest round about' (32.22) and made Hezekiah 'prosper in everything he did' (32.30). These four chapters of Hezekiah material offer few surprises for anyone familiar with Chronicles.

All the predictable hyperbole about Hezekiah, however, makes it easy to miss some untypical material in the Chronicler's portrayal. The extended account of the all-Israel passover, for example, has some odd features. These unusual elements raise the possibility that the Chronicler has reproduced, in altered form, a basically reliable tradition not reported by the Deuteronomist.

Scholars have spilled much ink trying to decide whether Hezekiah's passover celebration is historical. Chapter 30's account of this all-Israel feast gives clues which point in opposite directions. With no indisputable evidence, the historical judgment boils down to a question of opportunity and motive. Was it possible for a Davidic monarch late in the eighth century to call such a feast? And if he could do it, would he? Did Hezekiah have motive to call an all-Israel passover?

The question of opportunity has focused mostly on the history of cultic festivals in Israel and Judah. Specifically at issue is ch. 30's portrayal of a single festival of passover and unleavened bread. The people who have looked most closely at the history of cultic feasts in Israel say that the passover and the feast of unleavened bread have separate origins as distinct festivals. According to the usual reconstruction, the festivals were first joined no sooner than Josiah's reform.[1]

A feast of unleavened bread is mentioned in the presumably pre-exilic festival calendars of the Elohist (Exod. 23.14-17) and the Yahwist (Exod. 34.18-24), with ambiguous references to passover. Here, it is one of three feasts marking the annual harvest cycle (the feast of harvest and feast of the ingathering are the other two). It was a pilgrimage feast, all males being required to 'present themselves before the Lord Yahweh' (23.17), that is, to come to a Yahweh altar. The passover, by contrast, has non-agricultural roots and is celebrated in the home (Exod. 12.21-23; Deut. 16.5). In its biblical contexts, passover is always related explicitly to the exodus story. Some such as de Vaux, however, see an even more ancient origin for passover, among pre-Israelite pastoral nomads making a spring offering for the welfare of their flocks.[2] This reading, however, remains highly speculative and, in de Vaux's formulation, relies on a discredited social evolutionism which assumes a unilinear development of human

---

1. Cf., for example, de Vaux, *Ancient Israel*, II, pp. 485-88.
2. De Vaux, *Ancient Israel*, II, pp. 488-90.

societies from nomadic to settled (i.e. agricultural) formations.

The presumably distinct festivals remained separate until the law of centralization was enacted. The feasts had occurred at roughly the same time of year (the month of Abib), though passover was a household feast and unleavened bread was a pilgrimage feast. When the deuteronomists moved all worship to the central sanctuary, however, passover became a pilgrimage feast too. Since both were celebrated at about the same time every year and since passover already included eating unleavened bread, it was natural to celebrate the two feasts together.

Those who argue for such a conflation at the time of Josiah's reform find support in 2 Kgs 23.21-23. There, Josiah's all-Israel passover feast is characterized as follows: 'no such passover had been kept since the days of the judges who judged Israel or during all the days of the kings of Israel and the kings of Judah' (v. 22). Likewise, 2 Chron. 35.18 characterizes the Josianic passover as unprecedented in the monarchical period, as follows: 'No passover like it had been kept since the days of Samuel the prophet. None of the kings of Israel had kept such a  passover as was kept by Josiah...' What made Josiah's passover unique, the argument goes, was the joint celebration of passover and unleavened bread at the central sanctuary. This innovative merger of feasts is codified in Deuteronomy 16, which itself is dated around the time of Josiah's reform. Hezekiah's combination passover feast of unleavened bread is thus anachronistic, reflecting post-Josianic practice. Since Hezekiah could not have celebrated such a conflated festival, the Chronicler's account must be fictitious.

The logic of this argument is flawed. To begin with, the Deuteronomist's characterization of Josiah's passover as unprecedented for the monarchy is completely consistent with the deuteronomistic portrayal of Josiah as a king without precedent. The characterization is tendentious hyperbole, later repeated from the Kings *Vorlage* by the Chronicler. Furthermore, neither the Deuteronomist nor the Chronicler gives any indication that what was unique about the passover was its conflation with the feast of unleavened bread. As the Kings narrative now stands, the feast was unprecedented because it was celebrated in a completely purified and reunified Yahwistic cult. It comes as the culmination of Josiah's reform push into the North. The Chronicler only slightly alters the language of Kings, but here too, the uniqueness of the passover celebration does not lie in its joining with the feast of unleavened bread. The Chronicler finds no conflict between Hezekiah's passover and the report that Josiah's passover had no precedent since the days of Samuel. Hezekiah's passover, after all, had been celebrated according to the exceptional second-month calendar. Josiah's passover was celebrated 'on the fourteenth day of the first month' (35.1). Neither Kings nor Chronicles proves that Josiah's festival was the first joint celebration of passover and the feast of unleavened bread. To the contrary, both assert the antiquity of the festival as Josiah celebrated it.

Those who date the Chronicles passover account very late find further support for their position in the Chronicler's use of a late Numbers passage to explain the unorthodox date of Hezekiah's passover 'in the second month'. Verse 3 says, 'they could not keep it in time, because the priests had not sanctified themselves in sufficient numbers, nor had the people assembled in Jerusalem'. The verse appears to take its cue from the supplementary passover provision in Num. 9.1-14. In the Numbers passage, vv. 9-13 allow an exceptional celebration of passover in the second month for people who are ritually unclean because of touching a corpse or who are unable, because of long travel distances, to get to the first-month feast on time. Because the Chronicler utilizes this material from Numbers, the argument goes, the account of Hezekiah's passover must be late.

This reasoning runs aground on the question of literary dependency. Is the Chronicler's explanation really dependent on the Numbers exceptional passover, or did the two grow up independently? The Numbers story is generally thought to be a late, post-exilic addition to the P passover legislation.[1] The Numbers story and Chronicles originated in the same period. Roughly contemporaneous, the two passages cannot be dated with certainty.

Both are written to explain a variant calendar of passover celebration, but slight differences in the explanations suggest that the two passages may have grown independently. The Numbers legislation was generated by a case brought before Moses involving men unable to celebrate the passover, because they had recently touched a corpse and were ritually unclean. The legislative solution goes beyond the specific case to include an exemption for long-distance travel. The impurity

---

1.  Cf. M. Noth, *Numbers* (OTL; London: SCM Press, 1968), pp. 71-72.

exemption is limited, however, to those who are ritually unclean because of touching a corpse. The Chronicles verse, by contrast, says nothing about corpses. Here, the passover is delayed because the priests were unsanctified (no specific reason mentioned) and the people had not yet assembled in Jerusalem. It is not even clear that the Chronicler appeals to specific legislation here. It seems rather to be a practical solution to a practical problem. There is no appeal to Moses or the law or a prophet to justify the variant practice. The Chronicler mentions nothing about corpses or, for that matter, long distances. The priests were not yet sanctified in sufficient numbers and the people (whether nearby or far away) had not yet been assembled in Jerusalem. The Chronicles and Numbers passages appear to have a specific irregular passover celebration in mind. Their solutions are similar but not identical. Direct dependency of one passage on the other is impossible to prove.

It would be odd for the Chronicler to use the Numbers passage as the basis for a fictional Hezekian passover. When the Chronicler has taken great pains to portray Hezekiah as a new David–Solomon, why turn around and create a fictional passover celebration on an irregular date?[1] The Chronicler has no literary or theological motivation for making up an irregular passover for Hezekiah. The date of the passover 'in the second month' is implausible, unless the Chronicler here depends on a source which dated the passover at that time. The theological task for the Chronicler then becomes to explain the unorthodox date.

Another detail of the story makes it unlikely fiction. Verses 10-12 report the delivery of passover invitations throughout the North and South by courier. Verses 10-11 say:

> the messengers went from city to city through the country of Ephraim and Manasseh, as far as Zebulun. But they laughed them to scorn, and they mocked them. Only a few men of Asher, Manasseh and Zebulun humbled themselves and came to Jerusalem.

As shown in the discussion of Ahaz above, the Chronicler painstakingly shows a leveling out of North and South in preparation for the reign of Hezekiah. The repentance of the 'chiefs of the Ephraimites' (2 Chron. 28.13) indicates a softened attitude of Northerners toward

1. Cf. F.L. Moriarty, 'The Chronicler's Account of Hezekiah's Reform', *CBQ* 27 (1965), pp. 399-406.

Judah and the Davidic house. The way was prepared for their voluntary reunion with Judah under the faithful reign of Hezekiah. Yet in
30.10-11, the Chronicler reports that Hezekiah's messengers were
scorned in the North. The report runs against the literary grain in the
Chronicler's treatment of Northerners at the time of Hezekiah.
Neither is the report easy to explain given the Chronicler's view of
Hezekiah. The Chronicler has suppressed unflattering information
about Hezekiah's subservience to Assyria. Why, in a fictional account,
would the Chronicler introduce the unflattering report that Hezekiah's
passover invitation was mocked in the North? The details of the
passover account make it unlikely fiction. The Chronicler is passing
along a received tradition that Hezekiah celebrated a second-month
passover.

I have argued that the passover account is more plausible as history
than as fiction. I have suggested that such a passover celebration cannot be excluded as a possibility in the eighth century. Hezekiah had
opportunity. But did he have motive?

Hezekiah had good reason to call an all-Israel passover feast in
the face of rebellion against Assyria.[1] The appeal to the North is
historically plausible,[2] as is the North's lukewarm response. It is
especially fitting, however, that Hezekiah would call all Israel to a
passover feast, the principal theme of which is the deliverance of
Israel from the clutches of foreign oppression. Any kind of national
festival at Jerusalem would have boosted national solidarity behind
the king. It would have helped consolidate Davidic authority and
fortify the people for the struggle ahead. But a national passover,
with its anti-imperialist dimension, would be especially appropriate
as Hezekiah prepared the people for rebellion. It is even conceivable that, just as the Chronicler says, the passover celebration was the kick-off for cult centralization, another key part of

---

1. Williamson (*I and II Chronicles*, pp. 360-73) argues that the Chronicler's
passover account is based on an historical tradition, but that the feast he
celebrated was actually a feast of unleavened bread. As I argued above, however, the
assumption that unleavened bread and passover were separate until Josiah's time is
based on circular reasoning. A conflated feast is possible in Hezekiah's time, and a
passover feast, with its liberation theme, would make perfect sense in the context of
Hezekiah's rebellion.

2. Cf. Nicholson, *Deuteronomy and Tradition*, pp. 98-99; McKay, *Religion*,
p. 17; Williamson, *I and II Chronicles*, p. 361.

Hezekiah's preparations for rebellion.

As it now stands, the portrait of Hezekiah's passover in ch. 30 is painted in the style of the post-exilic period. Anachronisms are evident. Expansions and hyperbole abound. But at its core, the chapter builds on historical reality. Hezekiah celebrated a national passover to prepare his tiny kingdom to face off the ancient world's mightiest superpower, Assyria.

## Summary

Hezekiah made a bold, nearly fatal move when he rebelled against the empire. The probabilities of success lay in various factors, one of the most important being the widespread support of the Judean people. The symbols of Yahwistic faith, infused with new meaning by the conditions of imperial subjugation, provided a powerful motivation for Judean to support the rebellion. The ancient symbols of passover stirred Judeans to new hope and courage as they started the long, treacherous march from foreign oppression to freedom.

The extraordinary conditions of rebellion also led Hezekiah to take a strikingly unorthodox cult measure, closing down Yahweh's sanctuaries everywhere but Jerusalem. Cult centralization consolidated Davidic power by increasing the number of pilgrimages to the capital city. Requiring regular journeys to Jerusalem had the psychological effect on enhancing the status of the Davidic house, a potential effect perceived by Jeroboam I (1 Kgs 12.27). Centralization also offered substantial economic benefits to the capital city and its royal and priestly residents. When Deuteronomy's tithe legislation is figured into the equation, cult centralization is seen to have anti-Assyrian benefits as well. By shutting down the nation's internal revenue system of which the high places were integral parts, Hezekiah dried up the royal coffers and shut off the tax flow to Assyria. Cult centralization and the consumption of tithes by the tither provided an indirect non-revenue means of support for the royal bureaucracy, stimulating the capital city's economy, while providing for the ongoing support of royal dependents outside Jerusalem. Cult centralization had strategic benefits as well. It left no tax stores in the outlying areas for the Assyrian army to capture and use on its march toward Jerusalem. By removing Yahweh's cult objects from the countryside, centralization also thwarted Assyria's policy of capturing the idols of the enemy and enlisting the gods' assistance against their own people. For a number of reasons—psychological, economic, political and military—cult centralization, though radical, made sense as an emergency measure during the rebellion against Assyria.

In the years between Hezekiah's surrender and the collapse of Assyrian power in the West, the measures of Hezekiah's rebellion continued to inspire some people within Judah's cultic leadership. As symbols of Judean nationalism, Hezekiah's cult measures stood at the heart of an emerging system of thought, intensely nationalistic in character. However, as this deuteronomic thought grew, the primary significance of the symbols changed. So the full-grown deuteronomism finally embraced by Josiah stands in continuity with the embryonic 'proto-deuteronomic' cult measures of Hezekiah, but the two reforms are different. The long period of imperial accommodation under Manasseh was the gestation period of deuteronomic theology.

## Chapter 5

### MANASSEH: REFORM AND ACCOMMODATION

Manasseh was a faithful Assyrian vassal. Continuing the policy of his reluctantly penitent father Hezekiah, Manasseh paid heavy tribute to Assyria,[1] sent Judean troops on imperial expeditions,[2] and provided materials and labor for imperial building projects.[3] The Chronicler writes that Manasseh 'put commanders of the army in all the fortified cities in Judah' (2 Chron. 33.14), an indication that some of Judah's territory lost in the rebellion of 701 (2 Kgs 18.13) was restored by the time Manasseh was king,[4] perhaps as a reward for loyalty to the empire.

Expanded national borders and an enhanced trading relationship with the empire no doubt made life better for the top layer of Judean society than it was just after Hezekiah surrendered. A larger tax base made the national debt to Assyria easier to meet. For the laboring majority, however, nothing much changed. The contradiction of supporting a domestic monarchy and a foreign empire continued to make them highly vulnerable. Socially, politically and economically, Manasseh's rule marked a return to what had been the status quo prior to Hezekiah's rebellion.

Cultically too, Manasseh's reign returned Judah to traditional values. The high places were restored. The syncretistic cult he allowed was the orthodox First Temple cult, enhanced by Assyrian practice

---

1. *ANET*, p. 294; cf. also D.J. Wiseman, 'The Vassal Treaties of Esarhaddon', *Iraq* 20 (1958), pp. 1-99; R. Frankena, 'The Vassal-treaties of Esarhaddon and the Dating of Deuteronomy', *OTS* 14 (1965), pp. 122-54.

2. *ANET*, p. 294; M. Streck, *Assurbanipal und die letzten assyrischen Könige bis zum Untergang Ninevehs* (Leipzig: Hinrichs, 1916), p. 139.

3. *ANET*, p. 291; Wiseman, 'Vassal Treaties', p. 1; R.C. Thompson, *The Prisms of Esarhaddon and Assurbanipal* (London: British Museum, 1931), p. 25.

4. Ahlström, *Administration*, p. 75.

and belief, but the received tradition nonetheless. The era of cultic experimentation during the headier days of Hezekiah's rebellion had ended. Under Manasseh, the Yahweh cult got back to basics—at least, as those basics had been understood since Ahaz.

Yet, Kings tells us, Manasseh did evil in the eyes of Yahweh. During his reign, Judah acted more wickedly than the people Yahweh dispossessed before Israel. Manasseh rebuilt high places. He erected altars for Baal and the astral deities and put them right in the house of God. He made an Asherah, burned children as sacrifices, promoted wizardry, augury and necromancy, ignored Yahweh's prophets and filled Jerusalem with innocent blood. Manasseh provoked Yahweh to swear revenge against God's chosen city Jerusalem, to be wiped clean like a dish and turned upside down. The wickedness of this king could not go unpunished.

Manasseh died of old age after a peaceful, prosperous reign of about 50 years. Judah's Teflon king.

For the biblical historians, Manasseh posed a problem. Their views differed about how exactly divine justice works, but the Deuteronomist and the Chronicler both had a theology of retribution. God rewards the good and punishes the wicked. Often enough in Judah's monarchical past, history had thrown divine justice into question, but in the case of Manasseh, theology and reality almost missed each other entirely. The biblical historians had to adjust. For the deuteronomistic authors, Yahweh was vindicated first in the reform of Josiah, then in the destruction of Jerusalem. The Chronicler's theology demanded swifter retribution than history could provide. By the Chronicler's figuring, Manasseh's stunning success could only be the result of his faithfulness to God. The received record must have missed something, and the Chronicler had a good idea what.

Chronicles and Kings present slanted views of Manasseh. For the Chronicler, an otherwise unreported conversion and reform solves the theological problem of Manasseh's success, but in the process creates a big historical problem for Josiah's now redundant reform. Kings, on the other hand, uses the Manasseh narrative to set the stage for Josiah's deuteronomic reform, but in the process blames Manasseh for introducing cult practices he inherited. Though neither is entirely accurate, together Kings and Chronicles present a plausible characterization of a king who, like other Davidic kings, was a mixture of bad and good, and a keeper of Yahwistic orthodoxy as he and his monarchical predecessors understood it.

## 2 Kings 21.1-18

Kings' version of Manasseh's rule sets a theme of exile which runs through the chapter from beginning to end, climaxing in a prophecy of judgment against Judah (vv. 10-16). The exilic motif seems straightforward enough. A closer look, however, finds it harder and harder to pin down. I will argue that the exilic theme owes its slipperiness to a fairly late reworking which turns the Manasseh narrative to a different end from the one which it originally had. In the literary unpacking, I will argue that in the case of the Manasseh narrative, exile does not mean Babylonian exile.

Structurally, ch. 21 falls into rather neat blocks of material. Verse 1 presents a standard introduction and vv. 17-18 offer the expected source reference and death notice. The intervening material constitutes two main sections, an evaluative résumé of cult practices during his reign (vv. 2-9) and an anonymous prophetic judgment oracle against Judah (vv. 10-16).

The résumé of abhorrent cult practices in vv. 2-9, I will argue, is closely related to Deuteronomy 18 and 2 Kings 17, the treatise on the fall of the North. When the anonymous prophetic oracle is added, the literary structure of the Manasseh chapter mimics the structure of Deuteronomy 18. The oracle's exilic theme makes it appear to be a prophecy after the event, in this case, the Babylonian exile. The oracle is surprisingly vague, however, when it comes to describing Judah's fate under judgment. This lack of detail about the exile, and ch. 21's close connection with Deuteronomy 18 and 2 Kings 17 raise the possibility that the chapter took its definitive (though not final) shape in the pre-exilic period.

A close look at the anonymous oracle (vv. 10-16) opens my discussion of ch. 21. an editorial seam which ties the oracle to the 'Manasseh alone' explanation of the Babylonian exile. I will argue that the 'Manasseh alone' explanation, one of two explanations for the Babylonian exile offered in the closing chapters of Kings, appears late in the redactional history of Kings. Discussion of the double indictment in vv. 11 and 15 will follow my treatment of the 'Manasseh alone' passages and their connection with v. 16. Finally, I will move verse by verse through the announcement of judgment in the oracle's core (vv. 12-14). After discussing the oracle, I will look at the résumé of abhorrent cult practices (vv. 2-9) and its points of contact with Deuteronomy 18 and 2 Kings 17.

The prophetic oracle owes its present shape and placement to an exilic editor.[1] Verse 16 unambiguously connects the oracle with 24.3-4 and 23.26-27, which blame Manasseh alone for Judah's exile. Both are exilic, with 23.26-27 clearly rationalizing Josiah's death and the reform's failure to avert disaster. Neither passage elaborates much on why Manasseh bore such responsibility for the exile. Blaming Manasseh alone becomes even more puzzling when other passages at the end of Kings are considered.

The stereotypical and unqualifiedly negative evaluations of Jehoahaz (23.32) and Jehoiakim (23.37) offer a perfectly intelligible, though for Kings unprecedented, explanation of the Babylonian exile. The language of evaluation for these two kings shifts from previous regnal evaluations.[2] Earlier formulas typically compare a king to a particular predecessor. Jehoahaz and Jehoiakim, however, did evil 'like everything (their) ancestors did'. Jehoiachin, who acted wickedly 'like his father (Jehoiakim)' (24.9) and Zedekiah, who behaved 'like Jehoiachim' (24.19) are linked with Jehoahaz and Jehoiakim and thus implicitly with the evil deeds of all their ancestors. This pluralization, 'ancestors', introduces a new element in Kings: the collective guilt of the Davidic monarchs. Earlier Davidic kings were individually judged and, more often than not, judged favorably. Now, with Josiah dead and the dynasty in its final years, Kings paints the whole history of the Judean monarchy in a single unflattering color. Accordingly, the final four Davidic kings are summarily judged wicked with no bill of particulars offered—a surprising omission, since at least some of Josiah's reforms had been reversed by the time of Ezekiel (see especially chs. 6, 8 and 16). The last four summaries lump these kings together with all their ancestors, castigating the whole Davidic bunch for its wicked ways. The theological last word on the Babylonian exile comes just after the Zedekiah summary: 'Yahweh was so angry with Jerusalem and Judah that he put them out of his sight' (24.20). The exile was the

---

1. Cf., for example, Gray, *I and II Kings*, pp. 707-10; Jones, *1 and 2 Kings*, pp. 598-600; Dietrich, *Prophetie*, pp. 14, 30-79; Spieckermann, *Assur*, pp. 168-70; Hoffmann, *Reform,* pp. 155-62.

2. Nelson, *Double Redaction*, pp. 38-42.

result of the collective guilt of the house of David.

Over against this collective-guilt explanation stand 2 Kgs 23.26-27 and 24.3-4 which blame the Babylonian exile on Manasseh alone. The former passage sits uncomfortably toward the beginning of the long obituary of Josiah (23.25-30). The introductory particle *'ak* which opens v. 26 alerts the reader to a possible gloss in the material which follows. The theological judgment of vv. 26-27 is conspicuously unconnected to anything in the narrative around it. The verses also interrupt the normal literary pattern in the Deuteronomist's summary remarks on the monarchs. Ordinarily, the concluding source reference, 'the rest of the acts of X, are they not written in Y', is preceded by a stock theological evaluation or by notice of a significant event or characteristic of the reign.

Of the Judean kings, only the accounts of Jotham (2 Kgs 15.34-36) and Manasseh (21.16-17) attach the source reference directly to a theological evaluation. Otherwise, some outstanding event or political characteristic immediately precedes the source reference (1 Kgs 11.40-41; 14.25-29; 15.6-7, 22-23; 22.45-46; 2 Kgs 8.22-23; 12.19-20[Eng. 12.18-19]; 14.17-18; 15.5-6; 16.17-19; 20.19-20; 24.2-5 is a special case which will be discussed below). Among the Northern kings, the earlier accounts are more likely to attach the source reference to a standard theological evaluation (1 Kgs 15.30-32; 16.13-14, 19-20, 26-27; contrast 16.4-5; 22.38-39; 2 Kgs 1.17-18). The accounts from Jehu on, with the exception of 2 Kgs 13.11-12, all attach the source reference to significant political events (2 Kgs 10.32-34; 13.7-8; 14.14-15, 27-28 [here, Yahweh is described as pitying Israel and saving them by the power of Jeroboam II]; 15.10-11, 14-15, 20-21, 24-26, 30-31). In every case, Kings follows a tight pattern. The source reference comes immediately after a theological evaluation of the king or a record of an important event or characteristic of his reign.

2 Kgs 23.26-27 breaks the pattern, intruding into the Josiah summary to blame Manasseh for the exile and creating a literary structure unique in Kings. Without vv. 26-27, the source reference would immediately follow v. 25's theological evaluation of Josiah, 'and there was no king before him who turned to Yahweh with all his mind, soul, and strength according to the law of Moses, nor did any arise after him'. Such a structure would provide a nice contrast with the earlier Northern kings whose concluding descriptions normally attach

the source reference directly to a negative theological evaluation. Though remaining an unusual structure for Judean accounts, it would have literary precedent in Kings.

Verses 26-27 intrude upon the narrative conclusion of Josiah's reign. Theologically and literarily, they ill fit the context. These verses are secondary additions to Josiah's obituary.

The second passage blaming Manasseh for the exile (24.3-4) also breaks the pattern. It too comes immediately before the concluding source reference. Also introduced by '*ak*, this passage offers slightly different terminology than 23.26 (*ḥaṭṭāʾôt*, 'sins', rather than *kᵉʿāsîm*, 'provocations', in 23.26).[1] It repeats an earlier charge (21.16) that Manasseh had shed much innocent blood.[2] These verses show the same narrative awkwardness as the rationalization of Josiah's death (23.26-27) and appear theologically out of place in the Jehoiakim account. By including this attack on Manasseh, the author undermines the negative evaluation of Jehoiakim in 23.37, effectively exonerating him from any responsibility for the first deportation. Verses 3-4 also clash with the collective-guilt explanation of the exile implied in the final four regnal introductions. Removing vv. 3-4 would leave the bibliographical notice attached directly to the report of various raiding bands which plagued Jehoiakim. This would yield the normal literary structure for the Judean king summaries. Like 23.26-27 above, 24.3-4 breaks the larger pattern of the book and intrudes upon the narrative in which it appears. Both passages are secondary additions to already completed narratives which themselves originated in the exilic period.

The closing chapters of Kings, then, offer two different theological explanations of the Babylonian exile. One says the collective guilt of the Davidic monarchs throughout history brought the final destruction. This theory contradicts the pro-Davidic thrust of Kings as a whole. A second theory explicitly blames the exile entirely on Manasseh. The two passages late in Kings which advocate the 'Manasseh alone' explanation sit awkwardly in the narrative and are

---

1.	These two terms are frequently paired in the Northern regnal evaluations.

2.	J. Gray (*I and II Kings*, p. 757 n. d) says that this passage 'has all the appearance of a secondary expansion', though he does not elaborate. Commenting on 21.16, Hoffmann (*Reform*, p. 156 n. 48) states that such attachment of supplementary material, mostly with *wᵉgam*, is common throughout the reform texts (1 Kgs 14.24; 15.15; 2 Kgs 13.6b; 16.3; 23.[15, 19] 24).

best explained as secondary additions to a text which already had incorporated the collective guilt theory. How then should 2 Kgs 21.16 be read?

Among those who argue for a double redaction of the Deuteronomistic History (pre-exilic and exilic), there is wide consensus that v. 16 belongs to the first edition.[1] These scholars correctly argue that v. 16 is placed awkwardly after the oracle (vv. 10-15) and that its information appears superfluous in light of vv. 11 and 15. Nelson takes its syntax—simple *waw* followed by the perfect—as an indication that 'it must have been originally attached to some list of Manasseh's activities and not to v. 15'.[2]

The judgment that v. 16 is only secondarily attached to the oracle which precedes it is sound; however, the terminology of 16b argues strongly that the verse in its present form is at least as late as, and probably later than, vv. 10-15. The theme of Manasseh's causing Judah to sin, found with slight variation in v. 11b, makes an unambiguous comparison with the Northern kings. Throughout chapter 21 such comparisons function to foreshadow Judah's own punishment. Verse 16b thus is compatible with the theological judgment of the oracle, vv. 10-15. Based on its content and vocabulary, there is no compelling reason to suppose that v. 16b is earlier than the oracle to which it is attached.[3] As for 16a, which is sometimes taken to be archival,[4] one can only note that this theme of the bloodthirsty Manasseh appears elsewhere only in 2 Kgs 24.4, itself a secondary expansion of a  completed exilic edition. The murder of the innocents may find loose connections with the Naboth's vineyard episode (1 Kgs 21.1-24), drawing further parallels between Manasseh and Ahab, but the shedding of innocent blood is at best a minor theme in Kings.[5] If this account were archival or original to a pre-exilic edition of Kings, it is inexplicable that the Deuteronomist failed to pick it up again in the Josiah narrative.

---

1.   Nelson, *Double Redaction*, p. 66; Gray, *I and II Kings*, p. 709.
2.   Nelson, Double Redaction, p. 66.
3.   Cf. Jones, *1 and 2 Kings*, p. 600; Spieckermann, *Assur,* pp. 168-70; Hoffmann, *Reform*, pp. 157-58.
4.   Nelson, *Double Redaction*, p. 66.
5.   But note Dietrich's connection of the 'blood' theme with the 'nomistic' redactor, DtrN (*Prophetie*, p. 30). Spieckermann (*Assur*, p. 169) and Jones (*1 and 2 Kings*, p. 600) follow Dietrich's analysis.

In light of the above considerations, v. 16 is best understood as an expansion upon an already existing text which included the judgment oracle, vv 10-15. Verse 16a functions to tie 2 Kgs 24.3-4 and 23.26-27 to chapter 21 itself, thus better integrating the theory that Manasseh's policies alone caused the exile. Its placement immediately after the oracle as part of the accusation is necessary because of the prophecy–fulfillment schema which 24.3-4 sets up. In order to lessen the narrative disruption caused by the addition of this theme, the editor adds v. 16b, a somewhat expanded recapitulation of vv. 11 and 15, the verses which introduced and concluded the earlier literary form of the oracle.

Form-critically, both v. 11 and v. 15 are standard accusations, introduced with *ya'an* *'ašer* 'because. . .' The fact that there are two accusations is unusual but not without parallel in Kings, as Hoffmann notes.[1] Form-critically, v. 11 is better placed than v. 15, but the plurals of the latter verse better suit the announcement of judgment (vv. 12-14) which never mentions Manasseh and consistently implicates the whole people. Since v. 11 implicates Manasseh in the exile, it deserves consideration next.

Unlike v. 16 which sits with obvious awkwardness in the text, v. 11 is well integrated with what precedes it. Its vocabulary alludes to the résumé of Manasseh's cult practices in vv. 2-9. Mention of the 'Amorites' recalls vv. 2 and 9 which bracket the list of cult crimes, portraying Manasseh's policies as a return to the pre-Israelite practices of the Canaanites. In Kings, only Ahab is similarly compared to the Amorites (1 Kgs 21.26).[2] Like Manasseh in v. 11, Ahab reportedly worshiped 'idols' (*gillulîm*). Manasseh's crimes are described in v. 11 as abominations' (*tō'ēbôt*), while Ahab 'acted especially abominably' (*wayyat'ēb m<sup>e</sup>ōd*). Verse 2 also characterizes Manasseh's policies as 'abominations' (*tō'ēbôt*). Verse 3 explicitly compares Manasseh to Ahab. Finally in v. 11, the Deuteronomist unmistakably links this Judean king with Northern monarchs by the final clause, 'and he caused Judah also to sin. . .' *(wayyaḥ<sup>a</sup>ṭi' gam-'et-y<sup>e</sup>hûdâ).*

---

1. Hoffmann, *Reform*, p. 156. On the basis of this and the Huldah oracle, Hoffmann argues that an unorthodox, expanded oracular form is typical of the Deuteromonist.

2. Gray (*I and II Kings*, p. 443) suggests that this Ahab passage is a late deuteronomistic addendum.

This formulaic critique of Northern kings (1 Kgs 14.16; 15.26, 30, 34; 16.13, 19, 26; 2 Kgs 10.31; 13.2, 6, 11; 14.24; 15.9, 18, 24, 28) describes no other Southern king. Verse 11 thus is well integrated into the chapter and the larger book. Its theme and vocabulary are consistent with earlier verses and its assertions have grounding in the narrative which precedes it.

The narrative fit of v. 11 contrasts with the awkwardness of v. 16 discussed above. Yet these verses which introduce and conclude the judgment oracle against Judah seem to mount the same argument: Manasseh bears unique responsibility for the Babylonian exile.

Undeniably, v. 11 lays special blame on this king whose evil surpassed even that of the dispossessed Amorites. However, the portrayal models itself on the description of Ahab, a connection which has double significance. Ahab is portrayed as the Northern heretic *par excellence* (1 Kgs 16.31, 33). Jeroboam provides the paradigm of provocative behavior by which all Northern kings are judged, but Ahab occupies a place of unparalleled notoriety in the history of the North. Thus, on the one hand, v. 11's characterization of Manasseh in terms elsewhere reserved for Ahab indicates that this Judean king had a corresponding degree of notoriety among the Davidic monarchs. However, on the other hand, Ahab never shoulders sole responsibility for the fall of the North. To the contrary, 2 Kings 17, the Deuteronomist's most systematic treatment of the fall of the North, explains the disaster as the result of Israel's collective historical quilt. In the Manasseh chapter then, v. 11's presentation of Manasseh as a Judean version of Ahab assigns him a place of special notoriety in the history of Judah but stops short of pinning the exile on him *alone*.[1] Judah will be exiled 'because of these abominations which Manasseh king of Judah did', but, as the following prophecy makes clear, not because of him alone.

The oracle's second accusation comes in v. 15. It too is thematically well integrated into the chapter. The verse begins with standard deuteronomic vocabulary ('because they did evil in Yahweh's view') and, like v. 11, connects the judgment of Judah with that of the

---

1. In light of this, there is some merit in Spieckermann's observation (*Assur*, p. 168) that the title, 'Manasseh, king of Judah', which appears only in v. 11, serves to expand the judgment to encompass the Davidic monarchy as a whole.

Northern kings ('and they have been provoking me...').[1] The adverbial clause, 'from the day their fathers came out of Egypt until this day', recalls the Mosaic covenant theme which appears earlier in the chapter (v. 8), but more importantly refers the reader back to the exodus motif which introduces the treatise on the fall of the North (17.7). Like v. 11, v. 15 is well integrated into the larger narrative. At first glance, the plurals of v. 15 are better suited to the announcement of judgment in vv. 12-14 (which blames the people as a whole) than is the explanation of v. 11 (which focuses blame on Manasseh). Both, however, are well integrated into the larger literary plan of the chapter. That narrative fit indicates common authorship by the writer who gave ch. 21 its definitive shape.

The announcement of judgment in vv. 12-14 is a curious mixture of standard deuteronomic vocabulary and rather unusual sayings. The messenger formula of v. 12a ('therefore thus says Yahweh God of Israel') followed by the *hinnēh*-clause (*hinnēh* + participle), is typical in Kings (cf. 1 Kgs 11.31; 2 Kgs 22.16). The subordinate clause at the end of v. 12 ('so that all who hear it, both ears will tingle') is syntactically awkward.[2] The idiom appears in almost identical form in 1 Sam 3.11 to describe the impending downfall of the Elides and in Jer. 19.3 as part of a proclamation against the inhabitants of Jerusalem and Judah. It is not typical for Kings, but it does appear elsewhere in the Bible.

Verse 13's metaphor, 'to stretch the line and the plummet', appears in deuteronomic literature only here. Isa. 28.17 provides the only other biblical occurrence of the pair, 'line and plummet', though a different verb (*śwm*) is used. The idiom 'to stretch the line' (*nṭh qw*) occurs in Job 38.5 and Isa. 44.13 with neutral meaning, in Isa. 34.11 and Lam. 2.8 with negative meaning, and in Zech. 1.16 with positive meaning. Jer. 31.39 refers to a 'measuring line' (*qāwh hammiddâ*) in the context of judgment. Ezekiel envisions a heavenly being in the Temple with a *qāw* in his hand (47.3), a metaphor already introduced

---

1. Cf. v. 6b and 1 Kgs 15.30; 16.13, 26 for the connection of *k's* ('to provoke') with the theme of Northern kings causing Israel to sin. Ahab also 'provokes' Yahweh by his construction of the Asherah altar in 1 Kgs 16.33; cf. 2 Kgs 21.3. See also Jeroboam's Israel and their provocative Asherim, 1 Kgs 14.15.

2. The problem of the pronoun referent in *šōmᵉ'āyw* may be solved by emendation with Q and the Versions, substituting *šōmᵉ'āh* (cf. Jer. 19.3); though of course the ancients likely corrected a problematical text here.

in Ezek. 40.3 and carried through chs. 40–42, but with different terminology (*q<sup>e</sup>nēh hammiddâ*. As is often the case with this prophet's use of imagery, the significance of the measuring line metaphor in Ezek. 47.3 is difficult to fathom. Amos's vision of the 'plumbline' (7.7-8) also comes to mind, but the terminology is different ('*<sup>a</sup>nāk* instead of *qāw*: a dialectal variant?) Stretching the measuring line then is a common prophetic metaphor for Yahweh's intervention in history. Like the 'day of the Lord' motif, its implications can be either positive or negative. In the Manasseh oracle, Judah's measurement by 'the line of Samaria and the plummet of the house of Ahab' picks up the two major comparisons of chapter 21: the Manasseh era is like the disastrous history of the North and Manasseh is like Ahab.

The verb 'to wipe out' (*m ḥh*) in v. 13b is common in biblical Hebrew, though it occurs only five times elsewhere in deuteronomic literature (Deut. 9.14; 25.6, 19; 29.20; 2 Kgs 14.27). In non-deuteronomic material, it is usually 'sin' or 'transgression' which is being 'wiped out' (Isa. 43.25; 44.22; Pss. 51.3, 11[Eng. 51.1, 9]; 109.14; Prov. 6.33; Neh. 4.5). Thus it ordinarily has the sense of 'wiping the slate clean'. The more basic meaning, seen especially in Pentateuchal references, has to do with blotting something out of a book (Exod. 32.32, 33; Num. 5.23; Pss. 69.29[Eng. 69.28]; 109.13, 14; cf. Gen. 6.7; 7.4). This basic meaning underlies deuteronomic use of the verb. With the exception of this verse in the Manasseh-oracle, the Deuteronomist's use of *mḥh* is limited to a single idiom, 'to erase the name of X from under heaven' (Deut. 9.14; 29.20; 2 Kgs 14.27).[1] Verse 13b thus uses the verb in an untypical way for deuteronomic literature. The first part, 'I will wipe out Jerusalem', departs from the usual deuteronomic idiom for the sake of the comparison, 'just as one wipes out a dish, wiping [literally, 'he wiped'] and turning [literally, 'he turned'] it upside down'. The unexpected 3rd m.s. perfect form of the verbs 'he wiped' and 'he turned' gives v. 13b an awkward syntax.[2]

---

1. In minor variations, Deut. 25.6 has 'from Israel' instead of 'from under heaven', and 25.19 replaces 'name' with 'memory' (*zēker*). Elsewhere, only Pss. 9.6 [Eng. 9.5] and 109.13 speak of erasing the name. Neither contains 'from under heaven'.

2. The verbs could be read as infinitive absolutes rather than 3ms perfects (cf. BDB, p. 562). Otherwise disregarding the introductory words, 'and I will wipe out Jerusalem', the concluding words could be read as one half of the simile, 'just as one wipes a dish, he wiped and turned it upside down'.

Verse 13b's untypical use of the verb *m ḥh*, its syntactical awkwardness and its use of the unique dish-wiping metaphor suggest that this verse incorporates some kind of fixed saying or proverb which the audience is expected to recognize.[1] Verse 14 also presents a mixture of elements, some typical and some unusual for the Deuteronomist. Variations of the second clause, 'and I will put them under the power of their enemies', are common in deuteronomic literature. The first clause, 'and I will cast off the rest of my inheritance', is unusual, however. The verb *nṭš* is common, even in deuteronomic literature. In deuteronomic usage, it normally appears either as a military term referring to troop movement (1 Sam. 4.2; 2 Sam. 5.18, 22; Judg. 15.9) or as an idiom meaning 'to entrust something to someone for safekeeping' (1 Sam. 17.20, 28 of sheep; 10.2 of asses; 17.22 of a carriage). Twice in the deuteronomic passages, *nṭš* takes Yahweh as its subject and the people as its object (1 Sam. 12.22; 1 Kgs 8.57), both times connoting abandonment (1 Kgs 8.57 pairs this verb with *'zb*, 'to abandon'). 'Inheritance' (*nḥlh*) frequently refers to Israel/Judah, especially in prophecy and psalms (Isa. 19.25; 47.6; Jer. 10.16; 51.19; Joel 2.17; Pss. 33.12; 78.71; 94.14, etc.). But the idiom 'to forsake my inheritance' appears only here and in Jer. 12.7.

The use of *šᵉ'ērît* in this clause, 'I will forsake *the rest* of my inheritance', distinguishes this passage from its Jeremiah parallel. This 'remnant' terminology is uncommon in deuteronomic literature, appearing there only three other times, once in the woman of Tekoa story (2 Sam. 14.7), figuratively representing Absalom, and twice in the Hezekiah–Isaiah episodes (2 Kgs 19.4, 31), referring, in the first case, to the bleak historical reality of a subdued Judah and besieged Jerusalem and, in the second, to a brighter eschatalogical future for the Zion community. The root *š'r* occurs often in deuteronomic material, though only four times with reference to exile (2 Kgs 17.18; 21.14; 24.14; 25.22). Most likely, the use of 'remnant' here is meant to recall the treatise on the fall of the North: 'none remained, except the tribe of Judah alone' (17.18).

The third and final clause of v. 14, 'and they will become plunder and spoil for all their enemies', is also somewhat unusual for the Deuteronomist. The infrequently occurring word *mᵉšissâ* is used in

---

1.  Gray, *I and II Kings*, p. 709.

deuteronomic literature only here. In two out of four other biblical occurrences, it is paired with *baz*, 'spoil'. 'Spoil' appears only one other time in deuteronomic literature (Deut. 1.39) in some kind of discredited proverb about the children of the wilderness generation. The verbal form *bzz* is used a few times, always in the context of holy war (Deut. 2.35; 3.7; 20.14; Josh. 8.2, 27; 11.14; 22.8; Judg. 5.30, etc.). The phrasing of v. 14 is probably meant to portray the coming punishment as Yahweh's holy war against Judah. Such a theme resonates with earlier verses in the chapter which compare Manasseh to the nations dispossessed by Yahweh during the conquest (vv. 2, 9).

The announcement of judgment, vv. 12-14, is thoroughly worked by the Deuteronomist. Yet, its awkward syntax and uncharacteristic phraseology indicate that the author is incorporating fixed sayings and proverbs from other sources. This oracle then is a series of popular clichés threaded together by stock deuteronomic phrases loosely connected with the larger narratives of the chapter.

To summarize, v. 16 is added secondarily to vv. 10-15. It foreshadows the argument of 2 Kgs 24.3-4 and 23.26-27 that Manasseh's crimes alone caused the fall of Jerusalem and Judah's exile. These verses themselves are later additions to a narrative which explained the Babylonian exile as the result of the collective historical guilt of the Davidic monarchs. As for the rest of the oracle, the deuteronomic vocabulary of v. 10 links the oracle to the treatise on the fall of the North (cf. 2 Kgs 17.13, 14, 23). Verse 11, like v. 16, singles out Manasseh as an especially notorious king but, unlike v. 16a, uses theme and vocabulary well connected with the rest of the chapter and book. Its language compares Manasseh with Northern kings in general and Ahab in particular. Though its focus on Manasseh's guilt contrasts with the implication of the whole people in v. 15, both v. 11 and v. 15 are well integrated thematically into the larger structure of the chapter. The announcement of judgment, vv. 12-14, appears to be a deuteronomic production, drawing on fixed sayings and metaphors from popular and prophetic sources. The result is a hodgepodge of destruction imagery, loosely connected to the larger chapter's major themes and notable in its lack of concrete specificity. The announcement of judgment and v. 15's accusation condemn the people, not just the king. The oracle as a whole recalls ch. 17's treatise on the fall of the North, but only v. 16a ties it specifically to the Babylonian exile.

The surprising vagueness of this oracle cautions against a hasty assumption that it originally was a fictional prediction after the event.[1] The 'man of God' episode in 1 Kgs 13.1-10, a key deuteronomic prediction after the event, gives specific details about the Josianic reform it predicts. If the Manasseh oracle were such a prediction after the event, we would expect greater specificity. Though in its present narrative context preceding v. 16 the oracle has an exilic thrust, we must hold open the possibility that the basic literary form of the oracle is pre-exilic. How such an oracle of judgment might have functioned in a pre-exilic literary context is clarified by a look at the rest of the Manasseh narrative.

As already shown, the résumé of cult crimes in vv. 2-9 shares prominent themes with the judgment oracle, vv. 10-16. The Manasseh narrative as a whole shows numerous points of contact with the treatise on the fall of the North in 2 Kings 17 and the Ahaz narrative (2 Kgs 16). The interrelationship of these three chapters helps to interpret the Manasseh narrative and to determine its possible function for a pre-exilic audience.

Theological evaluations of Manasseh in vv. 2 and 9 bracket the list of his cult crimes. Verse 7b presents an expanded version of the relative clause which commonly modifies 'house of God/Yahweh' in Kings (as in v. 4, for example). Verse 8 ostensibly continues the Yahweh quote in v. 7b but shifts accent, serving as a bridge between the preceding list of cult crimes and the evaluation of Manasseh in v. 9. Verses 3-7a catalogue Manasseh's cultic policies, though vv. 4-5 and probably 7a simply expand the information given in the v. 3 summary. Only v. 6 clearly outlines crimes not already listed in v. 3.

The verses which introduce and conclude Manasseh's crimes are key in the Deuteronomist's evaluation of this king and, more broadly, the history of Judah. Verse 2 begins with the usual deuteronomic evaluation of a bad king, 'he did evil in Yahweh's view', but continues with deuteronomic language reserved for the most extraordinary cases of

1. Spieckermann (*Assur*, p. 169) places vv. 10-15 in his latest category, arguing that the use of deuteronomistic phraseology shows close affinities with the late 'nomistic' redaction also responsible for thoroughly reworking the Huldah oracle (see his pp. 58-72). However, a certain stiffness of metaphorical speech indicates that this piece was composed after a nomistic reworking of the chapter had already been accomplished. Thus, Spieckermann assigns this oracle to SD, that is, late deuteronomistic additions not correlated into a distinct layer. Also see Gray, *I and II Kings*, pp. 707-708; Hoffmann, *Reform*, p. 157.

corruption. Manasseh did evil 'like the abominations of the nations whom Yahweh dispossessed before the Israelites'. Nearly identical wording appears in the description of Ahaz's cult policy in 2 Kgs 16.3, there with reference to the Molek cult. In Kings, apart from Manasseh, only Rehoboam's Judah (1 Kgs 14.24), Ahab (21.26), Ahaz (2 Kgs 16.3), and the people of the North (17.8) are compared to the people dispossessed before the Israelites.[1]

Deut. 12.29-31, 17.2-7 and 18.9-14 are the models for the Deuteronomist's characterization of Manasseh's cult practices as 'abominations'. Deut. 12.29-31 warns Israel to stay away from the child sacrifice which it says is common among the dispossessed nations. Deut. 17.2-7 describes worship of astral deities (v. 3) as 'abominations' carrying the death penalty. Deut. 18.10-14 incorporates an exhaustive list of illegitimate ritual inquiry and divination practices, all of which are 'abominable'. Verse 12 says the indigenous people lost their land 'on account of these abominations'. When Kings compares Manasseh's cult practices to 'the abominations' of the 'people Yahweh dispossessed', it makes a very strong, very threatening statement.

Deuteronomy's 'abomination' passages also have influenced the verses between vv. 2 and 9. Manasseh commits the capital crime of Deut. 17.3 by worshiping and serving 'all the host of heaven' (v. 3) and by building them altars in the two courts of Yahweh's temple

---

1. Not surprisingly, the clause, 'to dispossess before [Israel]', always appears in connection with conquest themes (non-deuteronomic examples are Exod. 34.24 and Num. 32.21; 33.52, 55). With one exception (Deut. 18.12, discussed below), this language in Deuteronomy and Joshua always appears as part of a covenant promise (Deut. 4.38; 9.4, 5; 11.23; Josh. 3.10; 13.6; 23.5, 9, 13). Judg. 2.21, embedded within a deuteronomic typology of Israel's rebellious history under the judges, shows the flip-side of the promise formula. Here, Yahweh announces that Israel's transgression of the covenant means Yahweh will no longer dispossess a single person on Israel's behalf. Deut. 9.4 and 5 provide the first indication that the pre-Israelite natives suffered expulsion because they were wicked: 'Do not think, when Yahweh your God drives them out from your presence, "It is because of my righteousness that Yahweh has brought me to possess this land", when it is because of these nations' wickedness that Yahweh is dispossessing them before you. It is not because of your righteousness and your upright intentions that you come to possess their land, but because of the wickedness of these nations whom Yahweh your God is dispossessing before you and in order to confirm the promise Yahweh swore to your ancestors, to Abraham, Isaac, and Jacob.'

(v. 5). Verse 6 is a combination of the cult crimes listed in Deut. 12.29-31 (child sacrifice) and 18.9-14 (various forms of divination).

Verse 6 is heavily dependent on Deut. 18.9-14. With the exception of child sacrifice, all the crimes listed in v. 6 appear in Deut. 18.10-11.'Soothsaying' (*'ônēn*) is condemned by deuteronomic writers only in these two passages (cf. also Judg. 9.37). Outside of these passages, 'perform augury' (*niḥēš*) appears in deuteronomic literature only in reference to ben Hadad's ambassadors to Ahab (1 Kgs 20.33) and as a cult crime in 2 Kgs 17.17. The latter passage also makes reference to the Molek cult and mentions 'divination' (*qsm*), also outlawed in Deut. 18.10. 'Necromancer and knower', a fairly common pair,[1] appears in this form (*'ôb wᵉyiddᵉ'ōnî*) only in Deut. 18.11 and 2 Kgs 21.6 = 2 Chron. 33.6. The above parallels show that 2 Kgs 17.17 and 21.6 draw heavily upon Deut. 18.10-11. In some cases, the Kings passages contain the only deuteronomic parallels to the Deuteronomy 18 cult crimes. The v. 6 list of cult crimes thus has close ties with Deuteronomy 18 and the treatise on the fall of the North.

The literary structure of Deut. 18.9-14 also has influenced the literary shaping of 2 Kgs 21.2-9. The list in Deut. 18.10-11 is introduced with a warning to avoid the abominations of the nations (v. 9b), and is concluded with a statement that these abominations are the reason the people are being dispossessed before Israel (v. 12). This distinctive literary structure, with references to the practices of the dispossessed nations bracketing a list of cult crimes, reappears in Kings only in the Manasseh chapter (vv. 2-9).

The influence of Deuteronomy 18 on 2 Kgs 21 extends even further. The cult crimes of Deut. 18.9-14 are prelude to vv. 15-22. The cult crimes show how not to inquire of God. Verses 15-22 set up the only legitimate line of communication, the prophet like Moses. The Manasseh narrative is patterned in the same way. Verses 2-9, drawing structure and content from Deut. 18.9-14, introduce the prophetic oracle in vv. 10-15. Structurally, the deliverance of the prophetic word follows the résumé of cult crimes which shows all the ways not to seek Yahweh.

The Manasseh narrative is patterned closely on key passages in Deuteronomy, especially Deut. 18.9-22 and others dealing with the

---

1. The definite form, *hā'ōbôt* + *wᵉhayyiddᵉ'ōnîm*, occurs in 1 Sam. 28.3, 9 (Saul and the medium of Endor) and 2 Kgs 23.24.

'abominable practices' of the dispossessed Canaanites. The clear impact of this patterning is to characterize Manasseh as the opposite of Moses and Joshua, his leadership as the near undoing of the patriarchal promise. The language of the Manasseh narrative portrays a Judah set up as the object of Yahweh's holy war. What is curious about the portrayal, however, is its facing backward. Throughout the chapter, when destruction is implied, the metaphors point to Samaria, not Jerusalem.[1] The focal point of the chapter's vision is 722, not 586. It is the fate of the North, not the destruction of Judah by the Babylonians, which moves the Manasseh chapter along.

In 2 Kgs 21.1-18, Manasseh is being set up, not to take the fall for the Babylonian exile, but to be a foil for Josiah's reform.[2] The cult policies the narrative attributes to Manasseh are no doubt policies which he followed. They were the policies he inherited from his Davidic forebears. When evaluated by the terms of the deuteronomic lawbook, however, Manasseh's cult policies became 'abominations' which threatened Yahweh's holy war against Judah. Only a radical break with the past could appease the deity and stem the tide of destruction. Judah needed Josiah's reform.

## *2 Chronicles 33.1-20*

The Chronicler's version of Manasseh's rule, like Kings, is heavily stylized to reflect the author's key theological themes. Manasseh's surprising repentance and cult reform, supported by no other known source, raises historical questions to be sure. But the Chronicler's portrayal of Manasseh has more important significance as a metaphor for post-exilic Israel.[3] Manasseh's story shows Israel the efficacy of repentance.[4] Yahweh not only forgives, but brings prosperity to those who humble themselves and turn from even the most wicked ways.

The Chronicler's report of Manasseh's Babylonian exile and subsequent restoration has sparked a good deal of discussion about the historical record of his reign. Older works dismissed the account as

1. Cf. Noth, *DH*, p. 73: 'here he [the Deuteronomist] is clearly thinking of 17.7ff. and in v. 13 he explicitly sets up a parallel between the immanent fate of the state of Judah and the accomplished fate of the state of Israel'.

2. Cf. Spieckermann, *Assur*, pp. 160-70; Hoffmann, *Reform*, p. 162.

3. Ackroyd, *Chronicler*, p. 45; Mosis, *Untersuchungen*, pp. 192-94.

4. Williamson, *I and II Chronicles*, p. 389.

another example of the Chronicler's 'pure fiction'.[1] M. Burrows expressed the opinion of many scholars , that, when writing history, the Chronicler 'interprets the whole past in terms of individual retribution, even though this sometimes involves a radical reconstruction of what could be known from the more ancient sources'.[2] Other scholars, for example Eissfeldt[3] and W. Rudolph,[4] anticipated more recent arguments[5] which find a kernel of history for Manasseh's exile in the gathering of Assyrian vassals in 672 when Assurbanipal took the throne. The Chronicler either misinterpreted or magnified this meeting, turning it into a personal exile for Manasseh. Still others defend the basic historicity of Manasseh's detention in Babylon, relating it to the crushed rebellion of Assurbanipal's brother Shamash-shum-ukin (c. 652–648).[6] McKay interprets cult practices reportedly introduced by Manasseh (astral deities, Baal and Asherah) and his burial in the 'garden of Uzza' (which McKay ties to the Arabian god Al-'Uzza) as evidence of Manasseh's close ties with Phoenicians and Arabs who rebelled with Shamash-shum-ukin in 652.[7] This close relationship with the rebels caught Manasseh up in the conspiracy or else made him suspect enough to be summoned to Babylon to reaffirm his allegiance.[8] Reviv[9] even offers a rationale for Manasseh's eventual release: Assurbanipal wanted a buffer against the Egyptians. This explains the Chronicler's report of Manasseh's fortification

1. C.C. Torrey's words (*Ezra Studies*, p. 231).

2. M. Burrows, 'Ancient Israel', in *The Idea of History in the Ancient Near East* (ed. R. Dentan; New Haven, CT: Yale University Press, 1955), p. 126, cited by R.J. North, 'Does Archaeology Prove Chronicles' Sources?' in *A light unto My Path: Old Testament Studies in Honor of Jacob M. Myers* (Philadelphia: Temple University Press, 1974), pp. 375-401 (379). Cf. R.H. Pfeiffer, 'Chronicles', *IDB* I, pp. 572-80. H. Preller comments (*Geschichte der Historiographie unseres Kulturkreises: Materialien, Skizzen, Vorarbeiten. I. bis 330 a.D.* [Aalen: Scientia, 1967], p. 104) that the Chronicler is 'as fantastically unhistorical as possible'.

3. Eissfeldt, *Introduction*, p. 536.

4. Rudolph, *Chronikbücher*, p. 316.

5. Cf. Williamson, *I and II Chronicles*, pp. 392-93.

6. E.E. Ehrlich, 'Der Anfenthalt des Königs Manasse in Babylon', *TZ* 21 (1965), pp. 281-86; McKay, *Religion*, pp. 25-27; Oded, *'Judah and Exile'*, pp. 455-56; Reviv, 'History of Judah', pp. 200-201.

7. McKay, *Religion*, pp. 22-27.

8. Cf. Frankena, 'Vassal-treaties', p. 152.

9. Reviv, 'History of Judah', pp. 200-201.

projects when he returned to Jerusalem.[1]

It is possible that some historical event underlies the Chronicler's account of Manasseh's exile, but arguments that Manasseh was arrested for his actual or perceived participation in Shamash-shumukin's rebellion have nothing outside Chronicles to support them. Kings offers not an inkling of such a rebellion. The Assyrian records contain no such report.[2] To the contrary, imperial records show Manasseh to be a faithful vassal.[3] Manasseh's participation in a rebellion is out of character with the Judean monarch portrayed in the sources outside Chronicles.

The lack of external confirmation of Manasseh's exile is insufficient in itself to judge the account unhistorical.[4] The account's heavy patterning to reflect key themes of Chronicles, however, casts serious doubt on its accuracy. There are plenty of reasons to think the Chronicler has fabricated the story to fit the book's larger purposes and few reasons to believe that he has picked up the story from a reliable source.

Mosis[5] rightly has objected to older views that the Chronicler fabricated the Manasseh exile simply to meet the demands of a rigid theology of individual retribution.[6] Mosis and Williamson[7] point out that the Chronicler makes nothing out of Manasseh's longevity, a fact which 'tells against those who argue that the Chronicler invented the whole story in order to defend an alleged doctrine of rigidly individualistic retribution'.[8] It is not longevity alone, however, which presented a problem for the Chronicler's theology of retribution. It was

---

1.   M. Broshi, on the other hand ('The Expansion of Jerusalem in the Reigns of Hezekiah and Manasseh', *IEJ* 24 [1974], pp. 21-26), challenges the Chronicler's report about Manasseh's fortifications, arguing instead that construction was necessary at this time to accommodate Judah's rapidly growing population.

2.   North, 'Archaeology', p. 386; Williamson, *I and II Chronicles*, p. 391.

3.   See the first three notes of the present chapter.

4.   Cf. Ackroyd, *The Age of the Chronicler* (Auckland: Colloquium, 1970), p. 45.

5.   Mosis, *Untersuchungen*, pp. 192-94.

6.   Cf. also Williamson, *I and II Chronicles*, p. 389.

7.   Mosis, *Untersuchungen*, pp. 192-94; Williamson, *I and II Chronicles*, pp. 389, 393.

8.   Williamson, *I and II Chronicles*, p. 393.

also Manasseh's stunning success as a king, a point made in v. 14.[1] As
Williamson himself notes, Manasseh's building projects are 'regarded
as blessing' by the Chronicler.[2] The theology of individual retribution
does play a part in the production of this narrative. It is not, however,
the only or even the prominent theme which runs through the chapter.

Manasseh's cult reform (vv. 15-17), presented as a result of his
repentance in exile, is also spurious. Verse 22 of the same chapter
directly contradicts the portrayal of Manasseh as faithful reformer, as
follows: 'and [Amon] did evil in Yahweh's view just like Manasseh his
father did. He sacrificed to all the abominable images Manasseh his
father made and served them,'. Manasseh's removal of foreign gods
and abominable images also makes Josiah's reform redundant. The
Chronicler's reform of Manasseh cannot even be supported by
Chronicles.

More important than the historical discrepancies, however, is the
theological impact of the Manasseh story for the Chronicler's post-
exilic audience. In the Chronicler's portrayal, Manasseh becomes a
symbol of post-exilic Israel. His Babylonian exile is not coincidental.
Like the people of Judah, Manasseh suffered the pain of exile, because
he had committed hideous sins and refused to heed the warnings of
God (v. 10). More important than his exile, however, was his repentance, restoration and commitment to reform. For the Chronicler,
Manasseh is a clear example of God's mercy and willingness to for-
give those who truly repent.[3] His restoration and prosperity is proof
of God's surprising willingness to bless even those who must repent of
serious sins. His cult reform shows the righteous action which follows
true repentance. For the Chronicler, Manasseh stands as a paradigm of
righteousness for an exiled and now restored post-exilic community.
He is a key symbol of hope, based in trust that Yahweh forgives and
blesses beyond imagination those who truly humble themselves and
turn from evil. Manasseh then becomes the Chronicler's strongest

---

1.    See Welten's discussion of the textual and topographical problems of this
chapter (*Chronikbüchern*, pp. 72-78). Welten dismisses any historical value of the
passage, arguing instead that it reflects the Chronicler's own knowledge of post-
exilic Jerusalem.

2.    Williamson, *I and II Chronicles*, p. 394.

3 .    Williamson, *I and II Chronicles,* p. 389.

object lesson for restored Israel and their greatest reason to hope for the future.

## *Summary*

The Chronicler and the Deuteronomist both present highly stylized descriptions of Manasseh. For both authors he is a key figure, symbolizing something much greater than himself. The authors are diametrically opposed, however, in the way they understand Manasseh's significance.

For the Chronicler, Manasseh is a symbol of punished, repentant, restored and newly blessed Israel. The historical kernel of the story of Manasseh's exile and restoration is impossible to recover from known sources, but the historical veracity of the Chronicler's account is highly doubtful. Manasseh's exile, restoration and reform function to keep hope alive in the post-exilic Israel.

The Deuteronomist's Manasseh represents Judah's most dangerous threat. He is the mirror opposite of Josiah. The narrative description of Manasseh in structure and content reflects the influence of Josiah's lawbook. The assertions of Cogan, McKay and others that syncretism was on the rise in Manasseh's Judah are impossible to judge based on 2 Kings 21. The chapter is too heavily stylized. The cult crimes listed (Asherah, Baal, astral deities, child sacrifices, divination, sorcery, idolatry and high place worship) had been seen before in the Jerusalem temple. Manasseh inherited them. They were nothing new. What was new was their very tight correlation with the deuteronomic lawbook and its threats of doom. Yet the chapter remains surprisingly vague when it comes to characterizing the impending doom. This vagueness and the close dependency on the lawbook indicate that the Manasseh portrayal is intended not so much to explain an accomplished fact (the Babylonian exile) as to warn against an unrepentant path. It is not reflection on disaster. It is preparation for reform. The characterizations and threats of the Deuteronomist's Manasseh narrative prepare the reader for radical change, the radical change of Josiah's deuteronomic reform. The Manasseh narrative in its definitive form is Josianic-era literature of persuasion, supporting the necessity of Josiah's reform.

Chapter 6

JOSIAH: CULT REFORM AND CULTURAL REVOLUTION

If laid end to end, the scholarly pages written about Josiah's reform might well reach to the moon. Much has been written, because interpreters long have recognized that in Josiah's reform lies the key to Deuteronomy, and in Deuteronomy lies the key to much of the Old Testament.

Josiah reformed Judah's official cult with a scope and depth which was unprecedented for a Davidic monarch and never to be repeated. The deuteronomic reform he executed did not spring full-grown from the heads of Josiah and his priest Hilkiah. The high place–Asherah–sacred pillar reform of the rebel king Hezekiah stood at the heart of Josiah's reform. The reformist agenda picked up several additional elements, however, along the historical path from Hezekiah's rebellion in 701 to Josiah's reform around 621.

In these remarks, I will describe the changes and suggest reasons why Hezekiah's limited reforms might have grown into the comprehensive nationalist theology of Josiah and his supporters. My concluding chapter, immediately following, will describe how deuteronomic theology emerged as a combination of traditions and social interests under the conditions of Assyrian imperialism. Basic questions about the historical record and the purpose of Josiah's reform must be addressed first, however.

*2 Kings 22–23 and 2 Chronicles 34–35*

When Josiah took the throne in 640 BCE, Assyria's power had already diminished in the West.[1] With the death of Ashurbanipal a little over a

1. Cogan, *Imperialism*, pp. 65-71; contra F.M. Cross and D.N. Freedman, 'Josiah's Revolt Against Assyria', *JNES* 12(1953), pp. 56-58.

decade later,[1] the final disintegration of the empire began. Josiah ruled a kingdom free of the imperial yoke for the first time in a century.

From the perspectives of the biblical historians, the most important way Josiah used this new-found freedom was to reorganize and reform the official cult top to bottom, inside and out. Their reports are heavy on cult reform and very light on geopolitics. Hints of Josiah's political designs are given here and there, for example in his reform push to Bethel, and in his failed and fatal attempt to stop the Egyptian army at Megiddo. But these tidbits are few and usually indirect. Throughout their accounts, the biblical authors keep the clear and, I will argue, more appropriate focus on the fiercely nationalistic cultural revolution this king attempted from the top down.

The coincidence of Judah's independence and Josiah's reform raises a question about how Judah's vassal status relates to Josiah's overhaul of the cult. As the question has been put most typically, was Josiah's deuteronomic reform part of a rebellion against Assyria? The family resemblance between Josiah's reform and the cult reform of the rebel Hezekiah, Josiah's violent purge of 'foreign' cult practices, and the international political context of Josiah's reign are sufficient reasons to raise the question.

Oestreicher was the first to ask and answer the question about the political dimensions of Josiah's cult reform.[2] He started with 2 Chron. 34.3 and 8 which describe a reform in Josiah's twelfth year and a second reform after the discovery of the lawbook in his eighteenth year. Taking the Chronicler's version to be more accurate, Oestreicher argued that Josiah's deuteronomic reform took place in two stages. In 627, Josiah purged Assyrian cults from Jerusalem. He then extended the purge throughout Judah in 621 because of further disturbances in Assyria. The finding of the lawbook in 621 gave incentive to continue the reform but was not the reason Josiah started the reform in the first place.

Gressmann[3] supported Oestreicher's thesis by examining several Assyrian texts. He concluded that more than half of Josiah's reforms

---

1. Cross and Freedman (*'Revolt'*) put Ashurbanipal's death at 633 BCE. More recent studies, however, date his death in 627. Cf. Bright's chronology (*History*) and J. Reade ('The Accession of Sinsharishkun', *JCS* 23 [1970], pp. 1-9).

2. Oestreicher, *Grundsetz*.

3. Gressmann, 'Josia', pp. 313-35.

as recorded in Kings were purges of Assyrian deities (2 Kgs 23.4-7, 11-12). With this kind of supporting evidence from the Assyrian side, Oestreicher's theory that Josiah's reform was motivated by rebellion became the standard interpretation.

Among Oestreicher's many scholarly supporters,[1] Cross and Freedman attempted closely to correlate the 'stages' of Josiah's reform with specific events marking the disintegration of the Assyrian empire.[2] They envisioned a three-phase reform corresponding to the death of Ashurbanipal, the death of Ashur-etal-ilani, and finally the complete disintegration of imperial power in the West. Their chronology and their approach of trying to match Josiah's reform exactly with key upheavals in Assyria, are now generally rejected.[3] However, many scholars continue to find the Chronicler's multi-stage reform more plausible than the Deuteronomist's report characterizing Josiah's reform as one-time, all-out response to the finding of the book.

A. Jepsen,[4] for example, offers a three-stage reform but rejects a political interpretation of it.[5] Paralleling an earlier suggestion by D.W.B. Robinson,[6] Jepsen suggests that Zephaniah's preaching was the primary impulse for Josiah's reform.[7] Jepsen discerns a non-deuteronomic first-stage reform (c. 628) which removed Canaanite and Assyrian cults from Jerusalem. This reform was carried out independently of Deuteronomy. A second reform abolishing worship at the high places came after the discovery of the lawbook in 622, as Jepsen dates it. Later still, Josiah demolished the Bethel sanctuary, his third phase of reform.[8] Jepsen's reconstruction begs the question of political factors underlying Zephaniah's preaching. It also assumes the historical dependency of Josiah's centralization reform on the discovery of

---

1. Bright, *History*, pp. 318-19; Moriarty, 'Chronicler's Account', pp. 399-406; Weinfeld, 'Neo-Babylonian Analogy', pp. 202-12.

2. Cross and Freedman, 'Revolt', pp. 56-58.

3. Cf. for example, Jones, *1 and 2 Kings*, p. 607; Williamson, *I and II Chronicles*, pp. 397-98.

4. A. Jepsen, 'Die Reform des Josia', in *Festschrift Friedrich Baumgartel* (ed. J. Herrmann; Erlangen: Universitätsbibliothek Erlangen, 1959), pp. 97-108.

5. Jepsen, 'Die Reform', p. 98.

6. D.W.B. Robinson, *Josiah's Reform and the Book of the Law* (London: Tyndale Press, 1951).

7. Jepsen, 'Die Reform', p. 106.

8. Jepsen, 'Die Reform', p. 108.

the lawbook. Recent scholarship, however, correctly challenges such a rigid dependency.[1]

Jepsen's rejection of a political motivation for the reform has found a receptive audience from scholars such as Kaufmann[2] and Cogan.[3] To begin with, Cogan rejects the view of Bright, Noth, Malamat and others[4] that the assassins of Amon were anti-Assyrianist conspirators and that the people of the land who executed the assassins and put Josiah on the throne did so to prevent a confrontation with Assyria. Josiah's subsequent actions, aimed at purging 'foreign' elements from the cult and, presumably, at overthrowing foreign alignments, indicate that these people of the land had anything but restraining effects on Judah's foreign policy. Cogan cites Assyria's failure to intervene in Judah's coup and countercoup as evidence that 'Judah, as early as 640, had begun to free itself of vassal restraints, long before the final disintegration of the empire which set in with the death of Ashurbanipal in 627'.[5] Assyria had little influence in Judean politics by the time Josiah took the throne, Cogan concludes.

Having already argued that Assyria did not interfere with its vassals' cult practices, Cogan finds it unlikely that Josiah's reform was part of a political rebellion against Assyria. Instead, he argues that genuine cultic decay occurred during the reign of Manasseh. Judeans, rocked by the fall of the North, discouraged by Hezekiah's failed rebellion and disheartened by their continued subservience to Assyria, came to a crisis of faith and began to revert to indigenous Canaanite practices.[6] Josiah's reform comes as a genuine religious reform in a period characterized by a 'spirit of repentance and soul searching'.[7]

A slightly different slant on the political interpretation comes in the

1. Cf. Nicholson, *Deuteronomy and Tradition*, p. 16; Mayes, *Deuteronomy*, pp. 85-103.

2. Y. Kaufmann, *Toledot Ha'emuna Hayyisra'elit* (Tel-Aviv: Dvir, 1960), p. 2.

3. Cogan, *Imperialism*, pp. 5, 113.

4. Bright, *History* (2nd edn), p. 294; Nicholson, *Deuteronomy and Tradition*, p. 11; A. Malamat, 'The Historical Background of the Assassination of Amon, King Judah', *IEJ* 3 (1953), pp. 26-29; Oded, *'Judah and Exile'*, p. 462; Reviv, 'History of Judah', p. 201; Jones, *1 and 2 Kings*, p. 604.

5. Cogan, *Imperialism*, pp. 70-71.

6. *Imperialism*, pp. 88-96.

7. *Imperialism*, p. 113.

argument of Nicholson[1] and Moriarty[2] that Hezekiah's and, later, Josiah's cult centralization reforms were motivated by the desire to reunite the divided kingdom. In their view, the crisis occasioned by the fall of the North ignited a 'religio-political' movement in Judah toward reunification. This movement naturally had a strong centralizing tendency[3] which finally found expression in cult centralization. Hezekiah abolished the high places because foreign cults were gaining ground there and dampening the national will for reunification and independence from Assyria.[4] Josiah's reform, in turn, was motivated by his desire to conquer the North and reconstitute the old Davidic–Solomonic kingdom.[5]

When Nicholson and Moriarty identify the national will for reunification and independence as a moving force behind Hezekiah's and Josiah's reforms, they are on the right track. Their arguments are derailed, however, by their view of the high places as hotbeds of syncretism. The biblical authors describe high place worship as filled with illegitimate cult practices. However, as 2 Kings 23 itself attests, no Judean shrine came close to the Jerusalem temple in sponsoring foreign cult practices. The temple had it all. Yet Josiah did not close the temple because it was syncretistic. He purged it. He would have done the same for the high places, if his only concern were the presence of 'foreign' cults there. Josiah had some other reason for centralizing the cult at Jerusalem.

More than 60 years ago, A. Bentzen[6] suggested what that other reason might have been. For Bentzen, cult centralization had an economic motivation. The levitical priests of the smaller shrines in the country-

1. Nicholson, 'Centralisation', pp. 308-89;*idem, Deuteronomy and Tradition*, pp. 1-17.

2. F.L. Moriarty, 'The Chronicler's Account of Hezekiah's Reform', *CBQ* 27 (1965), pp. 399-406.

3. Nicholson, 'Centralisation', p. 384.

4. Nicholson, 'Centralisation', pp. 385-86.

5. For further discussion of the implications of centralization in the context of Josiah's Northern strategy, see the following: E. Junge, *Wiederaufbau*, pp. 28-93; Donner, 'The Separate States of Israel and Judah', in *Israelite and Judaean History* (ed. J.H. Hayes and J.M. Miller; OTL; Philadelphia: Westminster Press, 1977), pp. 363-66; M. Sekine, 'Beobachtungen zu der josianischen Reform', *VT* 22 (1972), pp. 361-68.

6. Bentzen, *Die josianische Reform*, pp. 68-72.

side legislated cult centralization as a way of integrating themselves into the more lucrative ministry at the central shrine. Shutting down the high places thus was a means of better providing for the material welfare of rural priests.

W.E. Claburn[1] picks up Bentzen's economic argument but runs it in the opposite direction. According to Claburn, the rural levites were a wealthy class of local cultic bureaucrats to whom the peasants paid taxes (tithes). The levites took their due and passed on the rest of the revenue to the central royal administration. These levites, however, became increasingly independent of the Jerusalem court, keeping more of the tax money than the monarchy could afford and building an ever stronger political base for themselves on the local level. In an attempt to re-establish monarchical authority, consolidate power, and especially to replenish the royal coffers, Josiah centralized the cult and brought tithe revenues directly to Jerusalem. Josiah's centralization of the cult this undercut the levites' economic and political authority in the countryside.

Bentzen's proposal ill fits the response of the rural priests to cult centralization as it is portrayed in 2 Kgs 23.9: 'However, the priests of the high places did not come up to the altar of Yahweh in Jerusalem. Rather, they ate bread in the company of their brothers'. If this verse is right, the rural levites did not benefit from Josiah's abolition of high places. They are unlikely proponents of centralization.[2] Claburn's proposal better accounts for the opposition of rural levites to Josiah's reform. It fails, however, to explain all the other aspects of the reform. Centralization is an important part of the reform, but Josiah did much more than abolish high places. Claburn's proposal does not explain, for example, what women weaving mats for the temple Asherah has to do with the economic status of rural levites.

Political, religions and economic theories about Josiah's cult reform fall short of explaining it, because their scope is too narrow. Deuteronomy and the Josianic reforms cover more than mere politics

---

1. W.E. Claburn, 'The Fiscal Basis of Josiah's Reforms', *JBL* 92 (1973), pp. 11-22.

2. The same reasoning applies, by the way, to von Rad's identification of the levites as the tradents of deuteronomic theology. Note, however, B. Halpern's recent defense of centralization as an economic program pushed by the rural levites ('The Centralization Formula in Deuteronomy', *VT* 31 [1981], pp. 10-38 [37-38]).

or economics or even religion. Deuteronomic theology is a comprehensive symbol system which incorporates all these.

Before attempting a more comprehensive explanation, it is helpful to highlight the history of scholarship on the origin and development of deuteronomic theology. After the survey, I will compare Josiah's and Hezekiah's reforms, briefly noting recent scholarship on the cult practices purged by Josiah.

The history of critical scholarship on the deuteronomic movement is properly traced from de Wette.[1] First, he noted that Israel's own tradition records that high places had been a key part of the Yahweh cult until Hezekiah's and Josiah's reforms. Since Deuteronomy is the only pentateuchal book demanding cult centralization, de Wette concluded that Deuteronomy must be the 'book of the covenant/law' found by Josiah's priest Hilkiah.

In the 1920's, Oestreicher[2] mounted an important challenge to de Wette's hypothesis, arguing that Deuteronomy does not even demand centralization. He dismissed the passages in Deuteronomy which obviously require cult centralization as late additions. In an important contribution, confirmed by more recent scholarship, Oestreicher observed that the report of Josiah's reform is literarily separate from the previous narrative concerning the discovery of the book. As mentioned above, he asserts that the entire reform was politically motivated by the desire to throw off Assyrian imperialism.

At roughly the same time, Hölscher[3] challenged de Wette's hypothesis from the other direction. Hölscher's argument is that Deuteronomy does demand cult centralization, but that Josiah's reform did not. The latter point he makes by deleting 2 Kgs 23.8-9 as a post-exilic addition to the Kings' reform account. His argument that Deuteronomy demands centralization is connected with his dating of the book in the Second Temple period. Doubting the practicality of cult centralization, especially in the First Temple period, Hölscher considers Deuteronomy to be a utopian document originating in post-exilic priestly circles.

Neither Oestreicher's claim that Deuteronomy does not require centralization nor Hölscher's dating of the book in the post-exilic

1. De Wette, *Dissertatio*.
2. Oestreicher, *Grundsetz*.
3. G. Hölscher, 'Komposition', pp. 161-255.

period gained wide acceptance. In the 1930s and 1940s, the direction began to shift in the scholarship of the deuteronomic movement.

Von Rad[1] observed the complex literary structure of Deuteronomy and posited a *Sitz im Leben* in 'a cultic celebration, perhaps from a feast of renewal of the covenant'.[2] Von Rad supported his contention by appeal to the covenant-making ceremony in Deut. 26.16-19. The cultic setting which underlies the book, however, has now been obscured by the didactic, homiletical form in which Deuteronomy is written. Taking a clue from Ezra's reading of the law in Nehemiah 8 where levites take a prominent role in publishing and preaching the law, von Rad identified the levites as representatives of 'militant piety' in the monarchical period.[3] These levites, according to von Rad, collected and interpreted the old premonarchical traditions, especially the holy war ideology, which came into vogue once more at the time of Josiah's program of political expansion. Agreeing with the earlier judgments of A.C. Welch[4] and A. Alt,[5] von Rad's assumption is that the deuteronomic movement had its origins in the Northern kingdom within a century before Josiah's reform. Although warning against overestimating the connection between Deuteronomy and the reform (one does not produce the other), von Rad views Josiah's reorganization of the cult as being carried out along the lines of Deuteronomy.

Lohfink[6] rejects von Rad's claim that the Mosaic traditions of Deuteronomy are limited to the levites. He accepts the identification of the 'book of the law' with Deuteronomy but suggests that this was the written 'federal document' (*Bundesurkunde*) of Jerusalem. Lohfink finds in 2 Kings 22–23 a four-section pattern of covenant renewal,

---

1. *Deuteronomy* (OTL; Philadelphia: Westminster Press, 1966), pp. 11-30.

2. *Deuteronomy*, p. 23.

3. *Deuteronomy*, p. 24.

4. A.C. Welch, *The Code of Deuteronomy* (London: Oxford University Press, 1924).

5. Alt, 'Die Heimat des Deuteronomium', *KS*, I, pp. 252-62.

6. N. Lohfink, 'Die Bundesurkunde des Königs Josias', *Bib* 44 (1963), pp. 261-88, 461-98; *idem* 'Deuteronomy', *IDBSup*, pp. 229-232. 'That this might be the language of sermon outlies or summaries of the restorative propaganda of rural Levites is only one possibility among many, and not even the most probable one. Rather the language of Deuteronomy shows many ties with the language of the court and with wisdom language, which were most widely known among higher officials' (*IDBSup*, p. 229).

consisting of repentance (22.3-11), an oracle of salvation (22.12-20), covenant renewal (23.1-13) and ritual feast (23.21-23). Lohfink believes the four-section document was put together during the reign of Josiah, since it is unaware of Josiah's violent death. In a later article,[1] Lohfink describes the two-chapter account of Josiah's reform, which now includes this Josianic era covenant renewal document, as a tightly written short story explaining the events leading up to the Babylonian exile. In his reconstruction, the documents of deuteronomic reform have their geographical locus in Jerusalem, not among rural levites.[2]

Rowley[3] and Nicholson[4] offer a very different reconstruction of deuteronomic origins. They find substantial Northern influence throughout the deuteronomic literature. Nicholson notes the heavy emphasis in Deuteronomy and Kings on the prophetic word, and argues that deuteronomic theology has its origins in Northern prophetic circles operating sometime before the fall of Samaria. After the fall of the North in 722, these Northern deuteronomists fled to Judah. There, they constructed a reform program. Cult centralization originally had Shechem rather than Jerusalem as its base,[5] but the idea was easily adapted to the Jerusalemite theology of the Davidic court.[6]

Northern influence on Deuteronomy and Kings cannot be denied.[7] Linkages can be seen between the preaching of Hosea, for example, and some aspects of the deuteronomic reform program, especially in Deuteronomy's use of the term 'love' to describe the Yahweh–Israel relationship.[8] However, the Northern prophetic theory of origin runs

1. Lohfink, 'Die Gattung der "Historischen Kurzgeschichte" in den letzten Jahren von Juda und in die Zeit des babylonischen Exils', *ZAW* 90 (1978), pp. 319-47.

2. *IDBSup*, p. 229.

3. H.H. Rowley, *From Moses to Qumran: Studies in the Old Testament* (New York: Association Press, 1963), pp. 187-208.

4. Nicholson, 'Centralisation', pp. 380-89; *idem, Deuteronomy and Tradition*.

5. Rowley, *From Moses to Qumran*, p. 198.

6. Nicholson, *Deuteronomy*, p. 95; *idem*, 'Centralisation', pp. 380-89.

7. See, for example, R.W. Wilson's discussion of deuteronomic ideas about prophecy as the clearest example of the Northern, 'Ephraimite' understanding (*Prophecy and Society in Ancient Israel* [Philadelphia: Fortress Press, 1980], pp. 156-225).

8. Cf. M. Weinfeld, 'The Emergence of the Deuteronomic Movement: The Historical Antecedents', in *Das Deuteronomium: Entstehung, Gestalt und Botschaft* (ed.

into problems at several points. Assuming Hezekiah's reform is historical, it is odd to think he would be influenced by a group of recent émigrés to overturn more than two centuries of Davidic tradition and centralize the cult. The emergency conditions of Hezekiah's rebellion, however, make sense of centralization. A plausible explanation for centralization can be found in the social-political conditions of late eighth-century Judah. If the need to find some kind of Northern setting for cult centralization is removed, Shechem has nothing to recommend it as the sole shrine originally envisioned by the deuteronomists. Finally, the generally positive view of the Judean monarchy and the adoption of Davidic election theology by the deuteronomic literature remain difficult to explain in an originally Northern setting. Northern influence does not mean a Northern origin. Several characteristics of the literature are better explained by reference to a native Judean context.

The scholarship of deuteronomic theology took a new turn following G. Mendenhall's correlation of pentateuchal legal traditions and Hittite vassal treaties.[1] McCarthy,[2] Frankena,[3] and others[4] tried to show Deuteronomy's dependence on common ancient Near Eastern treaty patterns. Underlying the literary form of Deuteronomy was an oral form in the covenant celebration, the ritual renewal of a treaty between vassal and suzerain, in this case, Israel and Yahweh. The vassal-treaty theories enjoyed a degree of favor in the 1960s.

The treaty pattern observations were modified by Weinfeld[5] in the early 1970s. Weinfeld's argument is that Deuteronomy's covenant-formula format was a common literary form in the ancient Near East. The form of Deuteronomy has a literary, not a liturgical origin. The

N. Lohfink; Leuven: Leuven University Press, 1985), pp. 76-98.

1.   G. Mendenhall, *Law and Covenant in the Ancient Near East* (Pittsburgh: Biblical Colloquium, 1955).

2.   D.J. McCarthy, *Treaty and Covenant* (Rome: Pontifical Biblical Institute, 1963).

3.   Frankena, 'Vassal-treaties', pp. 122-54.

4.   G.E. Wright, 'The Lawsuit of God: A Form-Critical Study of Deuteronomy 32', in *Israel's Prophetic Heritage* (FS J. Muilenburg; ed. B.W. Anderson and W. Harrelson; New York: Harper, 1962), pp. 26-67; K. Baltzer, *The Covenant Formulary in Old Testament, Jewish, and Early Christian Writings* (Philadelphia: Fortress Press, 1971).

5.   Weinfeld, 'Inquiry', pp. 249-62; *idem, Deuteronomic School.*

most likely tradents of deuteronomic theology then are the educated class of Jerusalem, the scribes and teachers at the royal court. Furthermore, Weinfeld discerns in the deuteronomic literature a process by which laws and institutions of substantially sacro-ritual character are rationalized and secularized. This 'secularizing' tendency in deuteronomic literature reflects a 'religio-national ideology which was inspired by the sapiential-didactic school' which inspired the scribes and the wise of Hezekiah's and Josiah's courts.[1]

Weinfeld correctly locates deuteronomic thought, at least in its definitive form, in the South near the seat of royal power. In a more recent article,[2] however, he also accounts for the strong Northern influences evident in deuteronomic theology, locating it in a national renaissance after the fall of Samaria as Hezekiah (and later, Josiah) tried to appeal to Northerners.[3] His notion of a 'secularizing tendency' in deuteronomic ideology is vague and too value-laden to be of much use. Similarly vague is the notion of a 'wisdom school' of thought which this 'secularized' deuteronomic ideology is supposed to reflect. Weinfeld is right to say that the deuteronomic literature has adopted some vocabulary and literary patterns from common ancient Near Eastern vassal treaties, though with nothing like the tight dependency envisioned in the 1960s.[4] The deuteronomists' familiarity with international treaty forms, however, does not itself prove that they were the court wise, unless literacy was limited to Jerusalem courtiers.

The quest for the tradents of deuteronomic theology is as confused as the search for a motivation for Josiah's reform. Surely, it is an odd literature which leads its critical readers to conclude that it is antimonarchical and pro-monarchical, Northern and Southern in origin, the product of rural levites, Jerusalem priests, royal scribes, recent émigrés, courtly insiders, wisdom teachers and prophetic circles. All these proposals have been put forward, however, because each of them has some warrant in the literature. A closer look at Josiah's reform sets the context for sorting out some of these contradictory

1.  Weinfeld, 'Inquiry', p. 262.
2.  'Emergence', pp. 76-98.
3.  'Emergence', pp. 89-91.
4.  Cf. B. Halpern, 'The Centralization Formula in Deuteronomy', *VT* 31 (1981), pp. 10-38. Halpern (p. 28 n. 20) argues the appearance of the treaty form in Deut. 28 does not suggest 'the origin of the code in its literary form in that time. Rather, it is a Hezekian or Josianic addition for treaty making purposes.'

characteristics of deuteronomic theology.

Whether to go with the Deuteronomist's version of a one-time law-book-inspired reform or the Chronicler's version of a two- or possibly three-stage reform over several years is an interesting question which cannot finally be settled. G.S. Ogden's fascinating comparison between the Kings and Chronicles accounts of Josiah's reform[1] shows heavy patterning in both narratives.[2] The Deuteronomist's focus on the discovery of the lawbook[3] telescopes Josiah's multi-faceted reform of the temple, abolition of the high places and defilement of the Bethel sanctuary into a very busy eighteenth year of Josiah,[4] an improbable level of activity for the time Kings allows. On the other hand, Chronicles, as Mosis has shown,[5] has its own agenda in the dating of the reforms. The Chronicler is anxious to show that Josiah started the cult reform as soon as possible (cf. Hezekiah's reform 'in the first year of his reign in the first month' [2 Chron. 29.3]). Therefore, the Chronicler dates Josiah's reform in his twelfth year, the first year of adulthood. Placing the discovery of the lawbook in Josiah's eighteenth year following an initial reform in the twelfth year also fits the Hezekiah pattern in Chronicles. Kings says the discovery of the book came during temple repairs. The Chronicler, following the pattern of the Hezekiah account (2 Chron. 29), presents temple repairs as part of a cult reform already begun.[6] Thus in Chronicles, reform precedes the temple repairs which result in the discovery of the book. That discovery prompts more reform.

There are good reasons to question the chronologies of Kings and Chronicles. In the final analysis, however, it is not of critical impor-

---

1. G.S. Ogden, 'The Northern Extent of Josiah's Reforms', *AusBR* 26 (1978), pp. 26-33.

2. Studying Chronicles, Ogden correlates the geography of Josiah's reform (2 Chron. 34.6) with similar geographical descriptions in 2 Chron. 15.9 (Asa) and 30.18 (Hezekiah) to argue that the Chronicler 'deliberately extends the geographical parameters to assert that Josiah's programme was superior to all other reform attempts' (*ibid.*, p. 30). In 2 Kgs 23.16-20, Ogden argues, the Deuteronomist has presented Josiah as another Jehu (*ibid.*, pp. 31-33).

3. Jones, *1 and 2 Kings*, p. 604.

4. Cf. Williamson, *I and II Chronicles*, p. 398.

5. Mosis, *Untersuchungen*, pp. 195-97.

6. Mosis, *Untersuchungen*, pp. 196-197; Williamson, *I and II Chronicles*, p. 399.

tance to settle which account is more reliable. The close correlation of Josiah's reform with Assyria's declining power in the West is the chief reason to prefer the Chronicler's chronology. Cogan, however, is thoroughly convincing that Assyrian power was virtually non-existent in Judah throughout Josiah's reign. Without the necessity of paralleling Assyrian chronology, very little is at stake in favoring Chronicles over Kings. Recent questions about Josiah's designs on the North, and his alleged intention to recreate a Davidic–Solomonic empire,[1] cast further doubt on any precise correlation of Josiah's reform measures with events limiting Assyria's power in the West.[2] A two- or three-stage reform to explain Josiah's political motives is unnecessary. On the other hand, neither is it critical to assert a one-shot, all-encompassing reform, as portrayed in Kings. Presumably, Josiah's deuteronomic reform took time. It may have been accomplished in stages over a period of years. It may have been carried out rather quickly. Without the need to fit Josiah's reform in with some external chronology, its social-historical impact can be seen to be essentially the same whether it happened in phases or all at once.

The actual account of Josiah's reform, 2 Kgs 23.4-20, has several characteristics which set it off from the surrounding narrative. The opening in v. 4, 'and the king commanded', and the closing in v. 20, 'and he returned to Jerusalem', bracket a coherent list of cult measures. The section makes no reference to the lawbook. Frequently, it employs the surprising simple *waw* verbal form, as opposed to the more expected *waw*-consecutive form typical of the rest of 2 Kings 22–23.[3] Many have found in the reform account, 23.4-20, annalistic material dating from the reign of Josiah.[4] Others see a complex redac-

---

1. Ogden, 'Northern Extent', p. 33; see especially, H.D. Lance, 'The Royal Stamps and the Kingdom of Josiah', *HTR* 64 (1971), pp. 315-32 (332); but note the opposite conclusion by A.D. Tushingham, 'A Royal Israelite Seal (?) and the Royal Jar Handle Stamps', *BASOR* 200 (1970), pp. 71-78; *idem*, *BASOR* 201 (1971), pp. 23-35; cf. also E. Stern, 'Israel at the Close of the Period of the Monarchy: An Archaeological Survey', *BA* 38 (1975), pp. 26-54 (27, 32, 37).

2. Jones, however (*1 and 2 Kings*, pp. 602-606), continues to argue against Mayes (*Deuteronomy*, p. 88) and others, by giving priority to the Chronicles narrative and correlating it with the decline of Assyrian power in the Levant.

3. Cf. Jones, *1 and 2 Kings*, p. 616; Spieckermann, *Assur*, p. 120; Mayes, *Deuteronomy*, p. 96.

4. Gray, *I and II Kings*, p. 715; Oestreicher, *Grundsetz*, p. 13.

tional history in the material,[1] continuing well into the exilic period. Spieckermann is closer to the mark, however, in his view that the basic narrative is essentially accurate and that it therefore has decidedly influenced later redactors.[2] I will treat vv. 4-20 as basically accurate information about Josiah's reforms.

What stands out about the cult practices purged by Josiah is that most of them are indigenous. They cannot be traced to Assyrian imposition. The clearest example of a long-standing Judean cult practice on the purge list comes in v. 7, with the destruction of the sacred prostitute quarters in the temple.[3] Known at least as early as Rehoboam (1 Kgs 14.24), cult prostitutes were a commonly accepted part of life in monarchical Judah (cf. Gen. 38.12-26).[4]

More controversial, but in the final analysis also indigenous, are the Asherah and Baal cults. Gressmann[5] argued that Baal, Asherah and the host of heaven are really Assyrian gods, a claim based on Ashurbanipal's statement that the Babylonians had to give offerings for Ashur, Ninlil and the gods of Assyria. Spieckermann[6] breathes new life into Gressmann's theory with his reinterpretation of Baals and Asherahs in Kings as Judean equivalents of the Akkadian pair *ilāni u ištarāti*, reflecting no longer, in the deuteronomic view, the Canaanite deities, but standing for all the religious impositions of the empire.[7] Spieckermann grants the Northwest Semitic origin of the biblical appellatives, but argues that their meanings were transformed as Israel and Judah came under the Assyrian domain. Indigenous names were used to describe imperial divinities. By the eighth and seventh centuries, the temple Asherah was none other than Ishtar of Assur, Ninevah and Arbela, the goddess of war who represented

---

1. Cf. Dietrich, *Prophetie*, p. 117; H. Hollenstein, 'Literarkritische Erwägungen zum Bericht über die Reformmassnahmen Josias 2 Kön. xxiii.4ff', *VT* 27 (1977), pp. 321-36. See also Würthwein, 'Die josianische Reform', pp. 412-23; Jones, *1 and 2 Kings*, pp. 616-17.

2. Spieckermann, *Assur*, pp. 158-59.

3. See my discussion of Asa's cult prostitute reform in Chapter 2.

4. Cf. B.A. Brooks, 'Fertility Cult Functionaries in the Old Testament', *JBL* 60 (1941), pp. 227-53.

5. Gressmann, 'Josia', pp. 313-35.

6. Spieckermann, *Assur*, pp. 200-25.

7. *Assur*, p. 212.

Assyrian power in Jerusalem.[1] She bore the name of her Northwest Semitic equivalent, but she was strategically placed to guard the interest of the eastern empire.

Gressmann's theory was made obsolete by new translations of Ugaritic texts which indisputably showed Baal, Asherah and even certain astral cults to be well established in the Levant, centuries before the establishment of Assyrian hegemony there.[2] Spieckermann's innovative reconstruction is more sophisticated and better able to absorb the Ugaritic material; however, the development he envisions depends at key points on the complex redactional structure he advocates for Kings. As I have said before, the redactional architecture Spieckermann builds is too top-heavy to be supported by the literature.

Asherah and Baal cults are indigenous, not Assyrian imports. Asherah is one of Judah's most ancient deities. Her frequent mention in connection with Yahweh's high places (1 Kgs 14.23; 2 Kgs 18.4; 23.13-14, 15; cf. Deut. 16.21) indicates that Asherah worship was considered a key component of the basic royal cult offered in all official cult centers. Baal is well attested at Ugarit and in Judah, at least from the time of Jehoshaphat's alliance with the Omride dynasty (cf. 2 Kgs 11.18). Furthermore, Spieckermann's identification of Baal with the Assyrian imperial god makes it hard to understand Jehu's fierce anti-Baal crusade (2 Kgs 9–10), in view of Jehu's submission to Assyria.[3] Baal and Asherah were common to the Northwest Semitic milieu long before the Assyrians came.

The deuteronomic purge of astral cults presents a trickier problem. McKay[4] is convincing that at least some of the purged astral cults, formerly thought to be Assyrian, instead had a West Semitic origin.[5] The uncertainty is introduced in v. 12, as follows: 'and the rooftop altars of the upper chamber of Ahaz which the kings of Judah

1.  *Assur,* p. 221.

2.  Cf. McKay, *Religion*, pp. 22-30; R. Patai, 'The Goddess Asherah', *JNES* 24 (1965), pp. 37-52; Montgomery and Gehman, *Books of Kings*, p. 529; *ANET*, p. 502.

3.  Gray, *I and II Kings*, p. 539; cf. M.C. Astour, '841 BC: The First Assyrian Invasion of Israel', *JAOS* 91 (1971), pp. 383-89.

4.  McKay, *Religion*, pp. 23-59.

5.  Cf. also Montgomery and Gehman, *Book of Kings*, p. 530; Cogan, *Imperialism*, p. 88; Jones, *1 and 2 Kings*, pp. 596, 617; *ANET*, p. 502.

made... the king [Josiah] tore down, crushed to pieces there and threw their dust in the Kidron wadi'. The Ugaritic Kirta myth gives a Northwest Semitic parallel for the rooftop altar.[1] The performance of rituals on rooftops is known elsewhere in the Bible as well (Jer. 19.13; Zeph. 1.5 for astral worship and Jer. 32.29 for sacrifices to Baal and other deities). Following the studies of McKay and Cogan, the tendency has been to dismiss any Eastern influence reflected in the rooftop altars.[2] The placement of the rooftop altars in a Northwest Semitic milieu, however, misses a more important question raised by the connection of these altars with the 'upper chamber of Ahaz'. The question is not whether rooftop alters were known in the Levant before the Assyrians came. It is why Ahaz should be so closely identified with this rooftop astral worship (cf. also 2 Kgs 20.11, 'the sundial of Ahaz'). Given the concern with astronomical phenomena in the late neo-Assyrian cult,[3] it should come as no surprise that Ahaz is thus connected with the Judean installation of cult objects and mechanisms for the worship and observation of astral bodies. It is no coincidence that Ahaz made Judah a vassal of Assyria and also came to be identified with at least some of the astral cult practices eventually purged by Josiah. The older consensus is correct that Ahaz brought some astral cult practices from Assyria.[4]

Other references to astral worship are equally compatible with either Assyrian or indigenous origins. As Montgomery and Gray have noted, the chariot associated with the sun in v. 11 may reflect the Assyrian sun-god title, *rākib narkābti*.[5] Parallels from pre-Assyrian Northwest Semitic culture are also known, however.[6] Verse 5's mention of incense burned 'to Baal, to the sun and the moon, the constel-

1. Krt 1, text 125 in C.H. Gordon, *Ugaritic Textbook* (Rome: Pontifical Biblical Institute Press, 1965), pp. 192-93. See Coogan's translation: M.D. Coogan, *Stories from Ancient Canaan* (Philadelphia: Westminster Press, 1978), pp. 58-74 ( 59, 62).
2. McKay, *Religion*, p. 10; Jones, *1 and 2 Kings*, pp. 588-89.
3. Spieckermann, *Assur*, p. 109.
4. Burney, *Notes*, p. 349; Montgomery and Gehman, *Book of Kings*, p. 508; cf. Gray, *I and II Kings*, p. 699; S. Iwry, 'The Qumran Isaiah and the End of the Dial of Ahaz', *BASOR* 147 (1957), pp. 27-33.
5. Montgomery and Gehman, *Book of Kings*, p. 533; Gray, *I and II Kings*, pp. 736-37.
6. McKay, *Religion*, p. 33; Jones, *1 and 2 Kings*, p. 623.

lations and all the host of heaven' likewise have Northwest Semitic parallels.[1] The word 'constellations' (*mazzālôt*), however, may reflect Assyrian astrological practice.[2]

The astral cults purged by Josiah could have origins in the native religion of Northwest Semitic culture or in the imperial religion of Assyria. The roots of Baal, sun and moon worship in pre-Assyrian Judean practice are clear. In the case of rooftop altars, Assyrian influence is likely. The following picture emerges. Astral worship was present in the pre-Assyrian Judean cult. When Ahaz brought Judah into the imperial orbit, he also introduced Assyrian astral cult practices, whether as an 'obligation' of Judah's vassalage or an 'imitation' of imperial culture. These astral cults fit easily into a syncretistic First Temple cult already accustomed to astral worship.

Josiah's reform most closely resembles Hezekiah's rebellion–reform in its abolishment of the high place shrines. The differences between the two reforms are striking, however.

As already noted in my discussion of Hezekiah's reform, Josiah took things much further than his grandfather did. Hezekiah shut down the high places. Josiah, on the other hand, 'tore down' the high places, 'defiled' them, 'burned human bones' on their altars, 'deposed' and even 'executed' their priests. The Deuteronomist does not give much detail about Hezekiah's high place reform, but neither does Kings give any indication that Hezekiah extended it beyond those sanctuaries which were part of the official first Temple system. By contrast, Josiah reportedly destroyed the official Judean sanctuaries and went on to attack the foreign embassies in the Jerusalem suburbs and the non-Judean temple at Bethel.

Josiah, like Hezekiah before him, abolished the high places, that is, the royal cult shrines in the countryside served by priests 'appointed' by the kings of Judah (v. 5; cf. vv. 8-9). The picture is confused about the fate of the priests who served there. According to v. 5, Josiah 'deposed' them (*hišbît*). Verses 8-9 imply, however, that Josiah called all the high place priests in to Jerusalem, presumably to serve at

---

1. McKay, *Religion*, pp. 37-39, 103; Montgomery and Gehman, *Book of Kings*, p. 530; Jones, *1 and 2 Kings*, p. 618.

2. Gray, *I and II Kings*, p. 733; but note McKay, *Religion*, pp. 38-39. Jones's suggestion (*ibid.*) has merit, in that the Hebrew word means 'planets', 'which were worshipped throughout the Near East'.

the central shrine, in accordance with the terms of Deut. 18.6-7.[1] Different terminology is used in v. 5 from that found in vv. 8-9. Verse 5 priests are 'prostrating priests' ($k^e m \bar{a} r \hat{i} m$) and 'incense burners' ($m^e qa \d{t} \d{t}^e r \hat{i} m$) while the clergy in vv. 8-9 are called by the more typical term, 'priests' ($k \bar{o} h^a n \hat{i} m$). The term 'prostrating priests' appears elsewhere in the Bible only in Zeph. 1.4 and Hos. 10.5, with clearly derogatory connotations.[2] In the Josiah narrative, it is in parallelism with 'incense burners', and the awkward gloss in the middle of the verse describes the 'prostrating priest' as one who burns incense. The 'priests' of vv. 8-9 also 'burned incense'. There is no reason to suppose that v. 5 and vv. 8-9 have different kinds of priest in mind. The prostrating priests are deposed. The high place priests of vv. 8-9 do not go up to serve at the central sanctuary. The net result is the same. Whether Josiah 'deposed' them or whether they refused to serve in the central sanctuary, these high place priests were out of a job.

With v. 9, Josiah's high place reform reached the outer boundaries of Hezekiah's earlier centralization program. In v. 13, Josiah turned on the foreign embassies, the 'high places' just east of Jerusalem along the south side of the Mount of Olives.[3] These cult places had sealed the marriage alliances of Judean kings from Solomon onwards (cf. 1 Kgs 11.5-7) and served to symbolize the ongoing international relationship.[4] The continued existence of these particular foreign 'high places' shows that Hezekiah's centralization reform did not include an attack on embassy row. When Josiah attacked these Mount of Olives 'high places', he was not centralizing the cult. He was breaking off foreign relations. Josiah may well have defiled these embassy–sanctuaries, as v. 14 suggests. The verse's statement that he 'smashed the pillars and cut down the Asherahs', however, is best explained as a literary reflex

---

1. Note, however, A. Cody's translation of v. 9, as follows: 'the priests of the high places could not go up, but ate bread. . .' (*A History of the Old Testament Priesthood* [Rome: Pontifical Biblical Institute, 1969], p. 135).

2. Cf. Albright, *From the Stone Age to Christianity* (Baltimore: Johns Hopkins University Press, 2nd edn, 1948), p. 234; Spieckermann, *Assur*, pp. 84-86 n. 111.

3. The Hebrew, 'mount of corruption', *har hammašḥît*, should be emended to *har hammišḥâh*. Cf. Gray, *I and II Kings*, pp. 737-38; Jones, *1 and 2 Kings*, p. 624; see differently, McKay, *Religion*, p. 41.

4. See my discussion of Jehoiada's 'anti-Baal' measures during the coup he orchestrated against Athaliah.

prompted by the Deuteronomist's description of these sites as 'high places'. Verse 13 is much more closely tied to Josiah's purge of 'foreign' cults than to his abolition of Judean high places. Whether in its own cult or in its international relations, Josiah's Judah was fiercely nationalistic and single-mindedly committed to its national God Yahweh.

As I said above, Josiah's designs on the North have been the subject of debate in recent years. The royal stamps and other material data show some expansion of Josiah's dominion,[1] but any systematic and large-scale control over the Northern province cannot be supported by archaeology.[2] Josiah's extension of deuteronomic reform to Bethel shows he might have had a reunited kingdom in mind. The unexpected execution of Northern high place priests (v. 20), if based in history,[3] gives credence to the view that he was attempting to reunite the kingdom. By executing the old regime's cult officials, Josiah eliminated a source of potential resistance to the new government.[4] Whatever his intent, however, Josiah was unable to exercise substantial control over the North. After the desecration at Bethel, Kings says, he returned to Jerusalem (v. 20).

Josiah's reformation built on Hezekiah's earlier reform but was not limited by it. Josiah purged indigenous cults and Assyrian cults. He even launched an attack on the foreign embassies near Jerusalem. Josiah's reform was the heart of a nationalistic cultural revolution which gained momentum after Assyrian rule ended in the West. Judah's new-found freedom called for a new direction. Royal policy had brought Judah to the breaking point under the strain of imperial obligations. Deuteronomic theology had grown in those conditions as a protest against the imperial status quo, in all its dimensions. Josiah, ruling a state free from imperial constraints for the first time in a century, found in deuteronomic theology a national identity fitting Judah's newly independent status. Appropriately, Josiah reportedly ended his reform with a national celebration of passover, the festival celebration of Israel's deliverance from foreign slavery.

---

1.   Stern, 'Survey', pp. 27, 32.

2.   Lance, 'Royal Stamps', p. 332; contra Tushingham, 'Seal'.

3.   Jones (*1 and 2 Kings*, p. 625) calls it 'an exaggeration written under the direct influence of 1 Kgs 13.2'.

4.   See my discussion of the murder of Mattan during Jehoiada's coup.

One further point must be made. Though deuteronomic theology and Josianic reform charted a new direction for Judah, it was not a creation out of whole-cloth. Communities do not simply 'invent' symbol systems. They receive them and transform them based on their concrete experience. Deuteronomic theology reached deep into Judah's past, bringing forward traditions which pre-dated the monarchy itself. But they were ancient traditions reinterpreted by the historical experience of foreign domination.

Josiah's deuteronomic reformation was part of a comprehensive view of the world deeply rooted in the ancient traditions of Judah, tempered by the historical experience of foreign domination, and reflecting the changed reality of national independence. Hezekiah's limited cult reform had been part of a strategy of rebellion. Deuteronomic reform built on that, but took it much further. Deuteronomists, including their monarchical patron Josiah, sought not so much to reform the cult as to transform the culture.

CONCLUSION

From start to finish, the official religion of Judah legitimated royal political claims and expressed royal interests. Cult reforms—in Judah, always led by kings—also were intended to serve the social-political interests of the monarchy. This is true even of Josiah's radically unorthodox and anti-imperialistic deuteronomic reform. The reform texts reflect a process seen throughout the biblical and archaeological records: the Davidic monarchy came to dominate the social and cultural life of Judah.

The monarchy's commanding social role was expressed economically in its right to tax and to draft able-bodied subjects for state projects and military service. These royal policies put many Israelites in a vice-like grip of economic hardship. In the best of times, farmers found it difficult to grow enough to feed their own families. Under the monarchy, they had the additional burden of producing surplus for state taxes, with a work-force depleted by statutory labor and the military draft.

These requirements transformed production. The diversified subsistence agriculture, which had been the norm in tribal Israel, shifted toward more specialized surplus agriculture. Environmental and technological constraints, however, made such specialization highly risky. Crop failure was always a disaster, but a diversified farming strategy provided a buffer against natural catastrophe. That buffer eroded, as farmers in the monarchical era turned increasingly to crop specialization for surplus production.

An ever more developed lending system, which included the option of land collateral and debt slavery, kept some land-holding farmers afloat under these difficult conditions. But borrowing only delayed the inevitable for many. High interest rates and the precarious nature of cash cropping led many to default, sacrificing collateral to creditors. The lending system became the chief mechanism by which land was alienated from small farmers and accumulated by the wealthy.

Biblical reform texts about Judah before the era of Assyrian imperialism show an increasingly centralized and powerful royal system. Taxation, statutory labor and an evolving national judiciary indicate that the monarchy exerted ever greater control over Judean society. The biblical texts even offer some indication that Judean kings may have conducted rather large-scale economic planning.

In the monarchical period, the rich got richer, the poor got poorer and the state became more more powerful.

Culturally, the monarchy legitimated its social dominance through an official cult which presented the king as the divinely chosen earthly representative of Yahweh, the national God of Israel. Yahweh's 'son', the Davidic king, exercised all the rights and responsibilities of an heir. As high God of Judah, Yahweh was true owner of the land and sovereign of the people. As vicar of Yahweh on earth, the king collected and invested the sacred rent and told Yahweh's people what to do.

Royal cult reforms in the period before the advent of Assyrian imperialism in Judah underscore the ideological function of First Temple Yahwism. Cult and court were inexorably bound. The king built sanctuaries, instituted and spent cultic taxes, used the temple treasuries as political events dictated, appointed and deposed priests, erected and demolished cult objects and defined priestly roles. The king was the single most important figure in the cultic life of the nation.

Reforms throughout the period of the monarchy reflect the syncretistic character of the First Temple cult. Yahweh indisputably headed the national pantheon, but other gods sat in Judah's heavenly court. Indigenous Judean gods, such as Asherah and Baal, had rituals performed for them as part of the royal cult. And, in accordance with the terms of international alliance, non-Judean gods were worshiped in the capital city's 'embassy row', along the Mount of Olives, opposite Jerusalem.

Ahaz's desperate submission to the Assyrian emperor Tiglath-pileser III had long-lasting social and cultural repercussions for Judah. The terms of Assyrian vassalage brought economic hardship for Judah's laboring majority. Unbalanced trading relationships with the Assyrian heartland hastened the centralization of production and unequal distribution of wealth, processes already well under way in monarchical Judah. Paying imperial taxes, providing troop and statu-

tory labor quotas for the empire and quartering the imperial army on
the march greatly exacerbated the already oppressive requirements of
supporting a domestic monarchy. Social conditions for the Judean
majority deteriorated further under the terms of Assyrian
imperialism.

Less clear than the economic impact are the religious implications
of Judah's vassalage. The biblical texts indicate that Ahaz changed the
First Temple cult 'on account of the king of Assyria'. But apart from
a dispassionate report about a new altar, the texts exhibit an astonishing lack of detail about what Ahaz's reforms were. It is very likely
that, in addition to Ahaz's unspecified cult innovations, imperial
beliefs and practices entered the Judean cult over time through the
process of acculturation.

Whether these Assyrian elements entered the official cult of Judah
by imposition or by imitation is not so important, however. In lopsided social-political relationships, such as that of imperial lord and
compliant vassal, the line between force and persuasion is very thin.
In such circumstances, 'imitation' is often difficult to distinguish from
'imposition'. What can be said with certainty in the case of Assyrian
imperialism, however, is that subject nations typically incorporated
into their own cults some of the religious rituals and symbols of the
imperial state. Judah was no exception.

The first major Judean challenge to Assyrian imperialism came in
Hezekiah's disastrous rebellion of 705–701. The extraordinary
circumstances of the rebellion led Hezekiah to take the radical, but
probably temporary, measure of closing down the sanctuaries of the
royal cult, everywhere but Jerusalem. This action consolidated royal
power and denied the approaching Assyrian army tax produce stored
at the religious sanctuaries. By removing Yahweh's cult objects from
the outlying areas, centralization also thwarted one of Assyria's
favorite battle ploys, capturing the enemy's cult objects to enlist the
support of native deities in the empire's conquest march.

Obviously, closing the high place sanctuaries carried risks. Since the
religiously legitimated state tax was collected, at least initially, at the
local high place, Hezekiah's cult centralization program, however
temporary, would have cut off state revenues. Deuteronomy's peculiar
tithe legislation, requiring the tither to consume the tax in Jerusalem,
may contain the plan of survival during the period of cult centralization. Deuteronomy's tithe law would stimulate the economy of

Jerusalem, chiefly inhabited by royal priests and other bureaucrats, while providing for the ongoing support of royal dependents outside Jerusalem, who were brought along for the capital city tithe feasts.

Once the rebellion was crushed, the strategic logic of shutting down the high places evaporated. It is most likely that Hezekiah reopened those high places which had not been destroyed by the Assyrian army en route to Jerusalem.

Hezekiah's son Manasseh apparently continued his repentant father's cultic policy and political course. By all Assyrian reports, Manasseh maintained a positive relationship with the empire. Relative prosperity, political stability and expanded borders were dividends of Manasseh's compliance. The Deuteronomist's report that Manasseh 'rebuilt the high places which his father Hezekiah had demolished' (2 Kgs 21.3) is plausible, or at least partly so. Manasseh, ruling a more stable and prosperous post-war Judah, would have been better able than Hezekiah to rebuild the country, including the royal cult centers. It is unlikely, however, that Hezekiah is the one who had demolished the high places Manasseh rebuilt. Hezekiah shut them down for a while, but the Assyrians destroyed many of them in their march across Judah in 701.

Heavily stylized, theologically loaded biblical portrayals of Manasseh make it impossible to judge what innovations, if any at all, were introduced to the First Temple cult during his reign. The cult crimes listed are nothing new. They had long been part of royal religion. What is striking about the Manasseh portrayal in Kings, however, is the strong conviction that the syncretistic 'orthodoxy' of the First Temple had led the nation to the brink of disaster. A radical, sudden about-face was Judah's only hope. Josiah's deuteronomic reform, the deuteronomistic text assures the reader, provided just the turn-around Judah needed.

Josiah's reform, as recorded in Kings, bears only faint resemblance to the reform of his rebel ancestor Hezekiah. Both kings reportedly shut down the high places, but Josiah took things much further. He 'tore down' the high places, 'defiled' them and 'burned human bones' on the altars. He removed and even executed their priests. Josiah extended the abolishment of royal high place sanctuaries to include an attack on the foreign embassies in the Jerusalem suburbs and the non-Judean temple at Bethel. In a further departure from Hezekiah's limited cult measures, Josiah purged non-Yahwistic ritual practices which had long been part of the orthodox royal cult. The full-grown deuteronomism finally embraced by Josiah stands in continuity with Hezekiah's embryonic 'proto-deuteronomic' cult measures, but the two reforms are very different. Judah's role in the geopolitics of the seventh century explains the important similarities and vast differences between the reforms of Hezekiah and Josiah.

Though Assyria had declined as a power in Judah a couple of decades before Josiah's reform, Assyrian imperialism provides the context for the development of deuteronomism in Judah. In the account of Ahaz's submission to Assyria, the Deuteronomist acknowledges imperial influence on the First Temple cult, but fails to outline which 'abominable' practices are Assyrian and which are indigenous to Judah. The text's failure to delineate, however, does not undermine its important assertion that imperial religion did influence the Judean cult. The deuteronomic campaign to purge the First Temple cult of non-Yahwistic practices was also a campaign to purge Assyrian cultic elements, whatever they were. In the context of Judah's vassalage to Assyria, the cry for sole allegiance to Yahweh had an unmistakably anti-imperialist ring.

Josiah's deuteronomic reform contains an ironic tension, however. Pre-exilic deuteronomic literature is strongly pro-Davidic. It adopts an election theology which legitimated the political claims of the Davidic house and expressed the interests of royal functionaries from prince to lowliest high place priest. At the same time, it condemns the vast majority of orthodox royal cult practices and advocates the abolition of royal sanctuaries throughout the country. Royal cultic orthodoxy and ecclesial structure are compared with the 'abominable practices' of the pre-Israelite Canaanites. The implied threat is clear: the Davidic monarchy will suffer the fate of the obliterated Canaanites unless it abandons centuries of official faith and practice.

Under normal circumstances, such an assault on the royal cult would be treasonous. Ordinarily, shutting down the royal high places, the initial collection point for the tax, would have hurt the rulers and helped the ruled. Assyrian imperialism, however, left Judah in extraordinary circumstances. Imperial obligations drained Judah, even the wealthy. Under Assyrian imperialism, the same cultic-political institutions which formerly had secured the Davidic monarchy's power now served Assyria's domination of Judah, a reality reflected in Hezekiah's high place measure.

Hezekiah's failed rebellion and temporary decommissioning of the outlying high places planted the seeds of deuteronomic reform. In the years between Hezekiah's surrender and the collapse of Assyrian power in the West, Hezekiah's rebellion continued to inspire some within the national leadership of Judah. As symbols of Judean nationalism, his limited and, in the case of the high places, temporary cult measures moved to the center of an emerging system of thought, intensely nationalistic in character.

As this sytem gestated during the long period of imperial accomodation under a defeated Hezekiah and compliant Manasseh, the primary significance of Hezekiah's cult measures changed. The practical utility of closing high places during a national emergency was forgotten, as high place abolition increasingly took on a life of its own. In the memory of anti-Assyrian leaders in Jerusalem, cult centralization had stood at the heart of the defiant Hezekiah's religious 'reform'. Now cult centralization became a magnet for reform traditions reflecting varied class and social interests, from Judah and the old Northern kingdom. The common thread now tying all these traditions together was the rejection of foreign cultural influence. The key political aim of the movement eventually was summarized in the fiercely nationalistic call to serve Yahweh alone.

In the emergence of deuteronomic theology, the deuteronomists were both passive and active agents. Without conscious guidance, the inconsistent goals of supporting the Davidic monarchy and attacking the royal cult became more compatible. In a sense, deuteronomism's curious pro- and anti-monarchical mixture just happened, as external political conditions altered the internal dynamics of social thought and action. Yet deuteronomic theology required careful, thoughtful crafting to assure both its effectiveness and its manageability. What the conditions of Assyrian domination made possible, the deuteronomists made real.

Deuteronomism works because the deuteronomists gave a nationalist, monarchist twist to the attack on the royal cult. Some of the reform measures now included in the deuteronomic reform very likely originated in anti-monarchical circles. The deuteronomists successfully coopted these anti-monarchical measures and made them anti-Assyrian. Opposing 'foreign' elements in the royal cults was transformed by the deuteronomists into a patriotic oath of allegiance to the Davidic monarchy. To oppose 'Canaanite' influences in the cult was to oppose Assyrian influence on the nation and, thus, to support a strong and independent Davidic king.

Though deuteronomic theology has an anti-imperialist concern, Josiah's reform should not be considered an act of political rebellion. Efforts to portray it as such are not borne out by the historical record of the empire's disintegration. Assyria's political control of Judah had ended by the time of Josiah.

Josiah's deuteronomic reform was not an act of political rebellion, as his grandfather Hezekiah's cult reform had been. Rather it was the core of a post-imperial cultural revolution by which the monarch sought to create a nationalist consciousness fitting Judah's newly independent status. Political independence from Assyria already had occurred via the demise of imperial power in the West. Josiah's reform sought cultural independence as well. Josiah adopted and extended key measures taken by Hezekiah. Only now, cult reform was intended to break the cultural, rather than the political, hegemony of the empire. Josiah built upon the failed reform of his heroic rebel ancestor to create a new nationalist consciousness among Judeans briefly free of imperial domination.

Pre-exilic deuteronomism emerged as a reaction against the conditions of Assyrian imperialism in Judah. These conditions had economic, political, social, religious and other cultural dimensions, addressed by the deuteronomists in theological terms. Many of the elements preserved in deuteronomic theology pre-date the Assyrian period and some no doubt pre-date the monarchy. They are drawn from the traditions of North and South. They represent the concerns of anti-monarchists and pro-monarchists, prophets, priests and common people. With one or two important exceptions, the key ideas of deuteronomic theology were nothing new. The distinctiveness of deuteronomism lay rather in its fresh ordering of old traditions. That ordering reflects an overarching concern about the ill effects of imperial subjugation and the new possibilities of Yahweh-centered freedom.

# BIBLIOGRAPHY

Ackroyd, P.R., *The Age of the Chronicler* (Auckland: Colloquium, 1970).

—*I and II Chronicles, Ezra and Nehemiah* (London: SCM Press, 1973).

Adams, R. McC., 'Common Concerns but Different Standpoints: A Commentary', in *Power and Propaganda: A Symposium on Ancient Empires* (ed. M.T. Larsen; Mesopotamia, 7; Copenhagen: Akademisk, 1979), pp. 393-404.

Aharoni, Y., 'The Excavations at Arad and the Centralization of the Cult', in *Reflections on the Bible: Selected Studies of the Biblical Circle in Memory of Yishai Ron* (ed. M. Hevav; Tel Aviv: Am Oved, 1974), pp. 13-31 [Hebrew].

—*Arad Inscriptions, Judean Desert Studies* (Jerusalem, Israel Exploration Society, 1981).

Ahlström, G.W., *Aspects of Syncretism in Israelite Religion* (Lund: Gleerup, 1963).

—*Royal Administration and National Religion in Ancient Palestine* (SHANE, 1; Leiden: Brill, 1982).

Albright, W.F., *From the Stone Age to Christianity* (Baltimore: Johns Hopkins University Press, 2nd edn, 1948).

—*Archaeology and the Religion of Israel* (Baltimore: Johns Hopkins University Press, 3rd edn, 1953).

—*The Biblical Period from Abraham to Ezra* (New York: Harper & Row, 3rd edn, 1963).

—'Further Light on Synchronisms between Egypt and Asia in the Period 935–685 B.C.', *BASOR* 141 (1956), pp. 23-27.

—'The Administrative Divisions of Israel and Judah', *JPOS* 5 (1927), pp. 17-54.

—'The Date of Sennacherib's Second Campaign against Hezekiah', *BASOR* 130 (1953), pp. 8-9.

—'The Judicial Reform of Jehoshaphat', in *Alexander Marx Jubilee Volume* (New York: Jewish Publication Society, 1950), pp. 61-82.

Alt, A., 'Der Anteil der Königtum an der sozialen Entwicklung in den Reichen Israel und Juda', in *Kleine Schriften zur Geschichte des Volkes Israel* (=*KS* [ed. M. Noth; Munich: Beck, 1953]), III, pp. 348-72.

—'Die Heimat des Deuteronomium', *KS*, I, pp. 252-62.

Anderson, G.W., *A Critical Introduction to the Old Testament* (London: Duckworth, 1959).

Astour, M.C., '841 B.C.: The First Assyrian Invasion of Israel', *JAOS* 91 (1971), pp. 383-89.

Baltzer, K., *The Covenant Formulary in Old Testament, Jewish, and Early Christian Writings* (Philadelphia: Fortress Press, 1971).

Baly, D., *Geographical Companion to the Bible* (London: Lutterworth, 1963).

Barlett, P., 'Adaptive Strategies in Peasant Agricultural Production', *Annual Review of Anthropology* 9 (1980), pp. 553-61.

Barnett, R., 'The Siege of Lachish', *IEJ* 8 (1958), pp. 161-64.

Bartlett, J.R., 'An Adversary against Solomon , Hadad the Edomite', *ZAW* 88 (1976), pp. 205-26.

—'The Moabites and the Edomites', in *Peoples of Old Testament Times* (ed. D.J. Wiseman; Oxford: Clarendon Press, 1973), pp. 229-58.

Ben-Barak, Z., 'Meribaal and the System of Land Grants in Ancient Israel', *Bib* 62 (1981), pp. 73-91.

Bentzen, A., *Die josianische Reform und ihre Voraussetzungen* (Copenhagen: Gad, 1926).

—*Introduction to the Old Testament* (Copenhagen: Gad, 1948).

Benzinger, I., *Die Bücher der Könige* (KHAT; Freiburg: Mohr, 1899).

Biram, A., *'Mas obed'*, *Tarbiz* 23 (1952) pp. 137-42 [Hebrew].

Bohlen, R., *Der Fall Nabot, Form, Hintergrund und Werdegang einer alttestamentlichen Erzählung (1 Kön 21)* (Trier: Paulinus, 1978).

Borowski, O., *Agriculture in Iron Age Israel* (Winona Lake, IN: Eisenbrauns, 1987).

Braun, R., 'A Reconsideration of the Chronicler's Attitude Toward the North', *JBL* 96 (1977), pp. 59-62.

—'Chronicles, Ezra, and Nehemiah: Theology and Literary History', *VTS* 30 (1979), pp. 52-64.

Bright, J., *A History of Israel* (Philadelphia: Westminster Press, 3rd edn, 1981).

Brooks, B.A., 'Fertility Cult Functionaries in the Old Testament', *JBL* 60 (1941), pp. 227-53.

Broshi, M., 'The Expansion of Jerusalem in the Reigns of Hezekiah and Manasseh', *IEJ* 24 (1974), pp. 21-26.

Buccellati, G., *Cities and Nations of Ancient Syria: An Essay on Political Institutions with Special Reference to Israelite Kingdoms* (Studi Semitici, 26; Rome: University of Rome, 1967).

Burney, C.F., *Notes on the Hebrew Text of the Books of Kings* (Oxford: Clarendon Press, 1903).

Burrows, M., 'Ancient Israel', in *The Idea of History in the Ancient Near East* (ed. R. Dentan; New Haven, CT: Yale University Press, 1955).

Carlson, R.A., *David the Chosen King. A Traditio-Historical Approach to the Second Book of Samuel* (Uppsala: Almqvist and Wiksell, 1964).

Chaney, M.L., 'Latifundialization and Prophetic Diction in Eighth Century Israel and Judah', Paper to the Sociology of the Monarchy Seminar, AAR/SBL Annual Meeting, 1985 (=*Semeia* 37 [1986], pp. 53-76).

—'Systemic Study of the Sociology of the Israelite Monarchy', *Semeia* 37 (1986), pp. 53-76.

Childs, B.S., *Isaiah and the Assyrian Crisis* (Studies in Biblical Theology, 2.3; London: SCM Press, 1967).

Claburn, W.E., 'The Fiscal Basis of Josiah's Reforms', *JBL* 92 (1973), pp. 11-22.

Clements, R.E., 'The Deuteronomistic Interpretation of the Founding of the Monarchy in I Sam. 8', *VT* 24 (1974), pp. 398-410.

—*God and Temple* (Philadelphia: Fortress Press, 1965).

—*Isaiah and the Deliverance of Jerusalem* (JSOTSup, 13; Sheffield: JSOT Press, 1980).

Cody, A., *A History of the Old Testament Priesthood* (Rome: Pontifical Biblical Institute, 1969).

Cogan, M., *Imperialism and Religion: Assyria, Judah, and Israel in the Eighth and Seventh Centuries B.C.E.* (SBLMS, 19; Missoula, MT: Scholars Press, 1974).

Coogan, M.D., *Stories from Ancient Canaan* (Philadelphia: Westminster Press, 1978).

Cross, F.M., 'A Reconstruction of the Judean Restoration', *JBL* 94 (1975), pp. 4-18.

—*Canaanite Myth and Hebrew Epic* (Cambridge, MA: Harvard University Press, 1983).

Cross, F.M. and D.N. Freedman, 'Josiah's Revolt Against Assyria', *JNES* 12 (1953), pp. 56-58.

Crüsemann, F., *Die Widerstand gegen das Königtum. Die antiköniglichen Texte des Alten Testaments und der Kampf um den frühen israelitischen Staat* (WMANT, 49; Neukirchen–Vluyn: Neukirchener Verlag, 1978).

—'State Tax and Temple Tithe in Israel's Monarchical Period', Paper to the Sociology of the Monarchy Seminar, AAR/SBL Annual Meeting, 1985. Published as 'Der zehnte in der israelitischen Königszeit', in *Wort und Dienst 1985* (ed. H.P. Stähli; Beilefeld: Kirchliche Hochschule Bethel, 1985), pp. 21-47.

Curtis, E.L., and A.A. Madsen, *A Critical and Exegetical Commentary on the Books of Chronicles* (ICC; New York: Scribner's, 1910).

Davies, E.W., *Prophecy and Ethics: Isaiah and the Ethical Traditions of Israel* (JSOTSup, 16; Sheffield: JSOT Press, 1981).

Dearman, J.A., 'Prophecy, Property and Politics', *SBLSP* 23 (1984), pp. 385-97.

Diakonoff, I.M., 'Main Features of the Economy in the Monarchies of Ancient Western Asia', in *Proceedings of the Third International Conference of Economic History, Munich, 1965* (Congres et Colloques, 10.3; Paris, 1969), pp. 28-29.

Dietrich, W., 'Josia und das Gesetzbuch (2 Reg. xxii)', *VT* 27 (1977), pp. 13-35.

—*Prophetie und Geschichte. Eine redaktionsgeschichtliche Untersuchung zum deuteronomistischen Geschichtswerk* (FRLANT, 108; Göttingen: Vandenhoeck & Ruprecht, 1972).

Donner, H., 'Art und Herkunft des Amtes der Königinmutter im Alten Testament', in *Festschrift J. Friedrich* (ed. R. von Kienle; Heidelberg: Winter, 1959), pp. 105-45.

—*Israel unter den Völkern* (VTS, 11; Leiden: Brill, 1964).

—'The Separate States of Israel and Judah', in *Israelite and Judaean History* (ed. J.H. Hayes and J.M. Miller; OTL; Philadelphia: Westminster Press, 1977), pp. 381-434.

Edelstein, G., and Y. Gat, 'Terraces around Jerusalem', *Israel—Land and Nature* 6 (1980), p. 73.

Edelstein, G., and S. Gibson, 'Ancient Jerusalem's Rural Food Basket', *BAR* 8 (1982), pp. 46-54.

Edelstein, G., and M. Kislev, 'Mevasseret Yerushalayim: the Ancient Settlement and its Agricultural Terraces', *BA* 44 (1981), pp. 53-56.

Ehrlich, E.E., 'Der Aufenthalt des Königs Manasse in Babylon', *TZ* 21 (1965), pp. 281-86.

Eissfeldt, O., *Erstlinge und Zehnten im Alten Testament. Ein Beitrag zur Geschichte des israelitisch-judischen Kultus* (BWAT, 22; Leipzig: Hinrichs, 1917).

—*The Old Testament: An Introduction* (New York: Harper & Row, 1965).

Elat, M., *Economic Relations in the Lands of the Bible c. 1000–539 B.C.* (Jerusalem: Mosad Bialik, 1977) [Hebrew].

—'Trade and Commerce', in *The World History of the Jewish People* (ed. A. Malamat; Jerusalem: Massada, 1979).

Fohrer, G., *Introduction to the Old Testament* (Nashville: Abingdon Press, 1970).

Frankena, R., 'The Vassal-treaties of Esarhaddon and the Dating of Deuteronomy', *OTS* 14 (1965), pp. 122-54.

Freedman, D.N., 'The Chronicler's Purpose', *CBQ* 22 (1961), pp. 436-42.

Frick, F., *The Formation of the State in Ancient Israel* (Social World of Biblical Antiquity Series, 4; Sheffield: Almond Press, 1985).

Friedman, R.E., 'From Egypt to Egypt; Dtr1 and Dtr2', in *Traditions in Transformation: Turning Points in Biblical Faith* (ed. B. Halpern and J.D. Levenson; Winona Lake, IN: Eisenbrauns, 1981), pp. 167-92.

Galling, K., *Der Altar in den Kulturen des alten Orients. Eine archäologische Studie* (Berlin: Curtius, 1925).

Gerbrandt, G.E., *Kingship According to the Deuteronomistic Historian* (SBLDS, 87; Atlanta: Scholars Press, 1986).

Geus, C.H.J. de, 'The Importance of Archaeological Research into the Palestinian Agricultural Terraces, with an Excursis on the Hebrew Word *gbi*', *PEQ* 107 (1975), pp. 65-74.

Gordon, C.H., *Ugaritic Textbook* (Rome: Pontifical Biblical Institute, 1965).

Gottwald, N.K., 'Contemporary Studies of Social Class and Social Stratification and a Hypothesis about Social Class in Monarchic Israel', Paper to the Sociology of the Monarchy Seminar, AAR/SBL Annual Meeting, 1985.

—'Israel, Social and Economic Development of', *IDBSup*, pp. 465-68.

—*Tribes of Yahweh* (New York: Orbis, 1979).

Gray, J., *I and II Kings* (OTL; Philadelphia: Westminster Press, 3rd edn, 1977).

Gressmann, H., *Die alteste Geschichtsschreibung und Prophetie Israels* (Göttingen: Vandenhoeck & Ruprecht, 1921).

—*Die Anfange Israels* (SAT 2.1; Göttingen: Vandenhoeck & Ruprecht, 1922).

—'Josia und das Deuteronomium', *ZAW* 42 (1924), pp. 313-27.

Gunneweg, A.H.J., *Geschichte Israels bis Bar Kochba* (Stuttgart: Kohlhammer, 1972).

Halpern, B., 'The Centralization Formula in Deuteronomy', *VT* 31 (1981), pp. 20-38.

—*The Constitution of the Monarchy in Israel* (HSM; Cambridge, MA: Harvard University Press, 1981).

Hanson, P., 'The Song of Heshbon and David's Nir', *HTR* 61 (1968), pp. 297-320.

Haran, M., 'Explaining the Identical Lines at the End of Chronicles and the Beginning of Ezra', *Bible Review* 2 (1986), pp. 18-20.

—'Temples and Cultic Open Areas as Reflected in the Bible', in *Temples and High Places in Biblical Times* (ed. A. Biram; Jerusalem: HUC–Jewish Institute of Religion, 1981), pp. 31-37.

—*Temples and Temple-Service in Ancient Israel. An Inquiry into the Character of Cult Phenomena and the Historical Setting of the Priestly School* (Oxford: Clarendon Press, 1978).

Herrmann, S., *A History of Israel in Old Testament Times* (Philadelphia: Fortress Press, 1973).

—'Operationen Pharo Schoschenks I im östlichen Ephraim', *ZDPV* 80 (1964), pp. 55-79.

Hoffmann, H.D., *Reform und Reformen. Untersuchungen zu einem Grundthema der deuteronomistischen Geschichtsschreibung* (ATANT, 66; Zürich: Theologischer Verlag, 1980).

Holladay, J.S., 'Religion in Israel and Judah Under the Monarchy: An Explicitly Archaeological Approach', in *Ancient Israelite Religion: Essays in Honor of Frank Moore Cross* (ed. P.D. Miller, P.D. Hanson, S.D. McBride; Philadelphia: Fortress Press, 1987), pp. 249-99.

Hollenstein, H., 'Literarkritische Erwägungen zum Bericht uber die Reformmassnahmen Josias 2 Kön. xxiii.4ff', *VT* 27 (1977), pp. 321-36.

Hölscher, G., 'Komposition und Ursprung des Deuteronomiums', *ZAW* 40 (1923), pp. 161-255.

Hopkins, D.C., 'The Dynamics of Agriculture in Monarchical Israel', *SBLSP* 22 (1983), pp. 177-202.

—*The Highlands of Canaan: Agricultural Life in the Early Iron Age* (Social World of Biblical Antiquity Series, 3; Sheffield: Almond Press, 1985).

Ikeda, Y., 'Solomon's Trade in Horses and Chariots', in *Studies in the Period of David and Solomon and other Essays* (ed. T. Ishida; Winona Lake, IN: Eisenbrauns, 1982), pp. 215-38.

Ishida, T., *The Royal Dynasties in Israel: A Study of the Formation and Development of Royal Dynastic Ideology* (BZAW, 142; Berlin: de Gruyter, 1977).

Iwry, S., 'The Qumran Isaiah and the End of the Dial of Ahaz', *BASOR* 147 (1957), pp. 27-33.

Jacobson, V.A., 'The Social Structure of the Neo-Assyrian Empire', in *Ancient Mesopotamia: Socio-Economic History* (ed. I.M. Diankonoff; Moscow: Nauka, 1969), pp. 277-95.

Jagersma, H., 'The Tithes in the Old Testament', in *Remembering All the Way... A Collection of Old Testament Studies Published on the Occasion of the Fortieth Anniversary of the Oudtestamentisch Werkgezelschap in Nederland* (OTS, 21; Leiden: Brill, 1981), pp. 116-28.

Jankowska, W.B., 'Some Problems of the Economy of the Assyrian Empire', in *Power and Propaganda: A Symposium on Ancient Empires* (ed. M.T. Larsen; Mesopotamia, 7; Copenhagen: Akademisk, 1979), pp. 193-221.

Japhet, S., 'The Ideology of the Book of Chronicles and its Place in Biblical Thought' (PhD Disseration, Hebrew University; Jerusalem, 1983) [Hebrew].

—'The Supposed Common Authorship of Chronicles and Ezra–Nehemiah Investigated Anew', *VT* 18 (1968), pp. 330-71.

Jenkins, A., 'Hezekiah's Fourteenth Year. A New Interpretation of 2 Kgs xviii 13–xix 37', *VT* 26 (1976), pp. 284-98.

Jepsen, A., *Die Quellen des Königsbuches* (Halle: Niemeyer, 2nd edn, 1956).

—'Die Reform des Josia', in *Festschrift Friedrich Baumgartel* (ed. J. Herrmann; Erlangen: Universitätsbibliothek Erlangen, 1959), pp. 97-108.

Johnson, A.R., *Sacral Kingship in Ancient Israel* (Cardiff: University of Wales Press, 1955).

Jones, G.H., *1 and 2 Kings* (NCB; Grand Rapids, MI: Eerdmans, 1984).

Junge, E., *Der Wiederaufbau des Heerwesens des Reiches Juda unter Josia* (Stuttgart: Kohlhammer, 1937).

Kaiser, O., *Das Buch des Propheten Jesaja. Kapitel 1–12.* (ATD, 17; Göttingen: Vandenhoeck & Ruprecht, 1981).

Kaufmann, Y., *Toledot Ha'emuna Hayyisra'elit* (Tel-Aviv: Dvir, 1960).

Kitchen, K.A., 'Egypt, the Levant, and Assyria in 701 B.C.', in *Fontes atque Pontes, Eine Festgabe für Hellmut Brunner* (Wiesbaden: Otto Harrassowitz, 1983), pp. 243-53.

—'Late Egyptian Chronology and the Hebrew Monarchy', *JANESCU* 5 (1973), pp. 225-33.

—*The Intermediate Period in Egypt (1100–650 B.C.)* (Warminster: Aris & Phillips, 1973).

Kittel, R., *Die Bücher der Könige* (HKAT; Göttingen: Vandenhoeck & Ruprecht, 1900).

—*Handkommentar zum Alten Testament* (ed. E. Kautzsch; Tübingen: Mohr, 4th edn, 1922–23).

Knierim, R., 'Exod 18 und die Neordnung der mosäischen Gerichtsbarkeit', *ZAW* 73 (1961), pp. 146-71.

Kraus, H.J., 'Die prophetische Botschaft gegen die soziale Unrecht Israel', *EvT* 15 (1955), p. 296.

Kuenan, A., *Historisch-kritische Einleitung in die Bücher des Alten Testaments* (Leipzig: Schulz, 1885–94).

Lambden, T.O., *Introduction to Biblical Hebrew* (New York: Scribner's, 1971).

Lance, H.D., 'The Royal Stamps and the Kingdom of Josiah', *HTR* 64 (1971), pp. 315-32.

Lang, B., *Monotheism and the Prophetic Minority*, (Sheffield: Almond Press, 1983).

—'Sklaven und Unfreie im Buch Amos', *VT* 31 (1981), pp. 482-88.

—'The Social Organization of Peasant Poverty in Biblical Israel', *JSOT* 24 (1982), pp. 47-63.

Leclant, J., and J. Yoyotte, 'Notes d'histoire et de civilisation ethiopiennes', *Bulletin de l'Institut francais d'archeologie orientale* 51 (1952), pp. 19-27.

Levenson, J.D., 'From Temple to Synagogue: 1 Kings 8', in *Traditions in Transformation: Turning Points in Biblical Faith* (ed. B. Halpern and J.D. Levenson; Winona Lake, IN: Eisenbrauns, 1981), pp. 143-66.

Lohfink, N., 'Die Bundesurkunde des Königs Josias', *Bib* 44 (1963), pp. 261-88, 461-98.

—'Deuteronomy', *IDBSup*, pp. 229-32.

—'Die Gattung der "Historischen Kurzgeschichte" in den letzten Jahren von Juda und in die Zeit des Babylonischen Exils', *ZAW* 90 (1978), pp. 319-47.

Loretz, O., 'Die prophetische Kritik des Renten Kapitalismus', *UF* 31 (1981), pp. 482-88.

Maag, V., 'Erwägungen zur deuteronomischen Kultzentralisation', *VT* 6 (1956), pp. 10-18.

Macadam, M.F.L., *The Temples of Kawa*. I: *The Inscriptions* (London: Oxford University Press, 1949).

McCarthy, D.J., 'Notes on the Love of God in Deuteronomy and the Father–Son Relationship between Yahweh and Israel', *CBQ* 27 (1965), pp. 144-47.

—*Treaty and Covenant* (Rome: Pontifical Biblical Institute, 1963).

Macholz, G.C., 'Zur Geschichte der Justizorganisation in Juda', *ZAW* 84 (1972), pp. 314-40.

McKay, J., *Religion in Judah Under the Assyrians 732–609 B.C.* (London: Allenson, 1973).

Malamat, A., 'The Historical Background of the Assassination of Amon, King of Judah', *IEJ* 3 (1953), pp. 26-29.

Martin, W.J., *Tribut und Tributleistungen bei den Assyrern* (Studia Orientalia, 8; Helsinki: 1936).

Mayes, A.D.H., *Deuteronomy* (NCB; Grand Rapids, MI: Eerdmans, 1981).

Mazar, B., 'Ancient Israelite Historiography', *IEJ* 2 (1952), pp. 82-88.

—'The Campaign of Pharaoh Shishak to Palestine', *VTS* 4 (1957), pp. 57-66.

Mendelsohn, I., 'On Corvée Labor in Ancient Canaan and Israel', *BASOR* 167 (1962), pp. 31-35.

—*Slavery in the Ancient Near East* (New York: Oxford University Press, 1949).

—'State Slavery in Ancient Palestine', *BASOR* 85 (1942), pp. 14-17.

Mendenhall, G., *Law and Covenant in the Ancient Near East* (Pittsburgh: Biblical Colloquium, 1955).

Menzel, B., *Assyrische Tempel*, 1.2 (Studia Pohl; Rome: Biblical Institute Press, 1981).

Mettinger, T.N.D., *King and Messiah. The Civil Legitimation of the Israelite Kings* (ConBOT, 8; Lund: Gleerup, 1976).

—*Solomonic State Officials: A Study of the Civil Government Officials of the Israelite Monarchy* (ConBOT, 5; Lund: Gleerup, 1971).

Millard, A.R., 'Sennacherib's Attack on Hezekiah', *TynBul* 36 (1985), pp. 61-77.

Miller, J.M., 'The Fall of the House of Ahab', *VT* 17 (1967), pp. 307-24.

Molin, G., 'Die Stellung der Gebira im Staate Juda', *TZ* 10 (1954), pp. 161-75.

Montgomery, J.A., and H.S. Gehman, *A Critical and Exegetical Commentary on the Books of Kings* (ICC; Edinburgh: T.& T. Clark, 1951).

Moriarty, F.L., 'The Chronicler's Account of Hezekiah's Reform', *CBQ* 27 (1965), pp. 399-406.

Mosis, R., *Untersuchungen zur Theologie des chronistischen Geschichtswerkes* (Freiburg: Herder, 1973).

Myers, J.M., *I Chronicles. Introduction, Translation, and Notes* (AB; Garden City, NY: Doubleday, 1965).

Na'aman, N., 'Sennacherib's Campaign to Judah and the Date of the *lmlk* Stamps', *VT* 29 (1979), pp. 61-68

—'Sennacherib's "Letter to God" on his Campaign to Judah', *BASOR* 214 (1974), pp. 25-39.

Nelson, R.D., *The Double Redaction of the Deuteronomistic History* (JSOTSup, 18; Sheffield: JSOT Press, 1981).

Neufeld, E., 'The Prohibition Against Loans at Interest in Ancient Hebrew Laws', *HUCA* 26 (1955), pp. 376-83.

Newsome, J.D., 'Toward a New Understanding of the Chronicler and his Purpose', *JBL* 94 (1975), pp. 201-17.

Nicholson, E.W., 'The Centralisation of the Cult in Deuteronomy', *VT* 13 (1963), pp. 380-89.

—*Deuteronomy and Tradition* (Oxford: Clarendon Press, 1967).

North, R.J., 'The Chronicler: 1–2 Chronicles, Ezra, Nehemiah', in *The Jerome Biblical Commentary* (ed. R.E. Brown, J.A.Fitzmyer and R.E. Murphy; Englewood Cliffs, NJ: Prentice-Hall, 1968), pp. 402-38.

—'Does Archaeology Prove Chronicles' Sources?' in *A Light unto my Path: Old Testament Studies in Honor of Jacob M. Myers* (Philadelphia: Temple University Press, 1974), pp. 375-401.

Noth, M., *Das System der zwölf Stämme Israels* (BWANT, 4.1; Stuttgart: Kohlhammer, 1930; repr. 1966).

—'Die Wege der Pharaonenheere in Palästina und Syrien, Untersuchungen zu den hieroglyphischen Listen palästinischer und syrischer Stadte, IV: Die Schoschenkliste', *ZDPV* 61 (1938), pp. 277-304.

—*Numbers* (OTL; Philadelphia: SCM Press, 1968).

—*The Deuteronomistic History* (JSOTSup, 15; Sheffield: JSOT Press, 1981).

—*Überlieferungeschichtliche Studien: Die sammelnden und bearbeitenden Geschichtswerke im Alten Testament* (Tübingen: Niemeyer, 1943).

Oded, B., 'The Historical Background of the Syro–Ephraimite War Reconsidered', *CBQ* 34 (1972), pp. 153-65.

—'Judah and the Exile', in *Israelite and Judaean History* (ed. J.H. Hayes and J.M. Miller; OTL; Philadelphia: Westminster Press, 1972), pp. 436-88.

Oesterley, W.O.E., and T.H. Robinson, *An Introduction to the Books of the Old Testament* (London: Oxford University Press, 1934).

Oestreicher, T., *Das deuteronomische Grundsetz* (BFCT, 47.4; Gütersloh: Bertelsmann, 1923).

Ogden, G.S., 'The Northern Extent of Josiah's Reforms', *AusBR* 26 (1978), pp. 26-33.

Olmstead, A.T.E., *History of Assyria*. III (Chicago: University of Chicago Press, 1968).

Patai, R., 'The Goddess Asherah', *JNES* 24 (1965), pp. 37-52.

Pfeiffer, R.H., 'Chronicles', *IDB* I, pp. 572-80.

Plataroti, D., 'Zum Gebrauch des Wortes *mlk* im Alten Testament', *VT* 28 (1978), pp. 286-300.

Pohlmann, K.F., *Studien zum dritten Esra. Ein Beitrag zur Frage nach ursprünglichen Schluss des chronistischen Geschichtswerkes* (FRLANT, 104; Göttingen: Vandenhoeck & Ruprecht, 1970).

Polanyi, K., 'The Economy as Instituted Process', in *Trade and Market in the Early Empires* (ed. K. Polanyi, C. Arensberg and H.W. Pearson; Glencoe, IL: Free Press, 1957), pp. 243-70.

Porter, J.R., 'Old Testament Historiography', in *Tradition and Interpretation* (ed. G.W. Anderson; Oxford: Oxford University Press, 1979), pp. 125-62.

Postgate, J.N., *Taxation and Conscription in the Assyrian Empire* (Rome: Pontifical Biblical Institute, 1974).

—'The Economic Structure of the Assyrian Empire', in *Power and Propaganda: A Symposium on Ancient Empires* (ed. M.T. Larsen; Mesopotamia, 7; Copenhagen: Akademisk, 1979), pp. 193-221.

Preller, H., *Geschichte der Historiographie unseres Kulturkreises: Materialien, Skizzen, Vorarbeiten; I, bis 330 A.D.* (Aalen: Scientia, 1967).

Premnath, D.N., 'The Process of Latifundialization Mirrored in the Oracles Pertaining to Eighth Century B.C.E. in the Books of Amos, Hosea, Isaiah and Micah' (Dissertation, Graduate Theological Union, 1984).

Rad, G. von, *Deuteronomy* (OTL; Philadelphia: Westminster Press, 1966).

—*Das Geschichtsbild des chronistischen Werkes* (BWANT, 4.3; Leipzig: Kohlhammer, 1932), pp. 18-37.

—*Old Testament Theology*. I (New York: Harper & Row, 1962).

—*The Problem of the Hexateuch and Other Essays* (New York; McGraw-Hill, 1966).

Radjawane, A.N., 'Das deuteronomistische Geschichtswerk: ein Forschungsbericht', *TRu* 38 (1974), pp. 177-216.

Rainey, A.F., 'Compulsory Labour Gangs in Ancient Israel', *IEJ* 20 (1970), pp. 191-202.

—'Wine from the Royal Vineyards', *BASOR* 245 (1982), pp. 57-62.

Reade, J., 'The Accession of Sinsharishkun', *JCS* 23 (1970), pp. 1-9.

Rendtorff, R., *Das überlieferungsgeschichtliche Problem des Pentateuchs* (BZAW, 147; Berlin: de Gruyter, 1977).

—*Studien zur Geschichte des Opfers im alten Israel* (WMANT, 24; Neukirchen–Vluyn: Neukirchener Verlag, 1967).

Reviv, 'The History of Judah from Hezekiah to Josiah', *WHJP*, pp. 193-204.

Richter, W., *Die Bearbeitungen der "Retterbuches" in der deuteronomistischen Epoche* (BBB, 21; Bonn: Peter Hanstein, 1964).

Riesner, I., *Der Stamm 'bd im Alten Testament. Eine Wortuntersuchung unter Berücksichtigung neuerer sprachwissenschaftlicher Methoden* (BZAW, 149; Berlin: de Gruyter, 1979).

Robinson, D.W.B., *Josiah's Reform and the Book of the Law* (London: Tyndale Press, 1951).

Rofé, A., 'The Vineyard of Naboth: the Origin and Message of the Story', *VT* 38 (1988), pp. 89-104.

Rosenbaum, J., 'Hezekiah's Reform and Deuteronomistic Tradition', *HTR* 72 (1979), pp. 23-44.

Rowley, H.H., *From Moses to Qumran: Studies in the Old Testament* (New York: Association Press, 1963).

—'Hezekiah's Reform and Rebellion', *BJRL* 43 (1960–61), pp. 395-461.

—*Men of God. Studies in Old Testament History and Prophecy* (London: Nelson, 1963).

Rudolph, W., 'Die Einheitlichkeit der Erzählung vom Sturz der Atalja (2 Kön. 11)', in *Festschrift für Alfred Bertholet zum 80 Geburstag* (ed. W. Baumgartner; Tübingen: Mohr, 1950), pp. 473-78.

—'Zum Text der Königsbücher', *ZAW* 63 (1951), pp. 201-15.

Saggs, H.W.F., *Assyriology and the Study of the Old Testament* (Cardiff: University of Wales Press, 1969).

—'The Nimrud Letters: Part 1', *Iraq* 17 (1955), pp. 21-56.

—'The Nimrud Letters: Part VI', *Iraq* 25 (1963), pp. 126-60.

Šanda, A., *Die Bücher der Könige.* I (Exegetisches Handbuch; Münster: Aschendorff, 1911).

Schmid, H.H., *Der sogenannte Jahwist: Beobachtungen und Fragen zur Pentateuch-forschung* (Zürich: Theologischer Verlag, 1976).

Scott, R.B.Y., *The Relevance of the Prophets* (New York: MacMillan, 1944).

Sekine, M., 'Beobachtungen zu der josianischen Reform', *VT* 22 (1972), pp. 361-68.

Silver, M., *Prophets and Markets: The Political Economy of Ancient Israel* (Boston: Kluwer–Nijhoff, 1983).

Smend, R., 'Das Gesetz und die Völker: Ein Beitrag zur deuteronomistischen Redaktionsgeschichte', in *Probleme Biblischer Theologie* (FS von Rad; ed. H.W. Wolff; Munich: Kaiser Verlag, 1971), pp. 494-509.

—'Das Wort Jahwes an Elia. Erwägungen zur Komposition von I Reg. xvii–xix', *VT* 25 (1975), pp. 525-43.

—'Der biblische und der historische Elia', *VTS* 28 (1975), pp. 167-84.

—*Die Entstehung des Alten Testaments* (Stuttgart: Kolhammer, 1978).

Smith, M., *Palestinian Parties and Politics that Shaped the Old Testament* (New York: Colombia University Press, 1971).

Smith, W.R., *Lectures on the Religion of the Semites: The Fundamental Institutions* (London: Black, 3rd edn, 1923; repr. 1969).

Soden, W. von, 'Sanherib vor Jerusalem', in *Atike und Universalgeschichte* (FS H.E. Stier; Münster: Aschendorff, 1972), pp. 43-51.

Soggin, J.A., 'Compulsory Labor under David and Solomon', in *Studies in the Period of David and Solomon and Other Essays* (ed. T. Ishida; Winona Lake, IN: Eisenbrauns, 1982), pp. 259-67.

Spieckermann, H., *Juda unter Assur in der Sargonidenzeit* (Göttingen: Vandenhoeck & Ruprecht, 1982).

Stade, B., 'Anmerkungen zu 2 Kö. 10–14', *ZAW* 5 (1885), pp. 275-97.

—'Anmerkungen zu 2 Kö. 15–21', *ZAW* 6 (1886), pp. 156-89.

Stager, L.E., 'The Archaeology of the East Slope of Jerusalem and the Terraces of the Kidron', *JNES* 41 (1982), pp. 111-21.

—'The Archaeology of the Family in Ancient Israel', *BASOR* 260 (1985), pp. 1-35.

Steck, O., *Überlieferung und Zeitgeschichte in den Elia-Erzählungen* (WMANT, 26; Neukirchen–Vlyun: Neukirchener Verlag, 1968).

Stern, E., 'Israel at the Close of the Period of the Monarchy: An Archaeological Survey', *BA* 38 (1975), pp. 26-54.

Streck, M., *Assurbanipal und die letzen assyrischen Könige bis zum Untergang Ninevehs* (Leipzig: Hinrichs, 1916).

Tadmor, H., 'Philistia under Assyrian Rule', *BA* 29 (1966), pp. 86-102.

Terray, E., *Marxism and 'Primitive' Societies* (London: Monthly Review Press, 1972).

Thiele, E.R., *The Mysterious Numbers of the Hebrew Kings* (Chicago: University of Chicago Press, 1951).

Thompson, M.E.W., *Situation and Theology. Old Testament Interpretations of the Syro–Ephraimite War* (Sheffield: Almond Press, 1982).

Thompson, R.C., *The Prisms of Esarhaddon and Assurbanipal* (London: British Museum, 1931).

Thornton, T.C.G., 'Charismatic Kingship in Israel and Judah', *JTS* 14 (1963), pp. 1-11.

Todd, E.W., 'The Reforms of Hezekiah and Josiah', *SJT* 9 (1956), pp. 288-93.

Trompf, G.W., 'Notions of Historical Recurrence in Classic Hebrew Historiography', *VTS* 30 (1979), pp. 219-24.

Tushingham, A.D., 'A Royal Israelite Seal (?) and the Royal Jar Handle Stamps', *BASOR* 200 (1970), pp. 71-78.

Vaux, R. de, *Ancient Israel* (New York: McGraw–Hill, 1965).

—*Les institutions de l'Ancien Testament*. I (Paris: Editions du Cerf, 1958).

Veijola, T., *Das Königtum in der Beurteilung der deuteronomistischen Historiographie. Eine redaktionsgeschichtliche Untersuchung* (AASF, 198; Helsinki: Suomalainen Tiedeakatemia, 1977).

—*Die ewige Dynastie. David und die Entstehung seiner Dynastie nach der Deuteronomistischen Darstellung* (AASF, 193; Helsinki: Suomalainen Tiedeakatemia, 1975).

—'Salomo—Der Erstgeborene Bathseba', *VTS* 30 (1979), pp. 230-50.

—*Verheissung in der Krise. Studien zur Literatur und Theologie der Exilszeist anhand des 89ten Psalms* (AASF, 220; Helsinki: Suomalainen Tiedeakatemia, 1982).

Weinfeld, M., 'The Counsel of the Elders to Rehoboam and its Implications', *Maarav* 3 (1982), pp. 27-53.

—'The Covenant of Grant in the Old Testament and the Ancient Near East', *JAOS* 90 (1970), pp. 184-203.

—'Cult Centralization in Israel in the Light of Neo-Babylonian Analogy', *JNES* 23 (1964), pp. 202-12.

—*Deuteronomy and the Deuteronomic School* (Oxford: Clarendon Press, 1972).

—'Deuteronomy—The Present State of Inquiry', *JBL* 86 (1967), pp. 249-62.

—'The Emergence of the Deuteromomic Movement: The Historical Antecedents', in *Das Deuteronomium: Entstehung, Gestalt und Botschaft* (ed. N. Lohfink; Leuven: Leuven University Press, 1985).

Weippert, H., 'Die "deuteronomistischen" Beurteilungen der Könige von Israel und Juda und das Problem der Redaktion der Königsbücher', *Bib* 53 (1972), pp. 301-39.

Weiser, A., *Samuel. Seine geschichtliche Aufgabe und religiöse Bedeutung* (FRLANT, 81; Göttingen: Vandenhoeck & Ruprecht, 1962).

Welch, A.C., *The Code of Deuteronomy* (London: Oxford University Press, 1924).

—*Post-Exilic Judaism* (Edinburgh: Blackwood & Sons, 1935).

—*The Work of the Chronicler. Its Purpose and Date* (London: Oxford University Press, 1939).

Wellhausen, J., *Die Composition des Hexateuchs und der historischen Bücher des Alten Testaments* (Berlin: de Gruyter, 4th edn, 1963).

—*Prolegomena to the History of Ancient Israel* (Berlin: Reimer, 1883; repr. Gloucester, MA: Peter Smith, 1983).

Welten, P., *Geschichte und Geschichtedarstellung in den Chronikbüchern* (WMANT; Neukirchen–Vluyn: Neukirchener Verlag, 1973).

—'Naboths Weinberg (1 Kön. 21)', *EvT* 33 (1973), pp. 18-32.

Wette, W.M.L. de, *Dissertatio critica-exegetica qua Deuteronomium a prioribus Pentateuchi libris diversum, alius cuiusdam recentioris auctoris opus esse monstratur* (Halle, 1805); repr. in de Wette, *Opuscula* (Berlin, 1833).

Whitelam, K.W., *The Just King: Monarchical Judicial Authority in Ancient Israel* (JSOTSup, 12; Sheffield: JSOT Press, 1979).

Williamson, H.G.M., *I and II Chronicles* (NCB; Grand Rapids, MI: Eerdmans, 1982).

—'An Adversary against Solomon, Hadad the Edomite', *ZAW* 88 (1976), pp. 205-26.

—'Did the Author of Chronicles Also Write the Books of Ezra and Nehemiah?', *Bible Review 3* (1987).

—*Israel in the Books of Chronicles* (Cambridge: Cambridge University Press, 1977).

Wilson, R.W., *Prophecy and Society in Ancient Israel* (Philadelphia: Fortress Press, 1980).

Wiseman, D.J., 'The Vassal Treaties of Esarhaddon', *Iraq* 20 (1958), pp. 1-99.

Wolf, E., *Peasants* (Foundations of Modern Anthropology Series; Englewood Cliffs, NJ: Prentice–Hall, 1961).

Wolff, H.W., *Hosea* (Hermeneia; Philadelphia: Fortress Press, 1974).

—*Joel and Amos* (Hermeneia; Philadelphia: Fortress Press, 1977).

Wright, G.E., 'The Lawsuit of God: A Form-Critical Study of Deuteronomy 32', in *Israel's Prophetic Heritage* (FS J. Muilenburg; ed. B.W. Anderson and W. Harrelson; New York: Harper & Row, 1962), pp. 26-67.

Würthwein, E., *Das Erste Buch der Könige* (ATD, 11.1; Göttingen: Vandenhoeck & Ruprecht, 1977).

—'Die josianische Reform und das Deuteronomium', *ZTK* 73 (1976), pp. 395-423.

—'Naboth-Novelle und Elia-Wort', *ZTK* 75, (1978) pp. 375-97.

Yadin, Y., 'Beer-sheba: the High Place Destroyed by King Josiah', *BASOR* 222 (1976), pp. 2-17.

Zunz, L., *Die gottesdienstlichen Vorträge der Juden, historisch entwickelt . . .* (Berlin: Ascher, 1832).

# INDEXES

## INDEX OF BIBLICAL REFERENCES

### OLD TESTAMENT

## INDEX OF AUTHORS

# JOURNAL FOR THE STUDY OF THE OLD TESTAMENT

## Supplement Series